13

Cotton
Field OF
DREAMS

Cotton Field of Dreams

A Memoir

Janis F. Kearney

Foreword by Former President
William J. Clinton

Writing Our World Press
Chicago

First Edition 2004
Printed in the United States of America

10 09 08 07 06 05 04   6 5 4 3 2 1
Cover design by Denise Borel Billups

Library of Congress Control Number: 2004098845
ISBN: 0-9762058-0-7

www.writingourworldpress.com

With love and gratitude to
the three men in my life,

James Thomas Kearney
Darryl W.K. Lunon II
and Bob J. Nash

In loving memory of my two best friends
and teachers in life,
Jo Ann Kearney and Ethel Virginia Curry Kearney.

Special thanks to Patrick Oliver, Denise Borel Billups,
Mellonee Carrigan-Mayfield, Gwendolyn Mitchell, Deatri King-Bey,
Mary Lewis and Yvonne Jeffries—
I couldn't have done it without you.

CONTENTS

FOREWORD
Former President William Jefferson Clinton

J anis F. Kearney's *Cotton Field of Dreams* paints a poignant picture of
an Arkansas black family's struggles to live the American Dream,
before and after the civil rights movement, with their only assets hope,
sweat, and a devout faith in God. This author's memories of growing up
black and impoverished in the South are the very memories white
Americans need to know and learn from.

The Kearney family was the poorest, largest family in their small
rural county in Southeast Arkansas, but their dreams were rich and large.
This amazing family is living proof that seemingly impossible dreams,
with hard work and persistence, can come true.

In part because of the South's history, our hearts are warmed by
stories as this one: under-educated African American sharecroppers
pushing their children to achieve academically, then seeing them reach
amazing pinnacles of success. From their parents, the children absorbed
a powerful conviction. They were neither better nor less than any other
human beings. This conviction gave them the self-confidence to move
far beyond their difficult beginnings.

Janis F. Kearney's poignant memoir illuminates the larger truth: That
it is the lessons we internalize in spite of our hurts and disappointments,
that remain with us; that enable us to dream beyond today and work
ourselves into a better tomorrow. With those lessons, Janis moved from
the cotton fields of Gould to the halls of the White House.

In *Cotton Field of Dreams* we learn that James Kearney expected his
children to contribute to this world, and he made them believe they could.

I have been privileged to know and work with Janis and four of her brothers. They followed their father's lead.

The Kearney family underscored what I learned during my 12 years as governor, and 8 years in the White House: there is a necessary role for government in citizens' lives—to empower people like the Kearneys to make the most of their lives—to defend and support the helpless—to stop discrimination. But the most important force in children's lives, whether they are privileged or impoverished, remains their parents. That force made all the Kearney children wealthy in a profound sense.

Fortunate are the children, white or black, rich, poor, or middle class, blessed with parents like James and Ethel Kearney, parents whose vision for their children is fired not by what is immediately before them, but by the deepest longings within them. Those longings got the Kearney kids beyond the long cotton rows, the hungry nights, and the taunts of schoolmates. These children, now grown, are beacons which will shine brightly enough to touch and light the way for others. The Kearneys' love and vision are a blessing for their children and for all the rest of us, too. I'm very glad Janis decided to share it with the world. ℚ

INTRODUCTION

I began this book with the full expectation of writing a story about my father's colorful, vibrant, amazing life. That effort began in 1973. Now 30 years later, my father is still a vibrant man at the age of 98.

As I began to shop my story 10 years ago, well-meaning editors showed great interest in my script. They told me I was chasing after windmills—that I couldn't write my father's story with the emotional depth it deserved. What I could do, they offered, was honor and celebrate his place in my life. That has taken another 10 years to do. In this vignette of memories, which I call memoir, I offer the world a photo sketch of this man whose greatest gift to his children was the permission to dream, knowing that our dreams would color our realities, soften our knocks and lift our reach beyond our stations in life.

My story is my truth—not the whole truth about my world, but a stringing together of dreams and recollections of growing up in a rural Arkansas town, of living a sharecropper's existence where cotton in many ways ruled our lives. This is a story that also celebrates a unique family that included 19 siblings who each possessed such rich personalities as to require a book of their own. It touches on my longing to know the two siblings I hardly knew as a child and on my parents' longings for something better than what Gould, Arkansas, offered. This collection of memories gives credence to my journey from the sharecropper's home on Varner Road to the White House on Pennsylvania Avenue.

In this ever-winding literary journey, I found that my memories—as vast as they may be—are not enough to call this my family's stories. I cannot offer their unadulterated truths. I can only attest to the small space that was mine, to my remembrance of the world that surrounded me and to my memories of Jo Ann, the beautiful and brilliant sister who tired of this world too soon. How would I tell the whole story of how our world drew us so close, yet served as a wedge between us during our childhood years? Jo Ann is not here to look deeply inside me and laughingly admonish me, "Tell the truth or hold your tongue."

Memories of my mother are both sepia-toned and stark brown with soft blue trimmings. This beautiful giver of life left us with her story still folded neatly inside her, never to be unraveled for public view. Nothing I write about Ethel Virginia Curry Kearney will even scrape the surface of who this open, but mysterious woman was. This woman who birthed me, taught me about love and hate and dreaming and who, in leaving, endowed me with strength and answers to questions I'd never had the courage to ask.

Varner Road, Fields Schools and the women and men who colored my life from the cradle to the present served a critical role in nurturing my childhood and defining my journey. Our lives, in so many ways, were threads in a crochet of the times, the place and the atmosphere of the pre-civil rights South. These are stories based on my journey for truth. ℚ

PART I

Going Home Again

(1987)

ONE

Coming Home
to Say Goodbye

My earliest memory of Jo Ann is somewhere between reality and dream—something Mama described as "a witch riding my dreams." Whether my younger sister was five or six or seven years old that day or if she truly wore the illuminating white dress my memory insists, I cannot say with certainty. For certain, my memory tells me she did.

It was summer out on Varner Road, of that much I'm sure. The kind of summer day by which you end up measuring all others. It was a day defined by its blistering, white sun and brilliant blue sky. There was a familiar and blinding light reflecting from places and things, as if the world was liquid-like the endless floor of sea-green grass that grew thick and defiant against the heat; the gargantuan trees, like beautiful monsters, floating upright in a melodic wave of their own; and the rainbow of birds flying toward the sun with only the sprite flapping of wings alerting me they were there.

Standing alone among the deaf-silent whiteness of the cotton field was the small chocolate princess. Jo Ann, young, beautiful and waiting. She stood in that picture of perfection, as if God or Mother Nature had tossed a weightless gauze there for effect. Jo Ann, oblivious to all and everything, was a maddening vision—a miniature Nubian beauty whose tinkle of a laugh caressed my ear, familiar and new, and forever.

The child's soft ringlets were blacker than tar and bounced as she laughed. It was the sound of a sweet child's bell. As she turned her perfect face toward mine, the laughter became that of an older, wiser Jo Ann holding secrets. I would never know or understand. Her flawless, chocolate face glowed under the sun, listening, and her eyes moved upward toward the man who blocked the brightness of the sun.

The tail of her beautiful white dress flounced wildly as she skipped with childish abandon and glee toward the man whose shadowed face was lit like the sun. Our father smiled down at Jo Ann, and I smiled, too, inside that dream reality. But it was Jo Ann's black, golden beauty and sweet child's laughter that held his vision. Together, the father and child walked, quietly speaking their thoughts, through the field of whiteness that matched her beautiful, blinding dress.

Daddy believed nothing in life compared to the pain of living on after losing a wife he had loved for nearly 50 years. It was a curse, he believed, for some unknown, long ago sin that had him burying his wife and the daughter for whom he had such dreams just five years apart.

Jo Ann was his chosen child, the one he was sure would represent his own dreams throughout life. Daddy never quite understood, nor would he find it in himself to completely forgive his daughter's decision to leave this world and his dreams untouched. It was even more of a struggle to forgive God, whom he'd served most of his adult life. What manner of loving, forgiving God would take the woman he loved more than he loved himself and, five years later, the child whose death closed the door to so many dreams?

In August 1987, I was going home to bury the child Daddy had believed hung the stars, until it became painfully obvious that she had no desire to do so. Jo Ann—my best friend, my archenemy, my secret-bearer, my secret idol—had said goodbye, forever. When we were children, most people who didn't know better believed the two of us were twins. Neither of us understood why. There was as much different about us as there were similarities. In our childhood, though, no one looked closely enough at two cute little girls to see the contrast in Jo Ann's deep stares into adults' eyes and my little-girl shyness.

4

As adolescents, Jo Ann and I found some weird thrill in walking our visiting neighbors down a darkened Varner Road after their visits. We'd walk and gossip and discuss boys halfway to the friends' home and, in turn, they'd walk back halfway to ours. We would go back and forth like this sometimes for hours. It was a form of country etiquette called "walking a piece of the way home." Neither of us would walk all the way to the other's home, and neither wanted to be the first to say good night. Jo Ann had beaten us all to the punch, the first of my siblings to say goodbye.

Five years ago my family had come home for a different goodbye. I would never be smart enough to understand God's reason for taking these two Kearney women who held such different roles in their family's lives. Did God merely let them slip away from us? From what I could see, Jo Ann and Mama were as different from each other as night and day. Sometimes, though, when I remembered hard enough, there were flashes of the woman and the girl that told me something different. Mama's death, even after five years, was still fresh-turned soil in our hearts. Jo Ann would be the one to push the soil aside, forcing us to remember.

Jo Ann had been one of the Kearney clan who converged on Varner Road two weeks ago. She was part of our celebration of our family, our annual reunion and Daddy's 80th birthday. Jo Ann celebrated for the last time with her family that she sometimes believed deserved no celebration.

My younger sister's passing away was my son D.K.'s first intimacy with death in his large, extended family. Jo Ann was a special aunt. She was closer to him than the others. She was visiting in my dorm room just hours after he was unknowingly conceived, and she was one of the first to visit him following his birth in Washington Regional Hospital in Fayetteville. The child's innocent questions about the aunt he'd lost reminded me of my sister's and my strained love over the years and of the unasked questions that would never end and the unfinished business left behind.

Daddy was depending on my strength today, and I would exhibit my ability to mask my own pain. I had learned that lesson, too, so well during my childhood on Varner Road. Though I had lost a sister and a friend, Daddy had lost a child and, as parents are wont to do, gained a serving of guilt and questions for which there may be no answers.

I guided the car through Boyle Park, home to my favorite walking paths and D.K.'s favorite playground. I whispered a selfish prayer that I hoped would help me through the next day. The drive from Little Rock to Gould would take 90 minutes if I avoided the highway troopers and drove at least 60 miles per hour all the way. I had 90 minutes, I thought, to remember and question Jo Ann's and my life and to dissect the crystallizing nugget of guilt rattling around inside me.

I stopped at the crowded gas station and made sure the needle moved to empty before heading for the freeway. I remembered the time 10 years ago—running away from a bad marriage—I'd run out of gas in the dead of night with my three-year-old son. Like an avalanche, other memories followed. I thought of Jo Ann's response when she learned of my pregnancy and impending marriage to Darryl during our sophomore year in college.

"But we love each other," I'd said weakly, avoiding my sister's stare. She'd laughed and simply shook her head. It was times like these that it was so hard to remember I was 18 months older than Jo Ann.

"You're making a stupid mistake, Faye," she'd said as she peered into my dorm room mirror and straightened her bangs. "I don't know whether you're foolish enough or in love enough to believe that you're doing the right thing. Either way, you're making a mistake."

That was one of the moments I'd hated my sister most. It was just like Jo Ann to ignore my need for comfort at a time like this, refusing to pretend with me that I was doing the right thing, the only thing I could do. But she had known she was right, and 15 years later I would admit she had been right. That had been so long ago. Somehow that memory reminded me of the day we buried my mother five years earlier and of how differently these two people had left us.

Mama had finally succumbed to the death that had pursued her for so long. Even with angry, changing cancer inside of her, she remained the picture of a woman at peace with her past and her afterlife. Her beautiful, unmarred face was that of a woman half her age. The pecan shell-colored face was framed by the wisps of fine, gray hair she had kept dark for as long as I could remember. Her smile remained until the end. Mama's was a silent, graceful goodbye—so much like her living.

Jo Ann's dying was a dash of cold water waking us from our sleep. Doctors had diagnosed her with paranoid schizophrenia seven years earlier, and we had known she'd attempted suicide before. Yet, we hadn't prepared for her death. Jo Ann had fooled us with her exhibition of her "old self" just weeks earlier. And the doctors made us believe our sister would "continue for years functioning almost as normal as you or I," if she only took her medicine and visited her doctor regularly. The fair-skinned female doctor's voice and words had been comforting, and we felt safe.

Today's trip home would likely include confronting the ghosts of our pasts—ghosts the Kearney family had long ignored. I settled in, steeling myself for this journey and trying hard to ignore the sadness and questions that might have no answers.

I opted for the downtown route which took longer but gave me a view of something other than my own memories. The city of Little Rock hadn't changed much during the 10 years I'd lived here. Like other southern cities during the mid-1970s and early 1980s, the downtown area had suffered as stores and businesses moved away or closed down. Many offices relocated to the outer edges of town, leaving the ghostly buildings to become home to the city's itinerant and poor.

White flight contributed to downtown Little Rock's demise, though leaders couldn't say for sure which came first. Developers worked tirelessly to hatch ideas to boost the downtown housing market, and the city's administrators exhibited little hope in turning their public schools around as white students moved to predominantly white county school districts.

City activists, religious leaders and well-intentioned citizens still wrestled with the racism that had cursed the South since the days of slavery. The civil rights struggle had come and gone. Black children had gone to school with white children. Stores and restaurants had been opened to black customers, but the ravages of racism persisted. White policemen still did profile checks throughout the black community, stopping and searching black motorists at an incomparable rate. While wealthy Bill Cosby was being touted as the number one entertainer in the country, black men were still generally regarded as "suspicious."

Even so, I had few complaints about my life. Arkansas and Little Rock were home, and I had no thoughts or intention of ever leaving. My life was comfortable, and Darryl and I were moving up in our careers. In 1978, I had been hired into a middle management job in state government, helping a friend run an employment training program that helped place workers in local governments. My husband, my son and my weekly visits home kept me busy outside work, and ever so often I was able to meet friends after work for "happy hour."

Little Rock's 150,000 population was just enough to make me know I was in a city, not a town like Gould whose population hovered around 1,600 people on its best days. There were enough cars on the freeway to cause a traffic jam on some mornings and Fridays after work. The city was also home to more than a handful of small and medium-sized manufacturing companies. There were two malls and enough gossip about another sprouting up in the suburbs to curb women's threat of driving eight hours to Atlanta or five hours to Dallas to find the latest styles. There were even a few four-star restaurants and small eateries that outsiders called "quaint" and Arkansas publications called "local gems." Arkansans were, by now, expanding our dining tastes to include ethnic cuisine: Italian, Mexican, Indian and even Caribbean foods.

Broadway was Little Rock's main conduit to anywhere in the downtown area and across the Arkansas River into North Little Rock. Quapaw Quarters, dubbed Little Rock's largest historical district, was my favorite part of the city. The area boasted the oldest homes in the city, the largest churches and the infamous "9th Street Business Corridor" that was once home to a burgeoning black business strip before integration made it irrelevant. Our impressive, typically southern governor's mansion was tucked away between Main Street and Broadway—a 10-minute drive from downtown.

Quapaw Quarters was known mostly for the beautiful antebellum homes handsomely decorating the neighborhood, offering history lessons about a Little Rock of days gone by. The all-white leaders of yesteryear would have never imagined the integration crisis at Central High School in 1957 or a U.S. president sending troops to the town to assure safety for nine black children integrating the auspicious high school. So much had changed in Little Rock over the last 30 years and far too much remained unchanged.

As I turned onto Highway 65, the man's deep voice coming through the dashboard told me it was 3 o'clock in the afternoon. I would arrive in front of Daddy's house two hours from now. I searched for an "oldies but goodies" station and imagined Daddy was likely scanning the oversized numbers on his watch and wondering what was keeping me. His voice had sounded distant and hollow over the phone.

I could always count on a warm reception when I visited Daddy each weekend. "I'm glad you could make it down," he would say, smiling, as if I didn't come down like clockwork each week. "How's Darryl?" he'd ask, half-apologetic that I'd left him at home but always happy that I at

9

least still brought D.K. He was usually already at the car before I got out, giving me a warm hug and telling me how glad he was to see me. In his loneliness and his old age, Daddy had become a doting father who felt no self-consciousness about his need to have his children around him.

The familiar "Welcome to Pine Bluff" sign reminded me I was just 32 miles from Daddy's house. I turned off at the Stop N' Go before driving through Pine Bluff on the last leg of my journey home. I tried to remember when this station had gone up. It had been here most of my adult life, serving as a corner grocer and a convenient gas stop for those traveling south or north. Travelers could buy everything from *The National Enquirer* to BC Brand Headache Powder here.

I browsed the crowded rows of snacks, drinks, paperback books and a mismatch of other conveniences before settling for a Dr Pepper and a package of pork rinds. The young clerk recognized my name as I slid a credit card across the counter.

"Oh...Miss Kearney," her young face lit up as she smiled. "You part of that big Kearney family from 'round here?"

I nodded and smiled. She totaled the two items, then swiped the card quickly. As she passed my card and the bill for my signature, she returned to her thoughts.

"Don't y'all have a reunion every year?"

I nodded as I wrote. "Yes, we do." I smiled as I handed her the slip of signed paper and grabbed my purchase to leave.

"I used to date a Kearney at Townsend Park High School—Jimmy Kearney," she blushed and giggled.

"Oh...yes, that's one of my nephews. My goodness, he must be in high school, now...."

She laughed, shaking her head, "No, ma'am, he graduated this year. He's about to go to college up in Jonesboro in the fall."

I was surprised but chose not to prolong the conversation. "Thanks a lot," I said, "and say hello to Jimmy if you see him." I quickly headed out to my car.

I patted my stomach lightly, as I felt the tug somewhere near my navel. I was fast approaching Varner Road. This time the comfort of knowing I was just a few miles from home was joined by something different. I knew what it was, but I refused to spend any time dealing with it right now. The sunlight reflected off the shiny, new Cummins State Penitentiary sign. The children riding the school bus with me years ago used to joke that Varner Road either took you to the Kearneys' house or to Cummins Prison Farm, depending on how drunk you were.

I was five miles from Daddy's home. The butterflies had completely awakened now and fluttered playfully in the pit of my stomach. I turned right down Varner Road, crossing the old railroad track and settling onto the familiar gravel road I'd driven so many times before. I rolled the car window down, and the smells of country life rushed in. The summer wind caressed my face like warm, soft hands. Tall weeds along the roadside ditch swayed lightly, and I listened to the harsh crunches of the gravel beneath the car wheels. It was a familiar sound, as if my life and Jo Ann's and Daddy's lives were the same as the last time I drove here.

I watched a family of geese fly up from the man-made lake opposite the houses and remembered our school bus passing that same lake when I was a child. My mind flashed back to how I would join the other kids as they hurried to the windows on that side of the bus, pressing our faces against the glass and pointing at the hundreds of turtles sleeping on the fallen logs.

There were four homes built right next to each other on the right, all inhabited by Cummins Prison Farm guards and other employees. The fields on either side of the road still reached further than the eye could see. In my youth, those same fields teemed with young black men in white uniforms, prisoners from Cummins, working the crops. Whenever we mentioned that we'd seen prisoners on our way home from school, a dark frown would appear in Daddy's face, and he would begin his speech about racial injustice in America's penal system.

"It's a shame you got all them colored boys down there working on the prison farm and jest a handful of white folks when it's more of them committing the crimes!"

Many an evening, prisoners worked in the fields as our school bus returned us safely home. The mostly young men would stand and watch as we passed. Some would smile and wave, others stood straight with hard, unsurprised looks covering their thoughts. The white men on the horses rarely acknowledged our passing. Most times, I sat near a window that allowed me to search the boys' and men's faces for traces of their lives. I created stories about the worlds they'd left behind—the childhoods they may have forgotten by now. What about their kin, their mamas or brothers or sisters?

Dora Bell Baptist Church sat just around the bend. I slowed the car, then came to a stop. I hardly believed the beautiful, quaint white church from my childhood was no longer there. The roof had almost completely collapsed. The windows were either cracked or laying on the ground. The large silver bell that had been visible miles away atop the church was now gone. Daddy said the church's congregation dwindled to almost no one over a span of five years. When families moved from Varner Road, it was years before some new family came to take their place. Here was another change I hadn't noticed the last time I visited. Dora Bell Church no longer existed.

I shook my head, remembering how the building had housed standing room only church services when I was a child. Robert and Nola Mae Jackson, the odd old couple who were our closest neighbors, had attended this church. I was glad they were not around to see what had become of their beloved church home.

The glaring white of Daddy's house forced it to stand out against the wall of trees and fields surrounding it. Minutes from home, I noted the mixed feelings of comfort and apprehension. The house looked just as it had two weeks ago, as if nothing in our lives had changed.

I remembered Jo Ann's visit two years ago and how she had shared, again, her deep anger with the world and the family with whom she had a love-hate relationship.

"Jo Ann, make up your mind! Are you part of the family or not?" I was again exasperated by Jo Ann's unkind words about our family. "I can't figure out what you want us to do. Is it our fault that people see merit in our family?"

While Jo Ann's visits always started out cordial enough, they usually ended in disagreement and strained temperaments. And, it always ended up in a discussion about our family's undeserved station in life. More often than not, she let me know she didn't consider herself a "true" Kearney.

Jo Ann snickered and shook her head as she always did when she thought I was being illogical.

"You really don't understand, do you, Faye? What makes us any better than any other family who were sharecroppers or lived in poverty? It's all a sham. We're pretending that we're something special—that we've done something great, when we've just been blessed."

Jo Ann, better than anyone in the family, could transform me into a babbling, angry child.

"Oh, so you don't remember how people made fun of us and made us feel like we didn't deserve to be sitting in the classrooms with the rest of the students just because we were so poor or the ones who called Mama the 'old woman who lived in a shoe'?

"We didn't make ourselves poor, but we sure had something to do with getting ourselves away from that environment.not just us, but Mama and Daddy. Can't you at least admit that if it hadn't been something special about them, we would probably still be down there making a living from that same farm?"

Jo Ann looked at me with that implacable smile that never seemed to change no matter what I said. After I finished, she shrugged and walked to the refrigerator to find something to drink. When she returned to the table where we sat, she went on:

"Faye, you get natural survival and having some special abilities mixed up. Don't you think that maybe we have God to thank for taking pity on us and plucking us out of that environment? You know, he even takes care of heathens and fools." She had laughed, and I couldn't help but laugh with her.

I was sure Jo Ann's thinking was that of someone with a twisted reality and a distorted idea of religion. I still didn't believe that deep down she disliked her own family the way she sometimes said. She had been stubborn and independent as a child, but she had loved her family, especially Daddy. Of course, she had been Daddy's model child, the one he held up to the rest of us as perfection personified. My jealousy had been something painful and the cause of the rift in our relationship over the years. But even that had mostly disappeared over the years as we shared more commonalities than differences.

Our best years were as teens, when we shared so many late-night confessions and secrets as we lay in bed fighting sleep. We hated and loved our parents together and swore we would get even with more than a few teachers and classmates who had treated us badly over the years. Even at those times when Jo Ann was most comfortable sharing her deepest feelings with me, she seldom expressed any deep-seated anger toward our parents or our family.

It was after our high school years that hints of a different Jo Ann began to appear. At that time, I connected the nonthreatening changes to Jo Ann's brilliant mind that was open to exploring new ideas. She discarded a number of religions over the years, but it seemed there were always others, even more radical, waiting in the wings.

As Daddy had hoped, I was the first of his children to arrive home. The rest would arrive later in the afternoon, including Cecil and Clara, my two half-siblings that neither Jo Ann nor I had grown up with. As I turned into the spacious yard, I felt some small bit of guilt that I wasn't looking forward to this time alone with my father. Mama's summer flowers, moving lightly to the pull of the wind, took my breath away. The giant, color-filled bouquet of buttercups, zinnias, morning glories, azaleas and peonies decorated the front edge of the yard. The smell and sight of Mama's flowers had so often brightened my mornings as I sleepwalked my way to Daddy's cotton field.

I blew the horn lightly before slowly stepping out of the car. It was Daddy's need more than my own strength that allowed me to place one foot in front of the other and move toward the gloomy white house. I believed Jo Ann was here, in this very yard that was our playground for so many years. I imagined her beautiful smile and wondered that she would choose to be here now. The last words we spoke to each other, just three days ago, had been in anger. Now, though, I heard my sister's soft, innocent laughter in the wind that moved the trees in Daddy's yard and in the songs of the birds that flew across Daddy's sky.

So many summer days we'd played hide-and-seek beneath the front porch. Jo Ann's uncontrollable laughter always gave her away. Except for my vibrant memories and Jo Ann's ghost, Daddy's house seemed bare of any life. For one moment, I worried. Daddy always stood in his door, smiling, as I walked to the house. A soft chill met me as I opened the door to a house that had always been 10 degrees too warm. A large fan whizzed in the open window, and the curtains kept out the sunlight.

15

The rattling cough that came from Daddy's bedroom made me worry how we'd get through these next hours. Daddy had kept summer colds throughout our childhood. I wondered, though, if Jo Ann's leaving had helped trigger this one. I stood now before the television set, peering for the hundredth time into the face of the 25-year-old Ethel Curry Kearney. My mother sat proper and demure in the photograph atop the television. How beautiful and serene she was! Her small, plump hands were clasped lightly in her lap, and a white flower held the thick, dark wave of hair away from her intense, pensive eyes. My eyes always ended up at the vague, mysterious smile offered to the photographer. Who was this young woman?

The slow scraping of Daddy's house shoes jolted me from my daydream. Before I could move to his bedroom, he was there in the doorway. "Daddy," I said, almost as a question. Though he seemed half drunk with exhaustion and grief, his weak smile was one of relief—relief that I was there and that he didn't have to listen to his own thoughts alone anymore. We hugged, a soft exchange, holding on to each other for strength.

"Hey, girl, you finally got here." Daddy's welcome was an effort at nonchalance.

The darker-than-usual circles beneath his eyes confirmed what I already thought. He hadn't slept a wink since my brother Jesse called with the news two days ago. I imagined the horror Daddy must have felt as the news sunk in—the cloying grief as he lay alone in this house awaiting daylight and someone, anyone, to share his grief.

"How're you doing, Daddy?" I absently rubbed his back as we walked together to the couch that took up most of the room. I wasn't strong enough for what he needed—a stoic heart to absorb his grief and an unflinching shoulder to lean on.

He shrugged his rounded shoulders and sighed before sitting back on the sofa. "Oh, I guess I'm all right. I guess I'll make it."

I sat gingerly beside him, and for the next moment we each settled into our own sadness. This was the second time in my life I'd come to grips with my daddy being just a man. He had been so much more for so long. He had been more than other men, straight and solid with a purposeful walk and a good reason for everything he did or said. As children, we would have followed him to hell and back, with his mouth spouting mesmerizing words and his mind making logic out of nothing. We sat still and quiet, unlike most children on Sunday mornings, listening to my father's eloquent speeches. He was an impressive man, near a perfect parent in our eyes.

James Thomas Kearney was what most women in town and on Varner Road called "a looker." His brown, piercing eyes were set close together above the "Indian" nose his daddy passed on to him. His hair was coal black, thick and wavy. His mother, proud of her child's "good hair," had combed it constantly, allowing it to grow down around his waist. Mother Nature had treated him kindly. All of his life, he had looked half his age. And though grief had slowed his pace, he was still an impressive man, and his movements were still purposeful. The sad, befuddled man sitting next to me was not the father I knew.

"I'm glad you here, Faye. I was hoping you'd get here before the bunch made it. I hadn't got nothing ready, yet. I just hadn't felt like myself at all—hadn't got nothing together for the service tomorrow either."

I nodded. "Oh, that's fine, Daddy. You just sit here and rest. I'll take care of everything." I walked into the kitchen, wondering if Daddy had enough food to prepare dinner for the family. "Have you eaten anything today?" I called back.

I felt his hesitation, and finally he said: "I ain't been real hungry. I tried, but just ain't been able to eat nothing."

"You got to eat, Daddy," I scolded. "You'll end up really sick if you don't. I'll fix you something light." I found canned vegetable soup pushed to the back of the cupboard and put it on the stove to warm. I was

17

surprised to find that Daddy had remembered to take a chicken out to thaw. I cut up the still half-frozen chicken before rinsing it.

"Where's your seasoning, Daddy?" He walked into the kitchen and opened the door to a different cupboard from the one I was peering into. "You used to keep it here, didn't you?" I asked, as I stretched to get the seasoning salt and pepper.

"Yeah, I used to." He returned to the living room.

As I floured the chicken, I found myself humming like Mama did as she cooked our meals. I stopped in disbelief. I dropped the floured chicken parts in the boiling grease and covered it before pouring the bubbling vegetable soup into one of Daddy's plastic bowls. "Here you go, Daddy...enjoy!" He chuckled, and I was remembering that I needed to hang up the black suit I'd brought for tomorrow.

I carried my overnight case from the living room, trying to decide which of the two guest bedrooms to claim. My oldest sister Jamie, who still took her role as firstborn too seriously, would be coming in later tonight. I left the first room for her and carried the suitcase to the back room which had two double beds. Daddy had said Judy would be in shortly. I decided we'd bunk together tonight.

Judy was the baby of the Kearney family, and it took Mama's passing for us to grow closer as sisters. Up until then, I remembered her as the baby that Mama carried with her during her summer trips to California each year. She had been no more than seven or eight when I went away to college, still writing letters to Santa Claus asking for bicycles that he never brought.

When Mama died in 1982, Judy had been enrolled at Brown University. She'd left the university just months before finals to attend the funeral and hadn't returned until the next year. Mama's death had changed my girlish youngest sister into a serious young woman. When she was born in 1963, she had been as much "our" baby as she was Mama's. To most of us, she represented an end to Mama's reign as "the woman who'd been pregnant 17 times" during her first 26 years of marriage. I don't know how we decided Judy was the last without Mama telling us. But somehow, we all figured it out. We guessed about lots of important things—especially things that our parents never found the words to explain to us.

It was Christmas Eve when Mama brought Judy home from the hospital. She was only the second Kearney child born in a hospital. The rest of us had been born in the same place we were conceived, our parents' bed. We all knew this beautiful baby must be extra special when Mama stayed in bed, cradling her to her breast for almost a week. It was as if a switch on Mama's body had suddenly turned off, demanding rest. Mama was 46 years old, two months short of being 47, and her body took its own dear time to heal.

———

When I walked back through the living room to the kitchen, Daddy had finished the soup and sat the bowl on the arm of the sofa. He was busy staring down at his hands when I grabbed the bowl up and headed into the kitchen.

"I'm going to throw a salad together, Daddy, then I think I'll make us a nice cup of coffee."

He nodded. "Yeah, that'll be nice. I guess I need to put some real clothes on before they get here, too." This was the first time it registered that Daddy was still in his pajamas and robe.

As he changed in his bedroom and the chicken simmered on low, I walked into what had been Jo Ann's and my bedroom for so many years before we both left for college—that long ago time. I looked through the window at the black walnut tree that looked so much smaller than it did during my childhood. Daddy had said a thunderstorm had hit down on Varner Road some years ago, and a bolt of lightning had struck the tree, leaving it just a shell of what it once was. So many nights I'd sat cradled in the lap of the walnut tree, dreaming about what my future might be. The strong tree had played such an important role in my childhood and my dreams.

Daddy hadn't gone in to change after all. Instead, he was walking through his back yard toward the chicken coop. He carried a bucket of feed in his hand and stopped at the fence to throw it inside. I heard the squawking chickens fighting over their evening meal. I remembered how just two weeks ago the family had been here to celebrate our 16th family reunion. When we'd made our annual trek to Rankin Chapel Church for Sunday morning service, the members had taken turns bragging about how Daddy kept himself young.

During our last reunion, the church members had tarried, not hurrying home but gathering under the shade of the large oak trees and chatting with Daddy and his oversized family. The old and young women gathered around Jo Ann as if they were happy to see her, hugging and kissing her and telling her how "good" she looked.

Jo Ann's beautiful smile was in full evidence that day. "I'm really glad to be here. I'm doing a lot better, thank you." Her delight in seeing her old friends was genuine.

They must have remembered Jo Ann giving each of them "a piece of her mind" at one time or another. But that day it seemed as if they had wiped the slate clean and forgiven Jo Ann's sometimes odd ways. They all whispered that Jo Ann looked and acted "almost" like her old self.

Daddy had finally changed into slacks and a white shirt. He now sat, waiting for the rest of his children to arrive. When the Kearney children had all left home and it was just the two of them, Mama had tried hard to convince Daddy to just sit and rest during the day. Very seldom was she successful. In the summers, as if to prove a point, Daddy worked outside through the hottest part of the day, returning at the end of the day to the fan. Since he no longer had a wife to tell him the right way to do things, he did things the way he thought they ought to be done and when he thought they ought to be done. His made it clear that we were still his children, not his caretakers.

The aroma of the instant coffee we sipped reminded me of winter mornings of years gone by, of how my parents huddled with us around the wood-burning heater after breakfast. I could almost hear their quiet voices, the coffee mugs clinking against glass plates, and smell the milky-sweet aroma of coffee during those cold mornings on Varner Road. With Mama gone, Daddy had lost his taste for the milk-sweet coffee in the winters, but he'd gained other things, including a love for the prolific garden out behind the house and the flower beds in his front yard. He'd also discovered a depth to his fatherhood that had lain dormant when Mama lived.

His garden was generous this summer because of, and in spite of, the many days of spring and summer rain. His peas and tomatoes had done well, and he'd carried buckets full down to the church each Sunday. The squash and okra fared just as well but dried on the stalks because no neighbors asked for those vegetables. Daddy perked up some when I commented on his beautiful garden.

"Yeah, it finally looks like I'll have a good watermelon crop again. These last few years I got nothing but knots," he said.

The house was quiet again, giving me time to think about why I was there and why Daddy's other children were coming. In the quiet, his uneven breathing blended with the whir of the window fan and he studied his hands again.

"Remember when you and Jo Ann were about to go to school and me and Ethel went to town and bought them satin dresses? They were just alike, except for the color."

I remembered. Daddy let a short laugh escape his throat. "We always made sure if we bought one of you something, we'd buy the other one something, too. Most times, they were just alike, just different colors. I swear, if y'all wasn't forever trying to outdo each other back then!" Another dry chuckle escaped, and he shook his head as if puzzled by the memory.

The tear formed in the corner of my eye. "I remember those dresses, Daddy. Mine was red checked gingham with a big bow in the back, and Jo Ann's was royal blue. We never forgot those dresses. That was one of the happiest days in both of our lives. We talked about that day just a few weeks ago."

Daddy's breathing stopped for one moment, and he shook his head. "Lord, I can't believe it was jest three weeks ago when y'all were all here for the family reunion. Everything seemed fine then. Jo, she seemed to be doing so good, and I was thinking how I wished Ethel had been with us...to see Jo Ann doing so good. She was really bad off when your mama passed."

I placed my arm around Daddy's stooping shoulders. "I'm sure Mama was looking right down on us at the reunion, Daddy. It was a good day. None of us could have guessed this would happen. Just like you always tell us, 'only God knows.' "

We sat silently again, allowing the sadness to roll over us, heavy and somehow comforting. I escaped into the back yard, walking in circles, breathing in Daddy's air and taking in this life he had continued since Mama's death—his beautiful garden and peach trees heavy with fruit.

By 7 o'clock that evening, Daddy's house began to fill with his children. By 8 p.m., all 16 of us were present and accounted for. There were no spouses or children there to distract our grief or to share

22

our sorrows. We were still possessive about our pain. The fact that we came together at all exhibiting our hurt was a stretch for the Kearney family. Except for our experience with Mama's death, this was a trial run for us. We hadn't learned to share emotions during all those years we'd been taught to share our food, our laughter, even our homes.

Our ages spanned several decades. In truth, some of us barely knew each other. We all knew the oral histories, the family stories passed down by parents or siblings. Clara, Daddy's oldest child, was 60—old enough to have great-grandchildren—while Judy had just turned 24.

I had seen my siblings' faces etched in such deep sadness only once before and wished foolishly that we'd never have this to go through again. Our voices, usually loud and strong, were lowered, subdued. After dinner, I offered Jude, a younger brother who was always the life of the party, a cup of coffee, hoping for just a glimpse of his bright smile. I moved through Daddy's now—crowded living room and dining area, offering coffee and cake, knowing there was nothing more I could offer this family.

As the family filed into Daddy's home, each one embraced him long and hard. The sadness in their eyes matched the fragile show of affection between them. It had been five years ago when I'd first seen Daddy embrace his sons. I wondered if it would be another familial death before we'd express our love and caring again.

The 19 children had separated over the years into three groups. There were 10 members of the older group, including my two half siblings, Cecil and Clara, who had lived in California since the early 1960s. Jamie, James, Jerrel, Janeva, Janetta, Joyce and Joseph followed them there, deciding that for many blacks California was the true land of opportunity. The first group of Kearneys to graduate from Fields High School went to AM&N College in Pine Bluff. Before finishing, however, some went off to California for greener pastures and an opportunity to help my parents. They all returned to college in their later years.

Jamie left home and migrated to California in 1960. Her first job there was with the Mattel Toy Factory. By the time her younger siblings started coming, one after another, she had secured enough connections to help each of them gain employment there as well.

The second group of Kearney's included Jesse, Jack, Julius, Jo Ann and me. We had dubbed our three brothers the "Three Amigos," given their close friendship during their teen years and the fact that you rarely saw one without the other two. Jo Ann and I always thought it strange that most people in Gould took us for twins. Maybe it was because of that fact, we would refuse to dress alike, and except for some obvious Kearney traits, we made sure we were quite different people.

While Jo Ann and I attended the University of Arkansas along with Jesse and Jack, Julius, who always said he would be the first black president, enrolled at Harvard University. He went to Phillips Andover Preparatory School during the summer of 1970.

By 1971, there were only four Kearney children left to keep Mama and Daddy company, and each one would be awarded scholarships to Western Reserve Academy. My parents, both past 60 when the last of their children left home, were more proud than sad to see their young children courted, then plucked from Gould High School with scholarships and promises of a better life. A better education for their children had always been their dream, and they thanked God they were able to live to see their dreams come true, one by one. Mama declared she didn't regret "for one moment" sending her children off to the prestigious prep schools when they were so young. She did, however, miss being a mother 24 hours a day. Being a mother was all she'd known for more than 40 years.

I sat at Daddy's wooden table across from my sister Janetta, my role model, and another sister, Joyce. James, my oldest brother, was especially quiet tonight—not that he was ever a chatterbox. He was the kind who said more in a few words than most people said in a hundred.

Tonight he wasn't bearing the usual beautiful smile he'd inherited from Mama.

I tried maintaining a stiff upper lip, but tears hovered inside my heart, waiting. Joyce's pretty face went from smiles to frowns. I remembered how neighbors now said the two of us could pass for twins. The last time we had seen each other two weeks ago, we'd stayed up half the night laughing about our families and old times. Today, though, her face was drawn and the familiar grin was nowhere in sight. Joyce had been daring and full of life in her young days—everything I didn't have the guts to be. I envied that in her and loved her infectious sense of humor.

She had a natural humor that most comedians worked their whole lives to achieve. As smart as she was pretty, she had graduated from high school at the age of 15 and left that same summer for California. She was 40 years old now, married and the mother of three boys. Since moving to California, Joyce had steadily moved up the career ladder at Los Angeles City Hall. She recalled Jo Ann's two years in California while attending the University of California at Berkley. Joyce had seen her quite often then, and they'd grown close for a time. After Jo Ann returned to Arkansas, the sisters had lost touch.

Humor was the Kearney family's way of expressing and suppressing our emotions. It was the closest anyone would get to seeing the inside of us. Few people, even our spouses, were privy to our hurts and pains. Each of us this night shared the need to understand why. Why would someone like Jo Ann, who was once so full of life, choose to pull the shades on her tomorrows? How in the world did we let such a thing happen?

As the night grew older, my stamina and spirits began to wane. The limited conversation with my family had helped. I was moving closer to accepting this harsh truth and internalizing the fact that my sister was gone. Jerome had been with me that last time, an unwilling accomplice. He sat quietly apart from the family. I imagined he was thinking what I had thought so many times before, that I'd give anything to erase the haunting mental snapshot of Jo Ann's lifeless body. We were all wrestling with memories, either the ones we no longer wanted or those we prayed would lessen the pain and guilt.

I needed to be alone with my own thoughts. I always told friends and my husband that growing up in a house full of siblings had made me prefer solitude. Some thought it should be the other way around and found it odd that a Kearney child would be introverted. But, in fact, most of my siblings grew up needing space as much as they needed other people.

As a child, I found quiet space in secret nooks and crannies, sometimes in the deep woods behind our house, disappearing for hours and returning to angry parents and sometimes punishment. "Crazy as a loon" was how my siblings laughingly described my strange ways. Their taunts hadn't stuck, and I never internalized them. I quietly kissed Daddy good night and hugged each of my siblings all crowded into Daddy's home on Varner Road.

I settled into the comforting bed, pulling the sheet up to my chin and closing my eyes. I felt the day's stress leak slowly from my body. I welcomed any lapse in thinking or feeling right now. I listened to my baby sister's even breathing in the next bed and was glad she'd found a way to sleep. I turned to peer out the window as I heard the scraping of Daddy's house shoes against the linoleum floor—another bathroom visit before he lays down for the night.

It was this room and this bed I had slept in two weeks ago. The stickiness in the air was the same. I folded the cool sheet under my chin. Like tonight, the moon had been full and round, seductive in its dull glow. Stars were strewn across the sky in perfect adornment.

But that had been a time of celebration—of my family's camaraderie, of our lives and our pride in our accomplishments. For Jo Ann, it was the last reunion. This gathering bore no resemblance to the gathering two weeks earlier. Jo Ann had died. There had been no jokes bantered around the table between family members tonight. Daddy's young man's laughter was hidden somewhere deep inside, forgotten during this dark time. This time two weeks ago, Daddy was regaling his grandchildren and great-grandchildren with lively tales about his childhood, stories that kept them entranced for hours and him nostalgic as he remembered.

The coroner quietly told us what we already knew. Jo Ann had ended her life with the very medicine meant to make her life better. She had committed the one unforgivable sin.

I heard Daddy's bed groan as he tried to settle comfortably. Even with the lulling sounds of the country night and the familiar hum of Daddy's refrigerator, sleep refused to come. I moved the worn, white curtains aside again. This time a lightning bug had settled on the window. Snapshots of my childhood loomed before my eyes, and Jo Ann was in every frame. My eyes fluttered, and as sleep rescued me, I wondered how deep Jo Ann's pain must have been to make an unknown world more attractive than the one she shared with us. ℚ

— TWO —

Jo Ann's Final
Goodbye

The Kearney family's brightest star extinguished itself. Jo Ann was the brilliant one, the one with the blinding smile and quick wit. She was Daddy's girl with unmarred beauty—before the ravages of her illness wrestled away what made her stand out above the rest of us.

On her last return home, Jo Ann had brought with her a master's degree in psychology, an encore to another master's and two undergraduate degrees from as many different colleges. Yet, looking back, it is clear that the degrees were merely ways to prove herself to us and to herself and maybe a way to pass her time on this earth.

Jo Ann's transformation was parallel to changes in my own life. As her illness was settling itself into her brain and she was becoming unpredictable, I was becoming normal and predictable. Darryl, D.K. and I had finally left "the hill," as Fayetteville is often called, and moved to Little Rock where we lived quasi middle-class lives and worked at quasi enviable jobs. Darryl was personnel manager at the local office of Tyson Foods, and I was a member of the middle-management team at a state government office. For me, it was a good life.

My weekend trips back home were still the highlight of my week. I never tired of driving the 72 miles between Little Rock and Varner Road, of seeing my mother's smiling face or of eating her delicious Sunday dinners. On one Sunday visit, however, I would leave feeling as if I'd driven into a dust storm. What I saw that Sunday broke my heart into pieces, and it would never be the same again.

Finally, I was forced to confront the truth I'd pushed way back into the crevices of my mind for so many years. Jo Ann was home from her years in California. My older sister had taken Jo Ann to a bus and pleaded with the driver to keep her on until she made it to Arkansas.

I walked toward my parents' house trying to decide who the woman sitting on the porch might be. I tried out different neighbor's names in my head, but none quite fit. The woman smiled and seemed to look clear through me. "Hi, Faye. You finally made it down," she said.

As I began to respond, the woman's smile told me what my brain refused to accept. Jo Ann was home, except she was hardly Jo Ann at all. When we attempted a sisterly hug I found her roundness precluded me from it.

"Mama's been waiting for you," she offered, returning to her seat on the porch, smoking a cigarette, extinguishing it, then lighting the next one.

As I walked into the house I watched my sister and suddenly remembered the conversations Mama had with her children in California. They'd all been worried about Jo Ann, but no one had a handle on exactly what was wrong. What was wrong was that something or someone had taken my sister away and left this caricature of the beautiful girl that once was so full of life.

Jo Ann's mind and body were someone else's—a woman twice my sister's age and size and who, unlike the old Jo Ann, had no concern about her appearance or hygiene. "What have you done with my sister?" I wanted to scream.

That was the beginning. This new Jo Ann would be the norm, not the exception, over the next 10 years. It was clear she was taking some kind of medication, given her listlessness and silence. On the good days, my sister knew she was ill and tried being as normal as possible. On those other days, she made all of our lives a living hell. My aging parents couldn't say "no" when one of their children asked for help. They paid for it with failing health and discomfort in their own home during the years Jo Ann lived off and on with them.

Jo Ann finally agreed to let our brother Julius take her to Drew County mental health clinic 20 miles south of us for an in-service checkup. The clinic kept her for two days for monitoring purposes. Doctors advised keeping her there longer. They offered to monitor her and regulate her medicine over the next month. We were hopeful, but it was finally up to Jo Ann. After her two-day stay, my sister opted to return to our parents' home with the promise that she would take her medication religiously.

My mother would later tell me that she never imagined one of her children having a mental problem. Neither had I. None of us knew how to deal with a sibling, or a child, with such serious problems. It was more than that. We didn't know how to accept a member of the family being "less than...." It was especially hard to accept that someone like Jo Ann, our brightest star, would be a victim of mental illness. It scared us, made us question the community's view of us as a "model" black family. How could we be a model when everyone now knew our sister was crazy?

My mother, a 10-year survivor of breast cancer, had finally been able to stop worrying about raising children and helping her husband in the cotton fields. She had spent the last 10 years enjoying her life with Daddy and with their now-grown children. She'd traveled across the country to visit her children and when she wasn't traveling, she stayed busy with local organizations in her church and community.

It was during this golden era of Mama's life that Jo Ann came home and began a see-saw of dropping in when she was at her lowest and staying months before she was off again. It was during this stressful time in her life that my mother went in to see her doctor about an upset stomach and was diagnosed with metastasized stomach cancer. The two family tragedies at one time were more than most of us believed we could deal with. While we loved our sister, or the sister we remembered, we resented what her illness was doing to our family. Some of us angrily and illogically held our sister responsible for my mother's recurring cancer.

30

After the short stay in the Drew County clinic and a new rash of medicine, Jo Ann's illness abated for a number of months. During that time, we were able to talk her into moving into a subsidized apartment in Pine Bluff where a number of my siblings lived. Along with the disability check she was by now receiving, the family would pitch in to help pay for the apartment. Most important to me, unfortunately, was that Jo Ann live apart from our parents—in case she decided, again, to stop her medication. Reluctantly, my sister agreed to the move.

During the next year my sister's disease ebbed and flowed. For months she would return to her old self, go through newspaper ads to find job leads and quite often would ace the interviews. She would work for a few weeks, usually before the pressure of the structured job sent her reeling back into her illness. She'd lose the job, and with that, her illness would be re-ignited. It was a vicious cycle that we watched in horror, pity and shame.

After a time we realized Jo Ann was falling behind on her rent even though she was receiving enough aid to take care of her basic needs. We would learn later that her disability assistance money was going to total strangers she met on the street. She borrowed money from family for rent and food and gave her aid money away to those she decided needed it more than she did.

Though her illness could be controlled with medication, like most sick people, Jo Ann would only take the medication until it began to work, then talk herself into thinking she was well. She had moved to a subsidized apartment complex in Little Rock after she decided she no longer wanted to live in Pine Bluff. I saw my sister more often then—and sometimes it was almost as if our relationship was as it had been so many years ago—that is, except for the times when I thought I was dealing with a completely different person.

One such instance was the day her neighbor called in the middle of the day to tell me: "You need to get over here. Jo Ann is standing in the middle of the street holding court—butt naked." According to the woman, Jo Ann was cursing out half the passers-by and offering the other half anything of value she possessed.

Jo Ann sometimes stayed a night or weekend with me. Sometimes it was my choice, other times it was hers—times she just didn't want to sleep in her own apartment. "Is Darryl at home?" she'd ask. If I said yes, she'd go on to another topic. If I said no, she'd offer to spend the night. I rarely slept before the early mornings when my sister stayed over. She either stayed up talking all night or she was experiencing one of her bad nights and I was afraid to fall asleep.

My fear was not only for my safety and my son's safety but also for what my sister might do to herself. I'd spend the hours before I picked her up hiding sharp utensils, poisons and anything that I thought Jo Ann might use as a weapon against herself or others.

I had never experienced the kind of deep fear as the night I surprised myself by wrestling a bottle of peroxide out of my sister's hands or the bottle of liquor she told me "helped kill the crawling things inside me." If nothing else, I probably improved my defense techniques during the years of visits from my sister.

Jo Ann was more than mentally unstable. She was angry at the world and especially at her own family. I didn't understand the anger and wasn't sure if it was real or something that came out of delusions. I learned later that it was both. Now I know we all would have dealt better with Jo Ann's death if we'd asked more questions of the psychiatrist. But, truthfully, I wasn't dealing so well with what I did know at the time.

It was after a second night of having to restrain my sister from flying out of the house—butt naked, again—that I decided it was time for another visit to a professional. The after effects of the earlier assessment and pills were long gone. We all knew my sister acted crazy, but unless a doctor examined her and told her she was crazy she'd never believe it. I

32

began making plans the very next day to get her to visit the state mental health center.

Whether it was a matter of her going through the routine before or tiring out after fighting with me, Jo Ann was cordial, though quiet as I drove her to Little Rock's state clinic. We were both in an amazingly sisterly frame of mind. When the nurse came out to escort her back and to explain that my sister would be staying a few days for evaluation, Jo Ann was quiet. The woman turned to me.

"If we decide she needs to stay longer than three days, we'll recommend it, but it will be completely up to her at that point."

I knew the spiel but had no better understanding of the strange mental health logic. What a stupid policy, I was thinking as I waved to my nonresponsive sister. Leave it up to the loonies to decide whether they need further help! Couldn't they see what shape the woman was in? Why did they have psychological and psychiatric degrees if they couldn't make a simple decision to do what's best for the patient and the family. I didn't care that I was being selfish. I was angry at the system, angry at my sister for being crazy and angry at myself for not feeling more empathy.

As I finally walked to the door of the patients' ward, I looked around to see Jo Ann still standing at the door she was to go into. Her face was that of a young girl's, crestfallen and confused. I was convinced at that moment that my sister wasn't so much against staying at places like this as she was afraid of being lumped into a place like this with crazy people. I walked back and hugged her for a long time. For the first time in my life I told my sister how much I loved her. The tears appeared from nowhere, blurring my vision as the nurse escorted Jo Ann through the door and out of sight. I hoped I'd made the right decision.

During the drive back to my office that sat directly across from the State Capitol, I longed for Jo Ann's and my childhood. I wanted to replay the tape, do some things differently, better. These new tears wouldn't stop, and I knew they were selfish. I would never again have the Jo Ann of my childhood. Instead, I'd have to learn to love this new person—to accept her illness as a part of who she was.

The next day was a busy one at work, but I had promised Jo Ann I'd come to see her. I drove faster than I should, wanting to get my responsibility over and arrive back at the office before my lunch hour was up. I was in a terrible mood, realizing that the time I usually spent as my quiet time was usurped by my visit to the loony bin to see a sister who might not even want to see me.

I was sitting in the mental health center's waiting room scanning the outdated magazines when I heard the nurse speaking to someone. I looked up in time to see Jo Ann walk through the door. Except for the drab gown she wore, Jo Ann was magically transformed from the woman I'd left there less than 24 hours earlier. She looked more like the old Jo Ann that I had not seen for some time. The brilliant smile was even a shoo-in for Jo Ann's once beautiful smile. I decided the doctors here had obviously figured out what medicine worked best for my sister.

"How are you feeling, Jo Ann?" I asked, surprising myself with my about-face in emotions. "I'm fine...I feel fine," she answered before sitting next to me on the hard sofa. We talked for almost 30 minutes before I began shuffling my purse, then my feet, in preparation for my goodbye. "I know...you gotta get back to work, Faye. I'm glad you came." She stood first, hugging me like she really meant it this time.

As I walked back to the clerk's desk with her, Jo Ann said, "I think I want to stay until I'm better...I really want to get better. I don't want you to have to take care of me all the time. You have your own life." I blushed, hoping my earlier feelings hadn't been that obvious.

"You're thinking of staying longer than the 48 hours?" I asked.

She nodded, "I want to get better."

I hugged her and told her I was glad about her decision. "We all want you to be better, Jo Ann, and I promise to come see you every day or almost every day."

Before I left she asked for change for cigarettes and asked if I would take her key and bring her a list of items she needed from her apartment. I looked around and saw that most of the other patients smoked. An effort to get Jo Ann to stop smoking at this point in her life was a crazy idea. Cigarettes seemed to be as much a part of their therapy as the medicine they took every day. I dug in my purse and came out with five dollars.

"Thanks, Faye," she said. She waved and walked back through the door that took her to her temporary home.

I was surprised at how clear the day looked to me now, how much happier and lighter I felt. I was more hopeful than I had been in years.

Jo Ann's monthlong stay at the hospital was nearly over when her psychiatrist called me in for a talk. My brother Julius went with me. The doctor was a young black woman who I was convinced already knew the answers to the questions she asked us. She asked simple questions about Jo Ann, about our childhood and our relationship over the years. Then she asked if we had any questions. We asked about Jo Ann's medication and for more detail about her diagnosis.

"Jo Ann has been diagnosed as paranoid schizophrenic," she answered matter-of-factly. "It is a progressive mental illness that must be medicated for the patient to function as a normal person. It gets progressively worse with age."

She told us there is usually few signs of the illness in youth, and we should have begun noticing small changes in Jo Ann's personality in her late teens to early twenties. I nodded, realizing that the strange behavior that worried me about Jo Ann during our early college years was likely the precursor to what we saw now. Before leaving the woman's office, the doctor made it clear there was no cure for Jo Ann's kind of mental illness, just a lifetime of medication.

"If there's anything you can help with, it's encouraging her to stay on her medication regime," the doctor suggested. "When she stops, she'll revert to illness, the way she was when you brought her here—or worse."

Fear works wonders. I promised I would do my best to help assure Jo Ann stayed on her pills. Before we left, the doctor touched on family responsibility and convinced us that family members have no responsibility in Jo Ann's illness.

"It's a chemical imbalance and has little or nothing to do with her family life. Doctors and scientists are still learning things about the human brain. We all hope one day to discover a way to prevent or eradicate diseases such as this." She said guilt by family members was normal but cautioned us that it was nonproductive. "You can't help Jo Ann if you don't take care of yourselves," she said.

After leaving the care of the mental health clinic, Jo Ann was almost normal for months. We rekindled our friendship. I often visited her at the two or three different apartments she lived in. She never seemed to settle down in one place very long. I also met a number of her new friends, all of whom tended to be struggling with one type of mental illness or another. They seemed to be leading fairly normal lives in spite of that.

Just as I began to feel that Jo Ann was almost back to normal, the inevitable happened. The medical explanation was simple. She had been doing so well; she'd decided she didn't need to continue taking her medication. That was hard for me to accept after spending so much time with Jo Ann, talking about her illness and listening to her swearing to remember that her pills were the only way she'd remain normal.

It was harder than any of us realized, I imagine, trying so hard to be sane. I was convinced my sister simply gave up. When it happened, I was at a new job as director of information for the state Department of Migrant Education. I loved my new job and was intent on impressing my new colleagues with my work. I was not very happy when the signs began that Jo Ann's illness was reasserting itself and that I'd likely be needed for regular babysitting duty soon.

My job included some travel, but even during my travel one part of my mind remained on Jo Ann. How was she doing? Was she doing some ridiculous thing that the whole world would learn about? Would I return to find her in worse shape than last time? I worried about my sister, certainly, but I was also worrying about my own little comfortable life.

Most days we talked on the phone at least once. I visited on weekends and sometimes during the week. On her good days, I breathed a sigh of relief that we could talk amicably. On her bad days, I might have to leave work to check on her, sometimes taking her to my home until she was okay again.

Finally, I breathed a sigh of relief when it seemed she was taking her medication again. There were times when the years and pain inside those years melted away for Jo Ann and me. We enjoyed laughing and joking about our days on Varner Road. She still spoiled D.K., bringing him too many gifts and treating him like a pal rather than a child.

During the times Jo Ann was not doing well, I tried to explain to my son as much as I could. "Your aunt's just not feeling like herself today. She needs to take her medicine, and she'll be fine." In his eyes, she was still his beloved "Aunt Jo," and I truly wanted it to stay that way.

Even with the logical explanation from the doctor, I often lay awake at night with questions rolling around in my head. How in the world did something like this happen to us? I knew what the doctor had to say about it, but still. Why couldn't we see it coming? At least we would have had time to prepare, to read up on it. Our parents had tried so hard to teach us how to survive in a harsh world, but those teachings hadn't prepared us for surviving a mentally ill sister.

Jo Ann was a living, breathing defect within the system. The Kearney family didn't know how to handle a real defect because we never acknowledged defects. We weren't equipped individually or as a family to admit that we were only human—that we were like other families with problems. If we were, then how could we explain what it was that got us from where we were to where we all had come in our lives? Ours had been a life of miracles, and mental illness didn't fit into miracles.

Though we all accepted the explanation for Jo Ann's problem, none of us wanted to own it. It would be years before any of us could discuss Jo Ann's craziness around people who weren't a member of our closed family. Mostly, I decided, we were afraid to believe that it could happen to any one of us. We had to admit helplessness—that we weren't smart enough to save someone we loved so much.

By the last weekend of July 1987, just two weeks after the Kearneys' 16th family reunion, Jo Ann had moved again, this time to a retirement center in North Little Rock. How she found it or came up with the money to pay for it, I didn't know. I'd always suspected Jo Ann was a miser who hid money away for rainy days. I simply couldn't imagine how she did it, given all the dark days in her life.

On that Saturday night, she called from her new apartment to invite me over and to ask that I loan her money. I told Jo Ann I didn't have it but that if it looked as if I could help her next week I would "see what I could do."

She didn't like that answer very much. What started out quietly rose to a crescendo of cursing and ranting about me, then the entire family. It had been a long day, and I wasn't up to listening to Jo Ann's usual berating of the Kearney family. When I said as much, she retorted, "I'll just call somebody else. I don't know why I even talk to anybody in this family—you're all a bunch of hypocrites anyway!" She slammed the phone down in my ear, and I decided that must mean the invitation to see her apartment was no longer there. I sat shaken for a while. But more than anything I was exasperated with my sister's on-again, off-again love for our family. "She's sick, Janis, she's sick," I told myself, forcing calmness.

On Monday, I called my younger brother, Jerome, at the state attorney general's office where he worked as an assistant attorney general. "Hey, have you talked to Jo Ann? Did she call you over the weekend?" I inquired. My brother chuckled and said he was lucky to have escaped her wrath for a whole two days.

I laughed and told him about our conversation on Saturday night. I noticed that he was half whispering, the same as I was. We were both afraid others would learn we had a crazy sister. "I expect she'll call in a little while," I said, lightly, before ending our conversation and returning to my work.

By noon, I checked with the receptionist to see if I'd missed a call from Jo Ann. I hadn't. I was feeling guilty by then. Maybe I should have taken a few dollars over and checked out her new apartment. I would assuage my guilt by taking over some money during lunch, I decided. I went through my purse counting the spare dollars I had. I put a 10-dollar bill inside a business envelope, then called Jo Ann to tell her I was coming over.

I had tried calling her several times when a feeling I couldn't shake crawled over my skin. I called Jerome again and asked if he'd heard from Jo Ann today. He sounded busy but said, "No." I told him I was a little worried. "She always calls me at least once during the day...whatever." He said maybe he'd try calling her in a little while. I tried again after hanging up with Jerome. No answer.

I took a deep sigh and called Jerome again.

"I know this is crazy, but can you pick me up at my office and drive to Jo Ann's apartment?" I could tell he didn't want to, but he didn't say so.

"Why now? She's probably sleep or something. Why don't you wait until later?" he suggested.

I couldn't wait, I told him. Something told me we needed to go right now. He thought I was overreacting but reluctantly agreed to pick me up. On our drive to the apartment, we talked and joked about our childhood, remembering what a tattler Jo Ann always was. I laughed half-heartedly but found it difficult to carry on the simple conversation. My hands were already feeling sweaty, and I was having even stronger sensations of panic.

I had called the apartment manager before leaving the office and asked her if she'd seen my sister. She had sounded disinterested but said, "No, not this morning." I went on to say that my sister called me every day, and I was worried that she may be sick. "The fact that I haven't heard from her tells me something is wrong," I said. I imagined the woman rolling her eyes and shaking her head.

"Well, if you insist, Miss Kearney, you can come by the office, and we'll go by her apartment to check on her."

Jo Ann had only lived at the newly built retirement complex a few days. As we drove to the well-manicured apartment complex, I wondered how she felt about living in a place built for old, retired people. She always had such strong opinions about just about everything. When I arrived at the office, I was amazed that the complex manager looked exactly like she sounded over the phone. She was tall with white hair and sharp features. She stood impatiently waiting in her office. Hardly offering a greeting, she guided Jerome and me through the walkways leading to Jo Ann's apartment.

When we arrived at apartment 203-B, the manager who was so brusque over the phone looked nervously at me now. She knocked on the door a few times, then spoke in a much louder voice, "Miss Kearney...Miss Kearney, you in there?" She looked at us, waiting for some response or directions. She shrugged and looked back at me.

I called out Jo Ann's name twice with no response. We both expelled a deep breath at the same time. I looked over at Jerome, who nodded for us to go in. "You can open the door," he suggested. As she did, I could feel a whoosh of cold air rush past us. Jo Ann always preferred cold temperatures and constantly stayed on me to turn my heat down, complaining, "It's unhealthy for people to sleep in that kind of heat." I stood there for a few seconds, and suddenly I knew what I would find.

I walked slowly around the small apartment's living room and kitchen, knowing I didn't need to hurry now. Jo Ann's apartment was immaculate, everything in its place. The bed was made up with a colorful bedspread—not a wrinkle in sight. The dishes and utensils in the kitchen were all neatly placed, and the floors were spotless.

As I walked into the bathroom, I saw the first thing in the house that was out of place. Jo Ann was half kneeling, half lying beside the oversized bathtub. The coroner would tell us later that she had been there, likely in that position, most of the weekend and that she died after taking a lethal concoction of medications.

"I'd say she's been dead two, maybe three days," the coroner would say just hours after we found Jo Ann. That would mean she might have died shortly after speaking with me or the morning after she spoke to me. I looked over at Jerome, but for the life of me I can't recall what his response was or the look on his face. I was likely the last person to talk with her, and that last conversation had been one of anger.

I don't remember even if we exchanged words, and I'm not surprised. Since I was a child, I had been able to immediately erase events that caused me pain or were too horrific to bear. My memory would automatically erase the ugliness of my life. I don't recall who called the coroner's office and got the ambulance there.

I sat dazed, outside myself, in the coroner's lobby with Jerome as we waited for the coroner's report. The tall, white man walked out of the closed door and asked if we would come in and identify Jo Ann. I don't recall Jerome walking in with me, so I might have gone in alone.

The bloated body lying on the coroner's table will not erase itself from my memory. In fact, it comes and goes at will. As I stared down at the woman who looked as if she was in a deep sleep, I tried to remember my beautiful sister with the blinding smile and the electric, vibrant personality. I looked up at the coroner and realized that I had to tell this man that the dead woman was indeed Jo Ann. ℚ

PART II

Life's Lessons in Black and White

(1958-1963)

THREE

Remembering When

As much as I've tried over the years, I can recall little about my childhood before the age of five. At times, I've wondered if something strange or hurtful happened during that period to make me purposefully forget. In truth, my life, for as far back as my mind will take me, has been an amalgamation of good and bad experiences—reality combined with something akin to dreams.

My memories of growing up on Varner Road evoke a myriad of emotions and responses. While many bring smiles and happiness, others bring feelings of nostalgia. Still others, in truth, evoke tears of regret. My earliest and only recollection of my toddler years is one that brings with it sadness. As if it happened yesterday, I remember the one instance that is stuck in my memory—the old tin pan that held hot coals and sat on the floor at the head of my parents' bed.

I still shudder to remember how the pan sat there through the night, both to warm the space where my parents slept and to serve as my father's ash tray and spittoon. I was no more than two or three years old at the time, still young enough to lie with Mama in bed in the early mornings when the rest of the family had left for work in the fields or gone off to school.

I have re-created that morning many times and imagined my mother in a hurry, leaving me lying in the middle of the bed wrapped in layers of sheets and quilts. Somehow, I must have been playfully rolling or scooting to the edge of my parents' bed. I might very well have let out a childish giggle as I toppled off the bed's edge until I landed in Daddy's tin pan of coals. Surely I toppled onto my side or my bottom in a seated position atop the burning coals.

Even now, I stare at the dark, blotchy scar on my hip and imagine the burning red embers and the pain. I wonder if it was Mama who ran into their bedroom from the kitchen or the clothes line or her children's room and grabbed me up from the burning coals, shushing my wails and attending the burned flesh. That is not a memory my parents and I have shared.

A memory that brings smiles is the day I turned five years old. It was September 29, 1958. On that day, my mother baked my first and only birthday cake. "You're five years old today, Faye," Mama said that day, using my middle name and nickname that all my family used. When Mama was happiest, her smile was wide and crinkles would form in the corners of her deep-set, hazel eyes.

"Would you like me to make you your very own birthday cake?" She asked this as if baking her child a birthday cake was as common as baking biscuits for breakfast, and I'm sure my heart leaped as I shook my head up and down.

Few Kearney children could claim such a treat—something as personal as a birthday cake. This was an unusual event in our home. Mama might have as many as 12 children underfoot at one time. She loved her children with all her heart but simply had neither the resources nor the time to bake individual birthday cakes for the houseful of children. At five years old, I was convinced that I was her special child...special enough to warrant a giant smile from Mama and a birthday cake.

While the buttery aroma of Mama's cake drifted through the house, I dragged one of her straw-bottom sitting chairs to the only full-length mirror in the house. I scrambled quickly upon the seat and looked at my five-year-old self. I had never seen a full view of myself before and was filled with awe and interest. The first thing I thought was, "I'm not very big." I had for some reason imagined myself bigger, taller.

Who was this small person with the round, paper-sack brown face, pouting lips and huge doe eyes? I touched the thick, coarse pair of braids brushing against my shoulders and remembered my older sister's impatience when she plaited my hair the day before. There must have been a myriad of other small details about five-year-old me, but I don't remember them—not even what I wore on the most wonderful birthday of my life.

As I grew older, snatches of memories presented themselves to me. I remembered things as I sat alone in a crowded room, still too shy to strike up a conversation; or as I played with my own child, my heart almost bursting with love; or during the dreamlike days I spent with my mother after I learned she was dying. Sketches of that young girl have appeared in my dreams, too, and sometimes I picture her during sleeplike moments. Some days, in fact, I am that little girl with the unsmiling face, quietly waiting and anticipating dreams to come true.

Growing up, I rarely slept when Mama directed her children to "get to bed and get to sleep—now!" I couldn't. I lived in morbid fear of the recurring nightmare Mama called a "witch riding your dreams." It began when I was no more than six or seven years old and continued throughout adolescence.

In the mornings, after just a few hours of sleep that ended with the witch riding my dreams, I'd rush breathlessly and horrified into the kitchen to tell Mama about the hellish experience. Mama would sigh and look quietly over at me as she rolled biscuit dough or stirred eggs or turned thick bacon strips. Then she would offer me a sympathetic smile.

"It's just that old witch riding your dreams, Faye. It's nothing to worry about."

Sometimes Jo Ann would stand watching from the corner, snickering. Mama often scolded her, "You stop it, Jo Ann," before my sister scurried back into the bedroom we shared, still grinning.

47

"It's nothing. You'll grow out of it," Mama assured me. Eventually I did grow out of it, after countless horror-filled nights.

Like all of the Kearney children, I was reserved and shy. My parents made it clear that their children were to be seen but not heard. Silence around adults was common. I talked to my sisters and brothers, and there were a few friends at school or on the school bus with whom I felt comfortable enough to carry on a conversation. But I never came very far outside my shell. Mostly I preferred conversing in my head with myself or with Jo Ann when we were getting along.

Daydreams took up much of my spare time, day and night. The black walnut tree in our back yard was the site of much of my daydreaming. When I couldn't fall asleep and the house had finally quieted, I would often steal outside. Tiptoeing with socks on in the winter or with bare feet in the summer and spring, I was careful not to let the screen door slam shut as I slipped out onto dew-drenched grass.

My love-hate relationship with the night began during that time when I began to experience a sense of safety in the darkness that embraced me. Perched under the walnut tree until my eyes began to droop, I would dream about the world around me and the world I imagined would be mine someday. There was something magical about how the moon and the darkness transformed my realities into something of beauty and possibility.

———

Until I was seven, my life pretty much mirrored that of other poor children I knew. In 1960, things changed dramatically when I was inducted into the world of Daddy's cotton field. At seven, I became one more field hand responsible for helping my father produce his yearly cotton crops. Like my siblings, I entered into an unwritten 10-year service contract that ended when a child graduated from high school and went on to college or started a life independent of the Kearney household.

My seventh summer was the same one in which my mother began patiently teaching me how to care for my baby brother, Jeffrey. Two years later, I learned the rudiments of cooking for my family. Breakfast usually consisted of toast and oatmeal or rice; and for many years dinner was meatloaf, cornbread and macaroni with tomato paste and potatoes. Dessert was pineapple upside-down cake. My brothers hated the days they came home and found me in the kitchen.

Without ceremony, one morning early in the summer, Mama paused in her sewing, looked over at me and said, "Well, Faye, your daddy thinks it's time you started going to the fields with the rest of 'em. Tomorrow, you'll need to get up with your brothers."

More than anything except dreaming, I liked spending summer days with Mama, watching her go through her unhurried day, feeling warmth and softness emanate from her curving body. But in the Kearney household, enjoyment of one's days was an extra. Like my brothers and sisters, I had a responsibility to contribute to the household, and the cotton field was how we made our contributions. There was a certain excitement about all of this—an anxiety about joining my older siblings leaving home early on summer mornings and returning late in the evenings. I anticipated joining them as they sat down together for breakfast in the mornings, and I looked forward to participating in the jokes and laughter that filled the air after their day in the cotton field. I was convinced it was something about their day in the field that produced such joy.

On my first day as a field hand I woke early. Hurrying to the front room, I heard my parents' voices and found Daddy already dressed, ready for the day's work. He looked over at me and smiled, continuing to sip his morning coffee.

"You ready to chop some cotton this morning?"

I smiled back and said, "Yeah, do I have my own hoe?"

My father nodded and said I did. Without knowing what the term meant, somewhere in the recesses of my being I understood that I was undertaking a rite of passage. After anxiously eating breakfast with the rest of the family, I heard Daddy hollering my name from the back yard. Mama smiled at me and nodded for me to go on out back.

Smiling, my father held a child's version of a chopping hoe. "Hold it and see how it fits. I might need to shave off some of the handle to make it fit."

I shyly took the hoe, holding it the way Daddy showed me. The shortened handle was of light, shaved wood with a brightly shining blade at the end.

"There you go, it's all yours," he announced. He looked up at the house and took a last few draws of a Pall Mall cigarette before throwing the butt into the chicken coop. "We'll be ready to go in a minute," he told me. "Just stand the hoe upside the chicken coop there 'til we ready to leave."

As I waited anxiously for the day to start, my siblings walked out to the back yard, claiming their individual chopping hoes. They all gave me either a giggle or a smile. One or two told harmless jokes about this new turn in my life. As they started down the gravel road toward the cotton field, I followed. I walked fast, taking long steps to keep up with them as we trekked the half-mile to the field.

"All right..." Daddy offered. I waited, looking from one brother to the next.

"Do we have to chop all this cotton today, Daddy?" I asked, looking down the long cotton rows that stretched as far as I could see.

"No, Faye. We just chop until it's time to go home. Wherever we stop is where we start the next day."

I was relieved. Daddy was grinning and shaking his head as he finished the last cigarette of the morning.

"Just watch the boys this morning until you feel you know what you doing," Daddy said, then motioned for me to pay attention for a minute.

Daddy crouched down on the ground beside the small plants and pointed out which plants were weeds and which was cotton.

"You want to chop all the weeds down with your hoe. The blade is sharp so you can cut it easily. Be careful not to cut yourself though."

He pulled up the weeds, leaving one small plant standing alone. As he threw the weeds down, he looked up at me. "This here is what the cotton plant looks like." He held the plant delicately between his fingers. "You don't ever want to chop down a cotton plant 'cause that's what grows and turns into the cotton we take to the gin in the winter."

I nodded. I knew Daddy took wagons loaded with fluffy white cotton to the gin and came back with groceries and money. I followed his directions and watched my older brothers at work for a few minutes, but then decided I could do it by myself. "I think I know how to do it, now." Daddy nodded but told me to just help Don with his row until noontime.

By quitting time that evening, I had earned my stripes, chopping several rows of cotton all by myself. The reality of what my days would be like was fast setting in. The sun's relentless heat and glare, now directly overhead, began to burn through my thick plaits and into my scalp. Daddy's ragged old shirt had been wet with sweat, then dried by the hot sun more than once that day. The sun was unrelenting—the only reprieve being the few clouds that passed under it, offering us moments of shade throughout the day.

To get through the summers I spent in Daddy's cotton fields, I learned the trick of transposing myself to another place and time as I worked. In my mind, I might be anywhere other than the cotton field. These moments of daydreaming helped me make it through the worst days of summer. In later years when my siblings spoke with a deep hate of those summers, I'd smile and shrug, saying, "They really weren't that bad." None of them understood.

D addy leased 45 acres of cotton, 10 acres of soybeans and two acres of land for a truck patch, or vegetable garden, from a white landowner. This was during the late 1950s and early 1960s, when cotton was indeed king in southern Arkansas. White landowners and black farmers, sharecroppers and day workers existed in a state of total interdependence. Prosperous landowners rented their land to sharecroppers like my father in exchange for credit for seeds and farm equipment and a yearly mortgage. These landowners also took advantage of black families' poverty and need for work by hiring them out as day workers and laborers at embarrassingly low wages for the jobs white workers wouldn't do.

These mostly black day workers were responsible for the many profitable crops these farmers produced. They were responsible for sowing, plowing, tilling, chopping and picking the products that made life for the landowners so much different from blacks' meager existence. The only role black day workers weren't saddled with was crop-dusting—using a small plane to spray the cotton and soybean crops with pesticides. That task was left to white men who owned their own farms and crop-dusted other farms on contract.

The world of cotton tied southern blacks and whites together in a way that nothing else could. Regardless of the history of racial separation that placed us on different sides of the social tracks when it came to school, church and, for the most part, personal relationships, black and white southerners during the preindustrial era and after could not survive without each other.

The cotton season was really three seasons. Springtime was for planting—the most important phase of farming for large farmers. Summertime was reserved for cotton chopping, critical to the economic well-being of black sharecroppers, day workers and field hands that often depended on this period of work. The fall was when we picked and ginned the invaluable white stuff.

For most of the years I worked in my father's cotton fields, autumn's success depended almost completely on the manual labor of field hands, itinerant workers and sharecroppers like the Kearney family. In fact, cotton picking was the most crucial link in the whole cotton farming process—for the farmers large and small, for sharecroppers like our family and for hired workers.

Cotton-picking season brought about a deep divide in the Kearney home. James and Ethel Kearney were in constant disagreement about their children and cotton picking. Ethel argued that her children's education was just as important as her husband's cotton. My father argued that he wanted his children educated but that during the first quarter of fall, school interfered with his cotton crop, and he couldn't afford to let it. "School won't put one crumb of food on this table, Ethel—cotton will," Daddy argued.

For Mama, the fight was personal. She was denied a high school education because she was a girl and wasn't allowed to travel to the next town to attend school. Ethel, more than any of her eight siblings, loved learning and was an excellent student. She had promised herself early on that she wouldn't make the same mistake her parents made. "You worry more about that cotton crop than our children's futures," she told her husband.

Daddy believed God blessed him with highly intelligent children for a reason, and he would recognize that blessing by making sure we grew up loving to learn. At the same time, he knew God understood about his cotton crop and his need to take care of his family's basic needs. To do that, he had to keep his children out of school during the first quarter. To assuage Mama's fears that we would fall behind, he made sure we were reading, writing and counting before we set foot in a school house. He would be our home tutor, but he couldn't turn his back on what had to be done to harvest his cotton crops. His children were his only assurance of that livelihood. Some of my brothers and even a couple of my sisters could pick as much as 300 pounds of cotton a day. There was no way Daddy could be assured of many bales of cotton without our help.

Both of my parents won, in a way. Though Daddy kept some of us out of school the full quarter, most of us went right to the top of our classes when we did attend-thanks to his home schooling. Most of us graduated at the top of our classes or as honor students. The "raggedy-ass Kearney children without a pot to piss in" were a mystery to the teachers and students at Fields schools. They could never figure out how we were able to excel academically in spite of our dire existence and missing so much of school.

During my 10 years as a part-time field hand, I witnessed the metamorphosis of the cotton industry. Manual labor, formerly so important to cotton production, almost disappeared in the late 1960s. Poisons and insecticides were used more widely by large farmers. It successfully killed off grass and weeds better than a chopping hoe's sharp blade ever could.

Monstrous cotton-picking machines took over the jobs that had, for decades, fed and clothed the families of black day workers and field hands. I saw the good and bad of progress. The changing cotton industry fueled a change in the economy. Black and white families suffered the loss of jobs and income. Gould's population, less than 2,000 at its peak, continued to dwindle as cotton's stature continued to diminish.

Even as changes were happening across the South, James Kearney continued to depend on his cotton crops to put food on his table, and he continued to depend on his children to bring in the cotton crops. For small farmers and sharecroppers such as James, the new mechanization boom would pass them by. They weren't given the option of no longer needing their children's labor. They could not afford the machinery, poisons and pesticides to reap their crops without touching a hoe or pulling cotton from its boll by hand.

Compensation became pitifully low for hard-earned bales of cotton.

There were many winters when our cupboards were nearly bare, and my large family lived from hand to mouth. Some winters one meal a day was the norm and rarely were we lucky enough to have a nickel or dime for lunch money to take to school.

My love-hate relationship with my life on Varner Road and my father's dependence on cotton deepened during those times. My family's happiness or unhappiness was directly related to the success or failure of Daddy's cotton crops. Because of that, my memories of Varner Road and the endless rows of the soft, beautiful cotton are inextricably tied. ℚ

Four

Living and Learning
the Rules

The year I turned 10 was a year of revelations and hard lessons that somehow made the thick yellow line between black and white America more real for me. The events during the anniversary of my 10 years on earth left me wiser and less innocent.

In 1963, America's South was just rounding the bend of the civil rights struggle. The next few years would be full of fits and starts. Black America's struggle for equality and white America's struggle to not fix what they believed wasn't broken left deep scars and irrevocable chasms across our flat, cotton-laden horizon. Americans, black and white, watched as this giant of a country, attempted to right itself after decades of simply doing what giants do—trampling the little ones outside the periphery of their vision.

In fairness to the many good-hearted whites and courageous blacks, the 1960s was a time of amazing progress and sorrowful retractions to that progress. There were large and small victories in towns such as Gould, Arkansas, oftentimes at far too high a price.

Little Rock, our state capital, just 72 miles north, turned famous overnight when nine black children integrated the all-white Central High School, changing the meaning of "education for all" in America's South.

The integration crisis at Central High was South Dixie baring its naked bottom to the world—exhibiting all our ugly stretch marks, bumps and sags of hate, racism and prejudice. The great lesson for the rest of the world was America's racial truths, and the truths during that time were a deeply ingrained racial divide in America. Black children for no reason other than the color of their skin were not welcome into white schools.

But southeast Arkansas, like the rest of America, was part of a wave that wouldn't be stopped. We were on the cusp of change, albeit a slow and stubborn change that was like Daddy's mule, Bessie, which he used for years to plow his crops before he could afford the John Deere tractor. Most whites in Arkansas, it seemed, were doing all in their power to turn back the hands of time—a time when blacks knew their place and feared change as much as whites clung to it. But, like a roiling river loosened without a dyke, change came, and the dirt poor sharecropping family of James and Ethel Kearney, like the white farmers and their families, were caught up in the middle of that change.

In November 1963, in the middle of America's tattered transformation, my parents, like every other black and white family in Lincoln County, questioned God's reasoning when he took the nation's dreamer, John F. Kennedy, away. Grown-ups feared for America's future; and children, for that moment at least, were confused by our parents' floundering in the wake of the white man's death. President Kennedy's death, in fact, meant as much to black Arkansans as the death of a parent or a much-valued grandparent.

Even though we were all affected by the death of this president, grieving for people outside our family and certainly for virtual strangers—even this familiar president—was something new and foreign to the Kearney children. Witnessing my usually stoic parents' open expressions of grief taught us what words couldn't—that John F. Kennedy evoked a rare hope in America. For James and Ethel Kearney, President Kennedy's death threatened that fragile hope.

I was in fifth grade at Fields Elementary when President Kennedy died. On the morning of his death, I was enjoying morning recess along with the rest of Miss Berba Brown's 29 black students. When the school bell rang halfway through our recess period, we all turned, looking for our teacher and an explanation. She was standing with another teacher, their bodies turned away from the students, sobbing.

The women parted, each walking toward their respective classes.

The tall, well-dressed Miss Brown signaled with her long arms and admonished in her usual high-pitched voice, "Quiet, students...we have an important announcement." The teacher's reserved manner was always calming for us 10-year-olds. We were suddenly as quiet as church mice. At least part of the children's discipline could be attributed simply to the times in southern history when children were blindly obedient to adults, and especially teachers.

Miss Brown stood still for a moment, except for her eyes, as she scoured the yard for stray students before she resumed speaking, now in a more somber voice. "I want you all to bow your heads for one minute and pray quietly...for our president...President Kennedy has been shot and may have been killed."

Each of our 29 heads-close-cropped, ponytails, plaits, cold-pressed curls-jerked up in unison followed by the sound of bewildered gasps. Tears began to stream down our young faces, as some semblance of realization set in.

"Let's pray, quietly, students," Miss Brown almost whispered, dabbing lightly at her own stream of tears.

As our heads rose from prayer, so did our whispering conversations. "Children, decorum...please! The principal has announced that school will be dismissed as soon as possible. The buses will be lining up in front of the school. I want you to go in quietly, get your belongings, clean your desks; and those of you who ride the bus should form a line and walk to the front of the school and wait for it to arrive. The rest of you are excused to go home. I will see you all in the morning."

Jo Ann and I stood together, speechless. We both still had tears standing in the corners of our eyes but were too embarrassed to openly swipe them away. "You think Mama and Daddy know?" was all I could think to ask. Jo Ann shrugged her shoulders and frowned lightly as if it was a question that demanded no response. My older siblings, already standing in line to board Varner Road's bus, waved for us to come up. No one cared today that we were breaking line to be near our older sisters. The Varner Road bus was quiet—the quietest I remembered since I started riding it in 1959. No one, it seemed, was up for conversations or knew how to express what we were feeling.

What we found when we all arrived home in the early afternoon was an anomaly in the Kearney home—James and Ethel Kearney sitting quietly in front of the television in the middle of the afternoon. I'd rarely seen my father sit at all during the day, and my mother would, any other day, be busy in the kitchen with our dinner. But there they sat, impassive, motionless in front of our small black-and-white television set. I wanted to ask Daddy what the president's death meant for us and for the world.

Mama shook her head from side to side, unable to stave her tears and daring not take her eyes from the newscaster's face or the news clips of the president and Mrs. Kennedy's famous motorcade ride down the Dallas street with Texas Governor and Mrs. John Connally. The horror of this death could be measured in my parents' openly grieving before their children. Except for the times of illness or childbirth, it was the first and only time my mother excused herself from preparing dinner for her family as we arrived home from school.

During the brief news break, she turned to one of my older sisters, "Go in the kitchen, Joyce, and find something to fix for these children." The amazing fact was that the Kearney children had relegated dinner to the back of our minds this evening. Mostly, we went through the evening in silence, few words passing among us as we watched David Brinkley, Chet Huntley and other newscasters discuss the traumatic events.

None of us noticed the time, and our parents either forgot or decided against hurrying us off to bed before nine o'clock.

In hindsight, Daddy must have decided this was an event that we all should "pay attention to" to help us along in life. Kearney children were strewn throughout the small living room. The crackling of burning wood inside the round, black heater sitting in the middle of the floor was the only sound except the newsmen's attempt at a monotone as they reported on the president's death. ℚ

FIVE

Indian Summers
on Varner Road

Mother Nature seemed indecisive that August in 1963 about whether she should amble into fall or extend the wretched heat of summer. Throughout the month, the sweltering heat and unrelenting glare of the sun made walking or working outside an exercise in misery. The heavy, still humidity dulled the world into a suffocating quiet. Even the small creatures seemed slighted by nature that year. The birds' summer songs were muted. The bees, butterflies and hummingbirds hid from the horrible heat and sun, and even Daddy's fun-seeking yard dogs lay beneath the porch, not a playful bone in evidence.

In spite of the heat, Mama had banished me from the cool comfort of the living room fan where I lay rereading *Uncle Tom's Cabin*—an end-of-school gift from my fourth-grade teacher—for the fifth time.

"Faye, I need you to pick that last batch of corn from that field before it all completely dry up and we can't eat it," Mama said, interrupting my temporary escape from reality. "If we don't pull it now, that corn won't be fit for the cows and hogs."

Though it was unheard of to question the wisdom of a parent's decision, my heart sank at the thought of the blistering heat and the drudgery of the chore.

After donning long pants and one of Daddy's throwaway shirts, I grabbed the 10-gallon tub Mama directed me to and headed for the cornfield, just feet from our home. The field was thick with tall, yellow-green corn stalks abundant with ears of corn. The cornfield made up half of the one-acre truck patch planted around our home.

"Start over there by the barn and come back this way," Mama had said, convinced it made more sense that way.

I sat quiet and still between the rows of corn for a while. Already, small beads of sweat were forming on my forehead, beginning their descent down my face. Within minutes Daddy's shirt was damp with cool sweat, even as the warm, faint wind blew across my face teasing me with the coming of fall.

I sighed, knowing that pulling the corn was just one part of a two-part process. I'd spend the next day helping Mama shuck, wash and blanch the corn kernels before filling plastic bags with the sweet-smelling kernels and packing the bags into the deep freezer for our cold and rainy winter days. All that wasn't frozen was either stored in the barn as animal feed or soaked in lye for hominy that Mama would cook outside in the huge cast-iron, boiling pot—which we used for everything from scalding hogs to bleaching clothes to frying cracklings and fish.

I shuffled lazily down the row, my mouth poked out, expressing weak anger at my mother's decision and at Jo Ann's not being there to help. I dragged the 10-gallon tub behind me, stopping at the end of the first row. I exhibited my disdain for the chore by pulling the almost-dried corn from their stalks as slowly as possible and tossing the ears callously into the tub. By the time I made it to the middle of the row, the tub was half full and felt tons heavier. I realized the foolishness of wasting energy on being angry—the sooner I finished my chore the sooner I could return to the window fan and *Uncle Tom's Cabin,* which I had hidden away under my mattress.

On most days, I was happy to spend hours all alone. Those were special times when I could travel to the place I most enjoyed—my dream world. I constantly sought ways and places to be alone, but this wasn't one of those times. I would have been happy to share my space and this chore with Jo Ann or another of my siblings.

The new school year was just around the corner; and just like every other year, I was excited to know that in less than a month we would be students again. August was second only to Christmas in joyous anticipation for the Kearney children. It represented the countdown to the beginning of learning again. We spent our August nights imagining what the new school year would be like, what new friends we'd make, who our new teacher might be, and, most important, what new things we'd learn.

In less than three weeks, our days would change from cotton fields, house work and farm chores to school work, chores and house work. We would hurry out to Mr. Hall's long, yellow school bus for the hour-long ride down Varner Road. He would pick up more than 50 children during his various stops—Mt. Moriah, Dark Corner, Nichols Road—before arriving at Fields school.

Our teachers always passed out our text books during our first or second day of class, leaving them to our safekeeping until the end of the year. We'd scribble our names in the front cover, beneath the lines that already had names of older black students or white students from across the track.

Though we knew our books were secondhand, they also represented the importance Daddy placed on dreams. "Books are like gold to the colored man. Reading lets us dream whatever world we want." Daddy believed the one thing no one could take from us was the knowledge we gained from books and learning.

As I moved slowly down the row of corn that August, the thought that the world of learning was just days away overshadowed the anger still lingering about the heat or the chore.

"Don't forget to separate the corn already gone hard, Faye, so we can store it in the barn for the cows and hogs," Daddy yelled, his keys jingling in his pants pocket as he hurried to his car. I sighed as I heard the door to the station wagon close and the whir of the engine as Daddy started the car.

When I heard the gravel grind under Daddy's car tires behind me, I sighed again, knowing that I could now daydream as much as I wanted to. Mama's small voice interrupted my first dream. She stuck her head through Daddy's car window.

"I left some beans on the stove, Faye. Check on them in about 30 minutes and make sure there's water still in the pot....And don't take all day out there. Get your head out of the clouds and get that work done before you have a heat stroke."

I was glad Mama couldn't see me shake my head and frown. I waved and watched the station wagon waddle slowly down the gravel road. I was soon humming the Supremes' "Stop in the Name of Love." I didn't know all the words because my parents didn't allow blues music in the house. I swayed to my own voice as I pulled a silky corn ear from the stalk and began caressing it. Jo Ann and I had perfected the art of styling the silklike hair that clung to the corn, sometimes spending hours combing, plaiting and curling the silky stuff, even naming the corn dolls for names we'd heard on TV.

I heard a truck speeding down the gravel road even before I saw the swirl of dust. The white truck was passing the thicket of trees where Mr. Lack and his wife lived before the tall white man died suddenly, and his wife moved away. I saw the truck slow as it neared our home, and I was hoping the red-clay dust didn't find its way all the way out in the cornfield when the truck passed.

I turned to see the whirlwind stop in front of my parents' house, still humming as the dust settled along the edge of our front yard. I'd seen the truck before when the white farmer had come to check on his soybean crop. He was part of a large family who owned thousands of acres of cotton and soybeans throughout Lincoln County, including the soybean field directly in front of our house. I returned to my chore and forgot the white man was there. His being there was no different from a hundred other times I'd seen white men pull up in front of our home. I was anticipating my return to the house and finishing *Uncle Tom's Cabin.*

I was halfway down another row of corn when I saw the white man was still sitting in his truck in front of our house. I always found it strange how the white men drove around checking on their crops, as if the fields would miraculously change from one day to the next. Most times, they'd get out and walk out in the fields, looking around for a while before hopping back in their trucks and leaving as fast as they'd come. It wasn't usual that I saw a white man sitting in his truck the way this one did. I knew if Daddy was here, he'd walk out to the man's truck and ask if he needed help. The real reason he'd walk out there, though, was to make the man drive away from in front of his house.

Daddy's two acres separated the white farmers' land. When he'd bought the two acres, a few years earlier, the farmers were forced to plant around the truck patch, chicken coop, hog pen and eight—room house that accommodated the large brood of Kearney children. We'd never found the white farmers to be terribly friendly, troubling themselves with anything beyond curt nods or "Good morning" slipped from under their breath. Daddy taught us that we didn't need their friendliness. We just needed to always make sure we were doing the right thing, even when other folks weren't. So the Kearney children neither sought nor hungered for acknowledgment from the white farmers and were comfortable with the lines they drew between us.

I was curious that morning about the white man's sitting in his truck in front of Daddy's house. I left the tub of corn and walked to the edge of the field where I saw the white man standing with one foot perched on the front of his truck. He was looking out toward the soybean field. It was a familiar picture, nothing to raise concern.

I stood for a minute, watching the man who looked to be in his 30s or early 40s. His half-buttoned shirt was dingy with dirty brown stains. His pants were wrinkled, dirty and too short...nothing out of the ordinary. Most farmers, whether black or white, gave little thought to their dress or hygiene during the work week. Their day-to-day work called for close association with dirt, oil, grime, machinery and animals. It wasn't until the weekends that might include Saturday night outings or Sunday church services that they turned their minds to "cleaning up."

The white farmer walked to the edge of his soybean field, stooped down and pulled up a few weeds before walking further out into the middle of the field. When I saw him turn to walk back to his truck, I hurried back to the shade of the tall corn stalks and my chore. As I walked, though, I felt the man's hard stare on my back and almost as quickly heard his gravelly voice calling out to me.

"Hey, girl, kin you tell me where there's a colored graveyard up that way?" He pointed toward Star City and Rankin Chapel Church. "Somebody told me it might be up the road somewhere."

I stood in the cornfield, not sure what I should do. My parents had talked about the cemetery behind Rankin Chapel, but I'd never been brave enough to venture out into the area. I was sure, though, that only Negroes were buried there and thought it odd that the white man wanted to know about the place.

"I think it's behind our church down there, alongside the soybean field," I answered, pointing toward the church eight miles away.

The man stood by his truck for another minute, then walked a few steps closer to the edge of Daddy's yard. "Well, I ain't so sure I could find it by myself...you thank you might ride up there with me and point it out?"

I frowned now and shook my head. "No, sir, my parents not here, and I didn't ask'em before they left...I have to finish my work before they get back."

The man's parched lips curled into what might have been a coy smile but made me think of the newspaper comic strips I sometimes read in Daddy's *Pine Bluff Commercial* newspaper. His smile reminded me of Prune Face from the "Dick Tracey" cartoon. He was looking over at the house when he said, "Shoot, girl, we'll be back 'fore you know it. I jest need to go down there and look at the place, then come right back."

My 10 years on Varner Road had afforded me limited knowledge of white people. What I thought I knew was restricted to what I saw on Daddy's 10-inch television set and my experience in the cotton fields during cotton-chopping season in early summer. After we finished our own cotton fields, we were hired out to white farmers around Lincoln County. The white men drove their mud-drenched trucks into my parents' yard on late summer mornings to haul us like livestock to their cotton fields.

Zombie-like, we'd climb into the bed of the white men's trucks, sitting quietly, huddled together for warmth as the truck's speed and the morning coolness collaborated to form a cold, harsh wind that chilled us even further. The white farmers—Mr. Jones or Mr. Harris or Mr. Grider—hauled us miles away from home to their cotton or soybean fields where breast-high plants just beginning to bloom awaited us. We moved in unison those mornings, expertly chopping the weeds from around those precious plants. As the sun rose in the sky, it dried the cool dew in our clothing, and we slowly began to awake from our sleep.

The first time I sat beside a white man in the front cab of his truck was during the summer of 1962 when I rode sandwiched between Mr. Shooks, an old white farmer, and my brother Julius. That was the summer Julius and I were picked as workers for the strange white couple in Cole Spur—a grocery store and small community—along Highway 15, 10 miles from Gould.

The Shooks were older and whiter than other white people I'd seen in Lincoln County. Mrs. Shooks' lined face and slight stoop made her appear years older than her husband, and her almost iridescent whiteness brought to mind the fat worms we sometimes dug up from underneath our porch for fishing. Mama called them "albino" because they'd never seen sunlight.

The Shooks were different in other ways, too, like the way they didn't notice we were Negro children, carrying on conversations with us as we rode to their home or down the buckshot road to the rice field, as if we could be their own. They were like the white television actors from "The Nat 'King' Cole Show" or "The Ed Sullivan Show" where the white folks treated Negroes as if there were no differences. I'd always believed it was all an act for television until we met the Shooks.

Julius and I spent the last month of summer in the couple's strange employ, pulling weeds from their rice paddy and picking up stumps from their uncultivated land. What was most memorable about the experience was how our mornings with the Shooks always began with breakfast in their home. They never asked if we'd already eaten, which we always had. Minutes after Mr. Shooks drove up to the house and let us out, Mrs. Shooks would come to the door and say, "All righty...breakfast's ready." The Shooks had no immediate neighbors, but I still wondered what they might have thought if there had been neighbors.

After breakfast, Mrs. Shooks gathered the plates and silverware and trotted off to the sink to clean up. Mr. Shooks looked over at Julius and me and asked, "Y'all ready...get enough for breakfast?" When we nodded and said, "Yes sir," we were on our way out the door and off to work.

Mr. Shooks never stayed after he'd deposited us at the swamplike rice field. I wondered how he possibly knew whether we'd worked or played or walked off. Julius was 10 and I was nine, and we were overseeing ourselves. We waded barefoot through the muddy water, pulling weeds and possibly dodging snakes that made the rice fields their homes.

At noon, Mr. Shooks drove up to the edge of the field and waited for us to trudge through the water and climb into the idling truck. "Lunchtime, children," he'd say, as he chewed on the tobacco pipe that was his constant companion. Lunch with the Shooks was another puzzling thing to us. We had always either packed our lunch or bought cold cuts and white bread from the nearest store when we worked with other white farmers. Mrs. Shooks, though, cooked enough food for twice the four of us sitting at her lunch table. "Y'all eat 'til you full, children," she'd say-a smile on her white face.

Mrs. Shooks looked to be in her 70s and reminded me of Granny from "The Beverly Hillbillies," except without the bonnet. She had a warm smile, though, and welcomed Julius and me into her home as if we were white.

"Put your stuff down over there and go wash your hands in the bathroom," she'd tell us, pointing to a small room down the hall. The only time we'd experienced indoor plumbing was at our schools, and there it was closer to a community stall that most times needed repair.

This foreign experience with the white couple became less foreign over time, but Julius and I never gained enough comfort to let our guards completely down. We still didn't have much to say, so the meal was a quiet one because the Shooks did little talking to each other. Other than the sound of forks scraping against a plate, pot or bowl, the meal was silent—something my brother and I rarely experienced at the Kearney home.

In truth, our table manners were functional, at most, but good enough for the Kearney family because meals were as much for sustenance as they were for enjoyment; and a full stomach was necessary to get through the hard work that was part of our everyday lives.

Mr. Shooks, like Daddy, offered the blessings before each meal. The difference was that Mr. Shooks prayer lasted less than a minute. Daddy's sometimes lasted five minutes. Both Julius and I were on our best behavior during these meals. We hoped the couple didn't see us watching closely as they picked up a fork or spread a napkin on their laps or sipped the tiniest bit of tea from their glasses. I mimicked Mrs. Shooks' ladylike etiquette and tried teaching what I remembered to my younger siblings.

I never forgot the kindness of that strange white couple and held on to warm recollections of that experience. But there was a stark difference between riding with Mr. Shooks and riding with this white farmer. Mr. Shooks was older, cleaner and I sensed much nicer. Besides, Julius wasn't here with me now.

My indecision about riding with this white man had a lot to do with how I thought my parents would react. The man looked on as I tussled with what I should do. Finally, I convinced myself that my parents wouldn't mind me helping the white man out.

"I promise I'll get you home before your mama and daddy get back," the man said, an attempt to be playful.

I talked myself into believing I was doing a good deed, showing this white man where the graveyard was. I slowly opened the door and climbed into the truck and let out an involuntary cry of surprise when the mixture of heat and the stink of hot sweat, tobacco and beer accosted me inside the truck cab.

The white man grinned and reached over to turn the air conditioner on. Dirt and oil had turned his stubby hands almost as black as mine. He rolled the window down some, saying, "This oughta give us a little air 'til the conditioner kicks in." He backed the truck from the edge of the yard, then headed down Varner Road. His eyes veered between the gravel road to the lush, green soybean fields. He whistled and rested his hairy arm on the open window ledge.

"I show appreciate you for showing me where this cemetery is, girl. I show wouldn't be able to find it by myself."

I nodded and eased myself closer to the door, looking out the window until the truck came to a stop. As Varner Road passed by, I realized I was experiencing something I had before...it was as if my body was one place while I was another place, watching. I murmured under my breath the names of all the families living along Varner Road: Mr. and Miss Wash

Calloway, Mr. Fletcher and Miss Mary Ella White, Mr. Frank and Miss Marzell Jones. Mr. and Miss Fred Grider were the only white folks on this end of Varner Road.

We passed the thicket of plum trees where my brothers ate so many plums every spring they would make themselves sick and the curve in the road with the sweetest blackberries of any berry patch along Varner Road. We would bring our gallon buckets to the patch after school some evenings to pick enough for Mama to bake her delicious blackberry cobbler the next day. I was still daydreaming about Mama's blackberry cobbler when the man turned off Varner Road and onto Rankin Chapel's yard.

"That's it back there!" I hollered, pointing past the church and toward the wooded area behind it. The man nodded and drove past the church and to the edge of the woods. It had taken the white man half the time to get to the church as it took Daddy on Sunday mornings.

"So, that's where it is, huh?" the man was talking to himself. He stopped the truck under a large maple tree, got out and walked along the edge of the field before moving just a short distance into the cemetery. He turned around and walked back toward my family's church. I sat in the hot truck watching the man and praying he'd hurry and finish what it was he had to do.

I was staring out into the cemetery, wondering what it was the man could've wanted here when the door suddenly opened and he hopped into his seat, now smoking a cigarette. "Well, that's it, all right." I wanted to ask what his business was here, but he was grown and white, and it was none of my business. "I show thank you for helping me find this place, girl." He sat sideways on the truck seat, squinting up at the sunlight while he finished his cigarette.

A long sigh escaped me, as I realized we would soon be on our way back home. I was sure we would make it back before my parents did.

"How old you?" the man asked, letting the smoke drift from his

71

nostrils as he spoke. He was still looking up at the sun through the trees.

I glanced sideways at him. "I'm 10." I added apologetically, "but...I need to get home now or I'll get in trouble."

"Okay...all right, girl...I'm gone get you home," he snickered. "Goodness sake, we ain't even been gone more'n five or 10 minutes."

He threw the cigarette butt in the church yard and turned his body around as he slammed the truck door closed. He was smiling some with his brown-stained teeth, and I smelled soured beer even before he reached over and touched me. I accidentally looked into the man's dead, yellow eyes and shrugged his hand away.

"I got to get home, mister...." I didn't recognize the girl's voice.

"Girl, I'm gone get you home in plenty time, just trying to be a little friendly to you." He pulled on my arm and cooed, "Come on and settle down, now."

I heard the whimper and hardly realized it was me. I knew I had made a mistake. The man tried grabbing me again, as I pushed myself closer to the door. The tears started falling, as I pushed his hands away.

"Girl, ain't gone hurt you none...I promise you." He caught hold of Daddy's shirt, pulling me toward him. "Girl, I told you, I'm gone get you home. Calm down, now," he half whispered.

I was standing outside myself again, looking on as the girl screamed and fought the man the way I fought my brothers. The man's eyes widened in surprise, and he doubled his own strength to hold the girl in place. Even as he protected himself, his calloused hands sought out places on the girl to touch and pull.

"You get your dirty hands off me, Mister!"

"Hold on, girl. Ain't gone do nothing to you!"

For what seemed like forever, the white man sat there staring over at the girl, watching as the girl stared back, breathing hard and letting the hot tears stream down her face. I could hear Daddy's harsh voice when he found out what I'd done. He wouldn't want to hear any excuses, and

Mama would likely say I brought it on myself.

"You get me home, Mister, or I'll tell my daddy, and he'll kill you for trying to mess with me!"

The white man snickered, still breathing hard. "Okay, girl, I'm gone take you home. I didn't do you no harm, now did I?" When I didn't answer, he looked over at me for a long time. "Girl, I hope your daddy ain't no fool, now." He started the truck, and I began to straighten my shirt and glued myself to the passenger door. I touched my hair and could tell that my plaits were askew. I smoothed them the best I could.

We rode along the gravel road in silence, except for my sniffling. The sour smell of the truck made me want to vomit, but I knew I couldn't. I imagined the smell staying on my skin where he'd touched me, even after I left the truck. When he crossed the bridge less than a mile from my house, I quickly wiped all trace of tears from my eyes and hollered, "Stop! Stop!" He slowed down enough to look over at me, and I snatched the door open and jumped out. Without looking back, I ran the half-mile home.

I was relieved to find my father's station wagon wasn't there when I reached the edge of my yard. Still breathing heavily, I turned and looked back down the road. The white man's truck sat within 100 feet of Daddy's yard. I ran in the house, locked the front and back doors, went to the window and looked out.

The man and his truck sped off, leaving whirls of dust behind. For a minute that seemed like forever, I sat on the living room sofa, looking out and letting the tears fall. When I ran out of tears, I wet a face towel and scrubbed my face, my arms, my chest—every place on my skin the man might have touched. Even so, I imagined I could still smell the sourness inside the white man's truck.

I slowly unlocked the front door and walked back to the cornfield. I would work doubly hard to finish my chore, make my parents proud and believe that nothing had changed in the hours they'd been away.

— Six —

Sundays in the Kearney House

James and Ethel Kearney were as rigid about religion as they were about work and school. It was what allowed them to go to bed each night believing the next day would be better than the one before. If there wasn't somebody up there looking out for them, that meant they only had themselves to depend on...and that just wasn't enough. As for the Kearney children, religion wasn't an option. We'd believe in God, or wish we had. James and Ethel didn't suffer fools lightly, and religious ignorance was no excuse in their household. There was no way around it.

When Sundays rolled around, the Kearney children knew they would be sitting in somebody's church, if not Rankin Chapel that day—or they better have a hell of an excuse why not. James and Ethel Kearney made every effort to make Sundays a real Sabbath, not requiring any real work on that day. Mama and us girls even cooked Sunday dinner on Saturday evenings—except for the light fixings we sometimes whipped up after church to supplement our dinner. During cotton season, Daddy would forego taking us to the fields on a Sunday, even if he desperately needed to finish a bale of cotton and get it to the gin to feed us the next week. Religion was a powerful force in the Kearney household.

Throughout my life, memories of Sundays at the Kearney home, mostly warm memories, would stay with me. I remembered how my father would fuss as his children got ready for church, complaining that they were "slower than molasses in the winter...and if you don't hurry and get ready, I'll leave without you."

My father never threatened or fussed with Mama that way, even though we all joked about her taking her own sweet time dressing on

Sunday mornings. She would finish breakfast before the rest of the family and take her bath while we finished eating. The smell of the dime—store talcum powder and too—sweet perfume would permeate my room and the narrow hallway. As I passed my parents' bedroom on my way to my own, I'd spot my mother sitting at the dresser, pulling her brown coffee stockings up over her ample thighs and securing them with a knot at the top.

Mama would sit before the mirror and smooth the nutmeg brown powder over her face—the smooth pecan-shell complexion, the thin lips, the aquiline nose and small eyes. The last touch was the Sunday hat. Ethel Kearney loved hats and had created a pattern for making the most stately, colorful Sunday hats of anyone at her church. She had one for every occasion sitting in the top of her closet and wouldn't dare leave home on a Sunday without one. She took special efforts not to disturb the carefully positioned curls as she placed the hat snugly on her perfectly round head.

I was mesmerized by this woman who was simply Mama all the rest of the week but turned into someone different—a beautiful church woman, the picture of grace and beauty—tilting her Sunday hat just so. A small smile lit up the pretty face moments before she looked away from her reflection and with a sing-song voice hollered, "I'm ready, James. It's time to go!" Out she walked, through the bedroom door, hugging the black Sunday purse close beneath her arm.

By then, we were all ready to leave. If all of us younger children weren't quite ready, my older sisters would sit in the back seat with us as Daddy drove down Varner Road. They'd finish plaiting hair, brushing heads, wiping faces or buttoning shirts as the long, yellow station wagon lumbered down the dusty, gravel road to Rankin Chapel. Even during our most impoverished times, Daddy kept a pickup truck or station wagon to transport our family to and from the cotton field and Rankin Chapel.

The 15-minute ride consisted of arguments, laughter and quiet discussions up front, as baby Judy cooed and lolled against Mama's breast. The stair-step Kearney children were a ragtag team, tumbling out of the station wagon onto the church yard. We walked into the church in an almost perfect line, avoiding Mama's eyes as she took a last, perfunctory review of us before we presented ourselves to the congregation.

As each of us walked by Mama, she would tilt her head slightly as she pressed down wrinkles from our dresses or wiped crumbs from one of the hastily washed faces with a spittle-dampened finger. After we had all gone in, she walked quickly through the church door that Daddy held open, her purse swinging slightly on her arm and wearing a small Sunday morning smile that stayed put throughout the service.

The Kearney family easily made up a quarter of the Rankin Chapel congregation and played critical roles in the regular services—mostly because we were all there, come rain or shine or sick stomachs or headaches, when other members simply didn't show many Sunday morning. On those days, visitors or newcomers to the church would snicker under their breath about the "one-family show" they'd seen that morning.

Daddy was Sunday school superintendent for almost as many years as we attended Church there. Mama served as Sunday school teacher for the adult class for almost as long. And the Kearney children, when we were old enough, would take turns teaching the young and the young adult classes.

My parents sometimes switched up teaching the adult class because the members were in awe of Daddy's amazing Bible scholarship. The older members, many of them illiterate or grossly undereducated, would never tire of his simple explanations of the Bible stories and his unbelievable ability to pronounce the strange biblical names. The old women bolstered his ego, telling him he was the best Bible scholar they had ever seen, "even better than the preachers we've had."

James Kearney basked in the adulation. He was a self-taught biblical scholar, reading and studying the Bible most of his life-long before he had joined church at Mama's behest. Like the many self-taught lawyers populating the South at the time, Daddy could spout God's law better than the most "educated" of theologians. He had taught himself every character, verse, chapter and story in the Bible and could pronounce names and words that most of his educated children had problems pronouncing.

Long before the federal government had funded preschool programs, Daddy taught his children the fundamentals of reading, spelling and arithmetic before they were ready for public school. He took that same approach with his adult Bible classes, teaching men older than himself the rudiments of the Bible and simplifying the stories that most preachers either didn't understand or mystified to elevate their own knowledge. During the 60-plus years James Kearney taught and served as Sunday school superintendent at Rankin Chapel, he had taught hundreds of the young and old inside and outside his community.

While Mama was smart "for a woman," she never flaunted her intelligence. She was reticent to speak out or against her husband, even when she believed something different. In spite of their once-in-a blue moon public disagreements, James and Ethel was an admirable and enviable couple in the eyes of our community. They were a good match—good looking, smart and morally upright, even if they did have a lot more children than some people thought the law should allow. ℚ

SEVEN

Miss
Nola Mae

The Kearney family stayed to themselves mostly. Neither James nor Ethel was the kind of folks who shuttled from one house to the next carrying and gathering news to share with neighbors. Neither of them could abide gossipers and kindly asked visitors not to leave their gossip when they left our home.

Some of the neighbors on Varner Road saw the Kearney bunch as standoffish and would scoff to each other, "Can you imagine—not a pot to piss in and they have the nerve to try to be proud!" Most folks liked my parents even if they didn't understand us. They felt sorry for my parents' predicament, being poor as church mice and having more children than the proverbial old woman in the shoe.

When she had no other choice—nothing in her cupboards and no money to buy anything-she sent me or one of the other Kearney children trekking across the soybean field or down the gravel road to a neighbor we hadn't borrowed from last time. One of us would innocently make his or her way to someone's home, empty sack or cup in hand to ask for whatever our mother needed.

Beforehand, Mama told the appointed child, "You be sure and say, 'Mama say she sorry to bother you, Miss Lane (or Miss Calloway or Miss Jackson), but she'll pay you back first thing next week.' " The kind neighbor would gladly send back a cup or sack or bucket filled with more than we'd expected, knowing my mama likely needed a lot more than she was asking for.

James and Ethel Kearney's aloof, independent ways were the very things that drew Nola Mae and Robert Jackson to them in 1963. Most people on Varner Road viewed old Miss Jackson, who really wasn't that old, as "a strange old bird." Her peculiar personality, plus the fact that she wore coke-bottle glasses over her crossed eyes, left no room for anyone to view the woman as normal.

What really got the goat of the people on Varner Road was how she ended up with Robert Jackson, a man at least 20 years her senior and married for more than 30 years when Nola Mae paid him and his wife a fateful visit.

According to Varner Road legend, Nola Mae and Mary, Robert Jackson's wife at the time, were friends during childhood. They'd grown up on neighboring farms in the small community of Wells Bayou, no more than 10 miles away. But Nola Mae had come on hard times after losing her first husband just months before she visited Mary. According to gossip, a visit that was supposed to last a few days turned into weeks, then months, then well into a year before things came to a head.

Nola Mae was well past her 50s. A squat man, Robert Jackson was at least a foot shorter than she was and some years past 70. This unlikely pair became the center of attention on Varner Road. The small community's rumor mill was buzzing like nobody's business by the time the 12th month of her "visit" rolled around. That's when Nola Mae rode with Mr. Calloway to her house in Wells Bayou. She gathered all her furniture, brought it back and settled into the Jackson home.

Women's evening strolls along the gravel road included the latest gossip about the strange triangle on the hill as they slapped each others' backs to smash "them damn mosquitoes," fanned away gnats from their ears and yelled at their children to stop throwing rocks "...'fore you get a cow killin'."

A few weeks after the rumors surfaced, Mary Jackson left the house she'd shared with Robert Jackson for so long. She paid Mr. Calloway five dollars to haul her nice, almost new furniture and belongings three miles up the road to her daughter's home.

Just months later, "soon as that judge signed the divorce papers," Robert and Nola Mae's marriage didn't put a dent in the rumor mill. It only added to the disdain folks felt for the strange couple's outlandish behavior. "And at their age" was the usual capper. The couple went about their business, pretended they didn't know they were the center of attention, though they did not leave the refuge of their home very often.

"Can you believe Nola Mae Jackson sneaking in and taking Robert Jackson from his wife of nearly 30 years?" That was how most people put it, shaking their heads incredulously. The nerve of such "a brazen hussy" was more than most people in the community—especially the women— could stand. It was a long while before the couple was welcomed into Christian folks' homes or invited to attend church services on Sunday. During the first few years of their marriage, folks on Varner Road blatantly ostracized the strange couple. The Jacksons became the closest thing to living legends—or outlaws—that community would ever know.

As the years went by, Robert and Nola Mae's sins were either forgiven or forgotten. Either way, they continued living as they always had, seemingly not phased by the community's opinion of them. They continued to stay mostly to themselves, living up the hill from us, separated by five acres of soybeans that we sharecropped each year.

The Jacksons maintained truck patches behind their house, working them most of the spring and living off them during the summer. The Kearney children, who spent most summer days outside rather than inside our house, watched the couple on Saturday mornings walking to the bayou, carrying their fishing poles. Miss Jackson led her little husband, who rarely looked up from staring at the ground. Later in the day, as we hung from a tree or dug a hole at its root to hide some shiny bright thing we'd found, we would nudge each other as the strange couple trudged slowly back to their house. As before, Miss Jackson still walked ahead of her husband, while he carried a five-gallon bucket that we guessed was full of catfish, carp or grinner.

On most Sunday mornings, we hurriedly dressed after breakfast so we could rush outside and watch the Jacksons pass our house on their way to Sunday school or church service at Dora Bell Church. We heard the clop-clop-clop of the horse and wagon before we saw them and stood too excited to be still as the Jacksons passed our home dressed in stiff black suits and hats, sitting proud and straight atop the horse-drawn wagon.

My five brothers, one sister and I would holler together, "Hey, Miss Jackson. Hey, Mr. Jackson." The couple would both look over, pretending surprise, and smile at our stair-stepped group. Miss Jackson would wave and chuckle and sometimes say, "Say hi to your folks for us." We seldom did.

We were as interested in the Jacksons' mode of transportation as we were in the couple. The old man and woman owned the last horse-drawn wagon in the community and didn't seem a bit bothered by that fact. James Kearney used his only mule in the fields and to haul wood during the winter. Some years before, he had saved up enough money from his cotton crop to buy a 1953 Plymouth station wagon. He used the long, yellow car to haul his oversized family around.

When things got really tough for them, the Jacksons would walk down the hill and across the soybean field that separated the two houses to ask my daddy to drive them to church or to town. Most times he did. But if he wasn't around, they'd trudge back up the hill, hitch their mule to the wagon and go places the same way they usually did. They rarely asked another neighbor for help.

The vision of the Jacksons riding high upon their wagon, pulling at their horse's tether, was part of the couple's allure. It was as much a part of their uniqueness as anything they did or said. And it was this fact which made a conversation I overheard between my parents that much stranger.

One night before bedtime, I heard Mama ask, "Where in the world did that woman get it into her head that she need to try to get herself a car, James?" Ethel's usually calm, sweet voice was raised a few decibels. I imagined my father's perplexed face, him shaking his head from side to side. "Who would be crazy enough to give her a car," Mama continued, "knowing she can't see worth a plug nickel."

James tried to stifle his giggle. "Ethel, it ain't that Miss Jackson can't see, she just see two of everything." However, his wife wouldn't be humored and continued to argue against the foolish idea.

"Ethel, you have to at least try to see her side of it. She say they jest tired of havin' to always depend on other folks to take 'em around to do their business, and the horses are gettin' less and less reliable as they get older."

I peeked into their bedroom in time to see Mama's deep-set hazel eyes narrowing. She shook her head. "They just asking for trouble, James. And you know good-darn well Miss Jackson don't need to be behind nobody's steering wheel. You need to tell her that. You show don't need to be encouraging her."

In the hallway, I could hear my father half-heartedly defending himself, swearing he hadn't encouraged the woman one bit. "That bull-headed woman's mind was made up long before she breathed a word of this to me."

I was sure the long sigh my mother gave was followed by her usual gesture of frustration, the folding of her arms.

"I'm through with it, James. All I got to say is, it's a sin and a shame for Miss Jackson to even think about learning to drive a car at her age—and to drag you into the middle of her foolish plan is more'n I can stomach!"

Maybe it was because James and Ethel Kearney were their closest neighbors. It might have been because none of the other neighbors had completely forgiven the Jacksons their sins and probably wouldn't assist them. Whatever the reason, the Jacksons had chosen James Kearney, figuring his good heart would see them through their plan. True, my father regularly allowed older people in the community to take advantage of his patience and Christian heart. But he promised Ethel he wouldn't be taken in by Nola and Robert Jackson. He told his wife he'd tell them point blank that he wasn't having any part of their plan, that they were pushing his religion to the limit.

After weeks of rebuttals, justifications and whining about the neighborhood, Miss Jackson wore down Daddy's reserve. It took weeks for Daddy to convince Mama that they would benefit from the independence the Jacksons' new car would bring. "Just think, Ethel. No more cartin' the nagging woman and her husband into town at the first of the month, to church on Sundays or into Wells Bayou so she can visit her crazy old family."

Mama half-heartedly relented. For weeks, after working in the cotton fields all day, Daddy spent his evenings driving up and down the dirt roads with Nola Mae Jackson. Robert Jackson sat in the back seat or he stood on the side of the road with a strange smile on his face. When my father returned home from those driving lessons, it was as though he'd just climbed down off a wild, bucking steer.

Mama smiled as she listened quietly to her husband's ranting about "that bull-headed, cross-eyed Miss Jackson." Mama was enjoying Daddy's misery, and she continued her chores without so much as a single comment while he fumed. Sometimes she'd even hum to herself, never allowing one word of response to pass her lips.

Knowing the root of Miss Jackson's driving problem was her crossed eyes, the Kearney children had fun at the woman's expense. "Our safest bet when we see Miss Jackson drive up is to stand right smack in the middle of the road!" This was not a joke we shared with our parents.

James kept up his driving lessons for nearly two months. His family knew it was over when he came home one day, threw his old brown felt hat on the table and said, "I jest pray that woman give up this foolishness. Heaven help the folks on the road if she don't!" We inched out of the room before our parents' laughter tumbled out into their balled up fists. Showing disrespect for elders, no matter how foolish they really were, always resulted in a whipping.

A few days later, when the Jacksons returned, asking for "Brother Kearney," we kids smiled demurely and said, "Yes, ma'am. Yes, sir. We'll go get him." Robert Jackson reminded me of a soft, brown bunny rabbit that one of us had gotten for Christmas the year before. He smiled down at us from the wagon and waved warmly. We smiled and waved back, wondering about the purpose of the visit. Miss Jackson scooted down from the wagon, pulled her dress straight and walked up to the front door to knock.

"Hey, chillun," Mr. Jackson said. His smile widened as he opened a sack of two-for-a-penny candy and began throwing it from the wagon. Watching us scramble for the unusual snack amused the old man to no end.

"Thank you, Mr. Jackson!" we hollered to him before running toward the back of the house where we compared our booty. The old man chuckled as we ran away. "Morning, Brother Kearney," he hollered as James Kearney walked out his front door.

Daddy stood halfway between his front porch and the wagon. For a short while, the three adults pretended the visit was merely a social one. They swapped small talk about the weather and the crops. Miss Jackson stood between the younger man, my daddy, and the older one, her husband, looking at each man and offering her strange grin from one to the other.

"Well, Brother Kearney," she said, "I know we jest about done worried you ta death, what with your trying to teach me to drive and all you do for us. I know I kin be some cross to bear!" She laughed with her husband at her own words, and James Kearney frowned and looked past the woman to the soybean field behind them.

"Brother Kearney, Mr. Robert and me talked about it, and we jest decided we need to go on and buy ourselves a car. I think I learned a lot from your lessons. I know it don't seem too much like it, but I did.

"We too old, Brother Kearney, to keep messing round with this ole horse here. We just don't think we ought to go out and get another one since even now we the only ones on the road with a horse and wagon, and it just get too dangerous sometimes.

"So, we really would be much obliged, Mr. Kearney, if you would see it in your heart to take us out to Trotter Ford in Pine Bluff and help us find us a little car we could run back and forth to town in."

James Kearney kept frowning and studied the ground. Maybe he didn't trust himself to say anything, and for a long time he just shook his head slowly. He probably hoped, foolishly, that Miss Jackson had given up on her car-buying idea. He looked from Miss Jackson to her old husband, who simply smiled down at him from the wagon.

"Miss Jackson, Mr. Jackson, I really don't think..."

The old woman cut him off before he could finish.

"Brother Kearney, I know just what you about to say, but I'm a Christian woman and I got faith in the Lord. He done told me I'm doing the right thing in this."

"I'll let you know later today," my father said, turning away without a formal goodbye, leaving the woman standing at his door.

She smiled faintly and nodded before climbing back up on the wagon, her old husband watching with a smile. She seemed sure my daddy would send one of us up the hill with an answer.

James Kearney stood at the window, shaking his head as the old couple drove off in the wagon. The look on his face suggested his dread at having to tell Ethel what the Jacksons were asking of him.

"What can you do, James? She put you between a rock and a hard place," Mama sympathized. "That hardheaded woman will get herself a car with you or without you. You might as well go on and take her out there to the Ford place to make sure she know what she doing."

So, that was that. James hemmed and hawed for a few hours, then told his son Ron to go up the hill and tell the Jacksons that Daddy would take them to town the next morning to try to find a car where he'd bought his, at Trotter Ford in Pine Bluff.

The next day, Jo Ann and I and some of the others were playing "My Car" in the yard. We'd count the cars that passed on the road in front of our house, and the first person to spot the next car could either call it or pass it on and claim the next one. Jo Ann had spotted a dark-colored car driving slowly past the house and claimed it for herself before realizing it was actually stopping in front of our home and Daddy was getting out.

We jumped up and ran out to the shiny, new car our father was driving. The excitement went a little awry when we saw Miss Jackson, stiff as a board, sitting on the passenger side of the front seat, and Mr. Jackson sitting in a corner of the back seat. We looked at each other, not believing what our brains were telling us. This was old cross-eyed Miss Jackson's car! It was the prettiest car we'd ever seen, shiny enough to see our faces in and midnight blue.

"This is old Miss Jackson's car?" I whispered to my father.

"Y'all gone back in the yard and stop putting your hands all over Miss Jackson's new car, now," he said.

My father had a funny squint in his eyes, and he kept looking up to the house as though he was waiting for someone. I followed my father's glance but saw nothing except a slight movement of the curtains in my parents' bedroom.

Daddy got out of the driver's seat and walked to the passenger side to open the door for Miss Jackson. He gave her the car keys before walking a few feet to where we were standing.

"Well, Miss Jackson, you got it from here." He walked back around to the driver's side to close her door after she got in.

"I show do thank you, Brother Kearney, for taking all this time up with me."

She smiled through the driver's window and handed James Kearney a small wad of dollar bills "for all your trouble." Tipping her head, she waved her dark little hand at us and drove away. We pointed and laughed at her little husband's head bobbing up and down in the back seat.

James Kearney moved toward the ditch as dust from the road whirled around him. He shook his head, as if in wonder.

"That woman don't even know the difference between the brakes and the accelerator," he said under his breath.

The pretty blue car was weaving from one side of the gravel road to the other, like a drunken sidewinder.

"Money ill-gained, James."

All eyes turned to see Mama standing in our front doorway, slowly shaking her head. Daddy walked up on the porch, chuckling as he handed Mama the crumpled dollar bills. They laughed quietly as they stood together in the doorway. And we could hear them laughing loudly after they'd walked to their bedroom. As we continued to stare down the road at the dust storm rising from the midnight blue car, we began to laugh, too, tickled to watch the car zigzag along the road.

Two weeks passed, and we waited impatiently for the times the Jacksons drove down Varner Road slower and straighter than that first day. But on a Sunday morning, shortly after breakfast and before I could have my turn to wash up in time for Sunday school service, a loud commotion outside drew everyone's attention.

Daddy was in his bedroom, standing at the dresser mirror shaving. He had on only his undershirt and pants when he heard Wash Calloway hollering down from the bridge for him.

"Mr. Kearney... Mr. Kearney! You need to hurry on down here, quick as you can!"

Daddy rushed to the door to look out. When he heard the neighbor's call again, he ran down the road with just his undershirt on and his belt hanging from his pants.

Mama and the rest of the Kearney clan weren't far behind, anxious to find out what was taking place down on Varner Road. The most memorable thing about this morning was that it was the first time I ever saw my father run, and I couldn't have imagined he could run so fast.

Daddy stopped a few feet before he made it to the wood bridge, bending over for a minute to catch his breath. He could already hear Miss Jackson's yelping. A sound, something like a scared puppy's howl, pierced the air. Mama was there now, and we huddled close by. Neighbors, some half-dressed in their church clothes, gaped down into the murky bayou.

Miss Nola Mae and Robert Jackson's shiny, midnight blue Ford sat nose forward in the muck, and the couple sat inside the sinking car. Robert Jackson sat in the passenger seat, seemingly calm and quiet, now looking up at Daddy. Miss Nola Mae sat behind the steering wheel, hollering and praying intermittently as if her high-pitched squeal might move her and her husband from the bayou to dry land.

The sight must have triggered something in my daddy, and he lashed out at the squealing woman. "Miss Jackson, you gone have to shut your mouth now, if you expect anybody to help you. Your hollerin' ain't gone help a bit!" He was trying to yell over her squeals, but it seemed his efforts were futile.

Finally, Miss Jackson quieted her squealing, turned her face toward Daddy and asked, "Mr. Kearney, you thank there's any way we can save our car?"

Neighbors frowned and shook their heads. Daddy didn't answer, and for a while the only sounds were the woman's pitiful sniffles.

Mr. Calloway hurried to his house to get his tractor and a chain. As we waited for his return, James spoke more kindly to the old woman and her husband. "Mr. Calloway gone be back in a minute, and we'll have y'all out in no time, probably in time for you to make it to Sunday school." The four old eyes stared beseechingly at my daddy.

After what seemed like hours of waiting, Daddy decided to see what could be done without a tractor. He called his sons Joseph, Jesse, Jackie and some of the neighbors' boys over and instructed them: "Ricky, Henry, the rest of you boys come on down here with me, and let's get these folks outta this car 'fore it sink all the way into this bayou."

Though the bayou was shallow, they had a hard time getting the old couple out of the car. Miss Jackson's window was cracked open, but the pressure of the water had sealed the doors shut. Finally, with Daddy and the boys pulling and prodding, the doors flew open with a guttural whoosh.

They moved quickly to get the Jacksons out of the car and onto the bayou bank. After a perfunctory check, they decided the Jacksons were fine. Though Mr. Jackson still hadn't uttered a word, a brisk wind let us know he had indeed been affected by all the commotion. Old Miss Jackson's sniffling had stopped, but she commenced to talking as my brother carried her to the bank, "My glasses...my glasses lost...I can't see a damn thing!"

Shaking his head, Daddy waded back out into the gray water to search the car for the woman's distinctive, wire-rimmed spectacles. Without a word, he walked onto the bayou bank and handed the glasses to the cross-eyed woman.

"Here your glasses, Miss Jackson. Why don't you and Mr. Jackson rest yourselves up there on the bank while we try to get this car outta here," he said wearily.

The rescue mission was an all-morning task. It was one of the few times the Kearney family missed Sunday school. Mr. Calloway's tractor arrived too late for rescuing the couple but in time for the heavier load—pulling the Jacksons' car out.

"Woo, there we go!" It was near noon when Daddy and Mr. Calloway let out a whoop at the same time. They laughed with relief as the car inched up the hill behind the tractor. All this time, the Jacksons had sat quietly watching, refusing Daddy's coaxing to go up to their house and wait.

"Mr. Kearney, we ain't leaving here till we see that car come outta that water. We gone set right here," declared the stubborn old woman.

For the first time that morning, Robert Jackson smiled as the still shiny but water-logged automobile rolled up onto the bank.

"Praise the Lord! Thank you, Mr. Kearney, Mr. Calloway. Praise the Lord!"

Mr. Calloway towed the car up the hill to the Jacksons' house. The old couple loaded into Daddy's station wagon, with us in the back seats, tired from so much early excitement. They smiled all the way home and their eyes never left the shiny blue car still dripping bayou water. ℚ

PART III

James Thomas and
Ethel Curry Kearney

(1905-1982)

EIGHT

The House
on Varner Road

My family's home sat five miles down Varner Road, west of Highway 65 and in the opposite direction of Cummins Prison Farm. "Turn wrong and you'll be eating mashed potatoes with the men in white," some of my parents' friends joked.

Ours was a large house. The eight rooms housed a changing number of residents as older siblings graduated from high school and left home for college or for greener pastures and new residents were added to the number. When I was 12 years old, I shared my home with my parents and 10 of my siblings: Joseph, Joyce, Jesse, Jackie, Julius, Jo Ann, Jerome, Jude, Jeffrey and Judy.

More than anyone else's, the home on Route 1, or Varner Road, was my father's house. He'd built it with his own hands in 1961, a fact he proudly shared with visitors to the impressive house in the middle of nowhere. Sometimes he acknowledged that his three teen-age sons and two neighbors from down the road had helped out, too.

A proud man in spite of his poverty, James Kearney had done what many a neighbor had told him he couldn't do and in less time than anyone would have imagined. More than proving his neighbors wrong, my father, however, was most proud of the fact that he kept his promise to his wife, that she'd cook Christmas dinner in her new home that year.

At night, when I sat in the crook of the old walnut tree, I could spot my room, the largest room in the house because I shared it with Jo Ann and two younger brothers. It was a wide-open, co-ed space with one window, unvarnished wood floors and paperless walls. Two wrought-iron poster beds were pushed into separate corners of the room.

I shared a bed with Jo Ann. Unfortunately, the corn shuck mattress demanded regular airing and drying, given my habit of wetting the bed. The other bed was occupied by Jerome and Jude, and sometimes Jeffery when they allowed him in.

Both beds were hand-stuffed with corn shucks from the year's crop. Once a year, Mama and the girls tore open the ticking, washed and dried it and stuffed it with fresh corn shucks. One of Mama's complexities was the fact that she never viewed domesticity as a male's purview. Thus, none of her sons were taught the basics of cooking, cleaning, washing and picking up after themselves. Though they all became exemplary homemakers as adults, it was nothing they could ever pin on Ethel Kearney. Jo Ann and I were responsible for our brothers' bed and their side of the room.

Our makeshift closet was a fishing string that stretched from the boys' side of the room to ours. Hung across the string were our school and church wardrobes. Mama had bought our white dresses at Goodwill to wear on Sundays when we helped out with ushering. We also had special Sunday dresses. Mine was a yellow, shirtwaist with a flared skirt, and Jo Ann's was a blue, straight shirtwaist with a matching belt. Mama had sewn both of them from a homemade pattern on her old Singer sewing machine.

Each of us had a white blouse that we wore over and over to school with every skirt we owned and black wool coats that lasted at least half of our childhoods. The nicer pieces were hung with wire hangers, while our brothers' few pairs of jeans, shirts and Sunday slacks were slung across the fishing string haphazardly. Jo Ann and I proudly washed and ironed our clothes as if they were expensive brand-name items. We wore hand-me-downs from older siblings, neighbors and secondhand stores with the pride passed on from our father.

Besides the beds, the only real furniture in our room was a wooden dresser that looked as if it weighed a ton and a matching straight-backed chair I'd hurriedly claimed. My grandmother originally owned the chair until she donated it to her neediest child, Ethel. "Big Mama," as we called her, had passed a few pieces of furniture down to Mama a week or so before she moved to Indiana.

I fell in love with the rich, dark wood of the dresser and chair and how it stood out in a house without one piece of furniture that wasn't from a discount or secondhand store. Mama agreed it could sit in my bedroom since there was more space there than in any other spot in the house. Sometimes my imagination ran away with me as I sat in the chair. An avid fan of Loretta Young, I sometimes imagined her sitting there, combing her long, dark hair before going to bed—never mind that my hair was thick and coarse and not half as long.

I dreamed that my life would be as glamorous one day, that I would somehow be transported from the dire poverty that I knew into something more. Someday, I dreamed. Ted Murray was the boy's name, and I adorned the hardwood dresser with his picture when I was just 13. The boy was much older, probably 17, but he called himself my boyfriend, writing me long love letters that I hid under the head of my mattress. Although I never used the term "boyfriend," I liked having the boy's picture on my dresser, the way I'd seen pictures of good-looking men adorn Loretta Young's dresser.

The house on Varner Road had four other bedrooms. One, at the front of the house and off-limits to the children, was my parents' bedroom. The rest of the rooms were all nearby, toward the back of the house. A wood heater, used to warm the back of the house, shared one of the back rooms with two beds. The heater kept the two adjoining rooms comfortable enough for us to wash off in the mornings and fall asleep at night. This was also where my older brothers congregated most nights to discuss secret subjects like girls and sex—and other taboo topics.

The living room served as the guest area for visitors. Attached by a door was a sitting room that held the larger of the two wood heaters. It was the one used to warm visitors who came during the winter. The kitchen and dining room was one large space separated by a long wooden partition. The dinner table was big enough to accommodate our outsized family. Many days the cooking stove stayed hot from morning till night as Mama prepared meals for her family. The last room of the Kearney home, 100 yards out back, was the outdoor toilet. ℚ

NINE

James Thomas
Kearney

Most people look into the kindly, smiling face of James Thomas Kearney and see a kindly, smiling old man, slightly stooping now but still rather distinguished-looking. Maybe it's something in the proud bearing and the way he holds his large black Bible tautly against his heart. The few friends still living know only some of what makes his life extraordinary to those of us who know him best, and even we know only part of his story.

For sure, James Thomas' childhood was full of magnificent horrors and miracles, and the combination of the two magically shaped him into the estimable husband, father and community sage he would later become. While my father has never claimed assurance of either the place or date of his birth, the place he has most consistently named is Tulsa, Oklahoma, or "Tulsey Town," before oil was discovered in 1901. He has settled on 1909 as his birth year—two years before Oklahoma became a certified state in 1907.

James Thomas' birth certificate was possibly burned in a fire around 1910 or 1911, less than a decade before the infamous Tulsa race riot and fire that destroyed 35 blocks of Tulsa's vibrant Greenwood district, dubbed "Little Africa." While no count has been established, as many as 300 black citizens might have died as a result of a young black man leaving his shoe shine stand to use a restroom and accidentally stepping on the foot of the white female elevator operator.

Daddy's age has long been fodder for humor and jokes at the annual family gatherings where we celebrate our family and my father's birthdays. At some point, we all realized that Daddy enjoys this guessing game at least as much as his children, knowing that it adds another layer of mystery to his past and more substance to the stories that meander somewhere between almost truths and maybes, depending on the day and the audience. The question of James Kearney's past, however, detracts nothing in his children's eyes from the miracle of his life.

James Thomas was actually born Thomas James. He changed his name some years after leaving his mother's home around 1920. He was the third child born to Thomas Clayton and Cynthia Kearney. Virginia and Sam, James' older siblings, were the couple's first. Cynthia's first child, Johnny, was born in Lake Village, Arkansas, when Cynthia was hardly past her teens. Though the father's identity was never divulged, the Chicot County residents whispered the boy looked more white or Indian than he looked colored. Her marriage to Thomas Clayton produced a total of six children, with Sallie, Harry, Lawrence, Willie, James and Evevia being the last batch. The couple chose James to carry part of his father's name.

Whether it was because he shared part of his father's name or because Thomas Clayton was a doting father, his son loved him unconditionally. From all accounts, young James' childhood during his years in Oklahoma started out extremely happy. In or around 1910, just weeks after the young colored farmer borrowed 1,500 dollars from the bank and bought over 100 acres of land and a herd of livestock from a white landowner, he lost everything in a suspicious fire. The fire consumed Thomas Clayton's modest but comfortable home and the livestock he'd recently branded "TCK." The merciless flames torched the healthy cotton crops, leaving acres of tiny blackened stubs peeping out of hot, black dirt. The fire was just the beginning of Thomas Clayton Kearney's misfortunes. Days after settling with the bank and the farmer who sold him the land and livestock, the Kearney family packed up what was left of their lives and returned to Lake Village where Cynthia's parents lived. Neighbors made a going-away gift of a horse and wagon, baskets of food and secondhand furnishings they would need to start over. Thomas and Cynthia Kearney moved with their three children to just within miles of the place where Cynthia had grown up, the place she had lived until she was old enough to start having children and to marry.

The good fortune Thomas Clayton had found in Tulsa would somehow elude him back in the south Arkansas Delta. He couldn't regain the farm, livestock or community status he had lost back in Tulsa. His father, an eternal optimist, accepted his fate of itinerant farming and sharecropping and moved his family throughout southeast Arkansas from one year to the next.

The long list of Kearney addresses in southeast Arkansas included Beth River, Round River, Chicot County and Long Lake, outside Grady. Thomas Clayton still believed a miracle might be right around the next corner. James and his brothers thrived on a kind of freedom in their way of living. And, though they were expected to attend school wherever they ended up, they also made the most of their freedom to roam the wood areas they called jungle land in southeast Arkansas.

Young James, lovingly nicknamed "Buddy" by his father, was just nine years old when what Daddy called the black flu claimed his father in 1918. Thomas Clayton, 47, was just one of the estimated 40 million throughout the world, including thousands of Arkansans, tapped by this swift angel of death. The black flu or bubonic plague had began its journey in the Great War of Europe and traveled across the globe within two years time, infecting a fifth of the world's population and 28 percent of America's population. While 1918 brought peace against war, the world faced an unmatched enemy in the black plague.

The cruelty, as James Kearney would later point out, was in how swift and mercilessly it took life. His father's death, he said, was without warning. Thomas Clayton had come in from his field work on Tuesday night a little more tired than usual, gone to bed for a restful night's sleep and woke up the next morning in the throes of the black flu. The horrendous death came as Thomas Clayton fought to clear his airways of a blood-tinged froth.

The black angel would strike the Kearney home a second time that week, taking the life of baby girl Evevia—thankfully in her sleep. The stories of the insipid death machine were rampant and horrifying with people dying in the streets or as they dined or played bridge into the night. There was endless speculation as to what had caused this curse. Most people believed the Great War played a role, whether it was the mass movement of men, a biological warfare weapon used by the enemy or the smoke and fumes from mustard gases soldiers used.

"It was the worst time in the world's history. People everywhere was dying and there was nothing doctors could do about it," Daddy recalled, somberly. He remembered a playground rhyme that children repeated when death became so common that it was acceptable to make fun of it:

> *I had a little bird, its name was Enza.*
> *I opened the window, and in-flu-enza.*

Young James Thomas had the dubious distinction of having experienced loss of family status, the security of home and now his much-beloved father and baby sister within his short existence. Though other memories of his blissful childhood would carry him through many a dark day, the loss of his father would haunt him throughout his life.

Even at 98, the memory of Thomas Clayton's passing reopens wounds, dulling the twinkles in his eyes. "Daddy's passing was about the hardest thing I ever had to go through—one day he was healthy, playing around with us and reading with us at night, and just like that, he was gone." When Thomas Clayton took leave of the world, he took a huge part of his son's childhood with him, leaving a deep hole that no one would ever fill—not James' mother or his devoted wife of 45 years, nor his 18 children who believed he hung the moon.

James Thomas survived all seven of his siblings and is the last of Thomas Clayton and Cynthia Kearney's children still living. Harry, who was both a brother and a best friend and shared so many of James' youthful experiences, died at 90 years old at a Pine Bluff nursing home. Most of Harry Kearney's last days were spent in a wheelchair. James had visited his brother regularly, bringing candy bars and cigarettes and memories of their childhood that brought a smile to his younger brother's face.

His sister Sally died in 1990 at 103 years old in Chicago, where she had lived a comfortable existence since moving there in the early 1960s with her husband, "a railroad man." James' other siblings, except for Virginia who died in her early 20s, lived into their sunset years. His brothers Willie, Sam and Lawrence—the minister in the bunch—and his half-brother, Johnny, all died decades earlier.

James' mother, Cynthia, died in 1959 after moving in with him and Ethel and their large brood of children five years earlier. Mama, who never spoke unless she had something kind to say about a person, admitted, "Your grandma and me didn't always see eye to eye."

Daddy has said he never imagined he would live as long as he has. He had been "sickly" for a long time with a weak stomach and sinus headaches and thought for sure he would leave other siblings behind. He was sure it was just plain common sense and staying away from doctors that had kept him alive.

James Thomas Kearney swore he didn't know one single instance where a doctor did more good than they did harm, beginning with the country doctor in Chicot County, who got there too late to save his father and sister. That also included his wife's doctor who checked her annually for 10 years, assuring her he saw no further growth of her breast cancer only to announce on the 11th checkup that they had missed the cancer spreading through her stomach. "Doctors ain't had nothing to do with my living, and I want to make sure they don't have nothing to do with my dying," he had said.

The most incredible era of his life, James Kearney said, began around 1920 when at 11 years old he accepted the fact that nothing could ever be the same after his father's death. That was the year he lit out on his own, leaving his home, his mother and his family. He never explained how such a thing could happen or what conversation might have ensued between the boy and his mother when he announced his leaving. "It was just time for me to go out into the world," he declared.

Daddy so often revisited that era in his life, as if there was something cathartic about the telling. He painted for us a life of unbelievable freedom and independence; stories of vivid and musical blues, yellows, greens and reds. As he shares his stories, however, it's clear that freedom and independence didn't always equal happiness in Daddy's world. There were real-life obstacles to his happiness. It was the era of racial segregation and Jim Crowism. The color of his skin, his age, his lack of a formal education and his somewhat voluntary aloneness in the world certainly all worked against complete happiness or independence.

The 11-year-old James' initial departure from home included hitching a 600-mile train ride from Pine Bluff to Chicago. He picked the city mostly on a whim after hearing his mother speak of a distant cousin living there. The young boy used his wit, his charm and his already-honed survival skills to find his mother's relative in Chicago's South Side colored neighborhood. James quickly ingratiated himself with the older woman and her family and convinced them that his migration north was part of a plan to make enough money to send back home. This distant relative hardly knew the boy's mother and certainly wouldn't write for confirmation of his story. James would live with the family on and off for the next few years.

His memories of Chicago in the early 1920s were both painful and wondrous. It wasn't just the cold winters, but also the harsh life and the unfriendly environment that were so different from the southern Delta. "Chicago living," he told his children, "makes a boy grow into a man whether he want to or not. You learn things a lot faster than boys do in the South, that's for sure." Though Daddy never explained exactly what that meant, we enjoyed guessing about the possibilities.

Daddy recalled how the Chicago winter snow sometimes reached the windows of his bedroom and how it nearly came up to his waist when he ventured outside to work. His first jobs in Chicago centered on the evil, cold white dust that turned his hands into brown stone as he raked hundreds of feet of snow from rich white families' sidewalks.

When James got up the nerve to write his first letter to his mother, he spent hours looking for a post office in the big city. By the time he found one in downtown Chicago and stuck the two-cent stamps on the thin envelope, his childish tears had first smeared, then frozen Cynthia Kearney's name and address so that he could barely read it. In Arkansas' moderate climate, Cynthia Kearney would have no sense of what her son went through to tell her he was "doing fine, working hard to make enough money to send home."

James remembered his first job as a dishwasher on Chicago's West Side at a strange-talking white man's restaurant. He would later learn much about gyros, Greek salads, pizza and other foods popular to the ethnic makeup of the community. The stout Greek man with white skin and coal black hair watched him work, then taught him the "right way to wash dishes." The man stood beside him, demonstrating. "Never lean on sink when wash dishes. Stand straight and tall," my father quoted the man. For as long as I could remember, Daddy had always stood straight and tall when he worked around our home, whether he was chopping cotton or repairing the fence of the cow pasture.

Daddy's stories never included answers to the one question that stuck in our young minds: How or why he'd left his mother's home and traveled the country? Why, at 13 years old, had he preferred the odd jobs in Chicago's harsh winters, not seeing the ground for months except when he removed the snow from driveways of expensive homes on the city's North Side?

When we sometimes complained about the cold, Daddy would share a memory he had of one Chicago winter day when it was 50 degrees below zero. "You complaining about cold!" he began. "I remember back in Chicago when it was so cold I spit and it turned to ice before it hit the ground—just rolled down the sidewalk like a glass marble. Now that's cold, and that's when I knew I was a long way from home." There was little in Chicago in the early 1920s—except other southern migrants who left the oppressive farm life for Chicago's promise—to remind James Kearney of Lake Village, Arkansas.

To his benefit, James had always looked older than his age because of his height and demeanor. Still, it was Chicago where he started changing his age, sometimes adding a few years to his real age to get the good-paying day jobs or putting his age back when it benefited him in other ways. "In that city, you always had to be on your p's and q's."

The one slice of Chicago life James Kearney remembers fondly was his participation in the rebuilding of the amazing Union Station in Chicago. The first railway station, the Grand Passenger Station, had been built in 1881 at the corner of Canal and Adams Streets, but due to the increased business and crowds, The Chicago Union Station Company decided to construct a replacement station. Pennsylvania's marquee trains which made a stop at the New York City Pennsylvania Station was the most famous to travel through Union Station at the time. Daddy was surely one of the youngest of the crew laying rail for Chicago's new train station.

"I remember when they opened the new Union Station in 1925," he would say with a gleam in his eyes. "They say it was the biggest and best train station built in the whole century. It was 10 whole blocks long, and man was it pretty! People use to just come there to see the place and meet folk. That station had its own jail, police station, a nursery and a hospital. It was a good feeling knowing I was one of the people who helped lay the rail for the tracks there before that station was built."

In spite of his love-hate relationship with Chicago, Daddy chose the city as the one place he traveled to more than any other. He rode the Greyhound bus there, anticipating the stop by the West Side station and the opportunity to tell fellow passengers of his role in building the tracks. It was the one bright memory of his years in Chicago.

"The longer you stay away, the easier it is to stay away," Daddy said, about his indecision about going home. "After a while, if you don't get a letter telling you bad news, you don't worry about home. I never was scared of hard work, but when I started out I was particular about what work I wanted to do....

"...Shoot, after a while I got to where I could make myself enjoy any job I ever done, even in the middle of them Chicago winters." He passed that trick of the mind on to us—that ability to transpose himself from the world he inhabited to the one he wanted for himself. "Most times nobody gone give you what you want in life, so you just as well start deciding what it is you want and spending your time figuring out how you get it. If you hate picking cotton, but you know you got to do it, fill your mind with something other than what you got to do. Figure out how you gone get it." While manual labor was a reality in our lives, none of us spent our days thinking about the work more than we did about what we wanted to be doing five years later. James Kearney encouraged our dreaming as the first step in getting what we wanted in life.

———

I could never visualize Daddy being the way he described himself as a young man. I had only what I saw in front of me to compare his stories. In my eyes, he was one of the most handsome, smart, serious men I knew. His roles as husband and father were the most important jobs in the world to him, but his stories told of a young, carefree and sometimes irresponsible man who lived for adventure and travel.

After hearing his stories, I envied Daddy's childhood freedom and the almost 20 years he spent waking up and going to bed when he wanted to. What child didn't wish for that? At the same time, I wondered, how easy was it for him to give up the security of home and family that he left so early in life?

Most amazing for me and my siblings were his stories of his days as a genuine hobo. While we were all convinced that there was nothing to be ashamed of, when it came to his past we certainly learned fast enough that everyone didn't share that view. We boasted at school to friends about our Daddy's exploits. "My Daddy use to jump freight trains and travel all over the county and hitchhike with strange people and spend the night around fires with hobos...." Our friends' eyes told us that they viewed Daddy's past differently from us. Their views never changed the way we looked up to our father or the pride we had in his rich, colorful past.

I often imagined him sitting around the night fires with fellow travelers, most of whom were older men; some with sadder stories to tell. "There was all kinds of people out there...you'd be surprised," he'd told us, "white men and colored sittin' around those fires at night not having a home to go to. They took turns telling stories and most of them drinking from one bottle of whisky somebody's begged off somebody or even stole. I couldn't believe how good a life some of the men had left behind."

His story about his travels to the Fiji Islands and his few hours stop in Liverpool, England, on giant sea vessels took our breath away. When we got to school, we searched the classroom globe to find the faraway countries he talked about. He was just into his 20s, he said, when he made those trips.

"I almost didn't go to the Fiji Islands 'cause the captain said they already had enough help on the ship," he recalled. "Then, at the last minute, just before they left the dock, the captain told the crew supervisor to bring me aboard." Though he was usually hired for anything from cooking to cleaning and handiwork, Daddy ended up doing whatever the captain needed including washing, sewing and repairing the crew's torn clothing.

"Most of the work wasn't real hard," he remembered, "but some of the lifting and toting jobs got to be pretty hard. When I was doing that, it seemed like we'd never get to shore." He described his trip to Fiji as "just like I'd read about, just like the pictures I'd seen. It was the most beautiful place I ever saw, and the people treated me like I was just as good as anybody else."

Daddy spent about a month on Fiji, long enough to learn enough of the language to talk to some of the pretty girls. Before leaving, he said, he had gotten so interested in one pretty Filipino girl, he asked her if she wanted to come to America and marry him. For reasons he chose not to share with his children, that relationship ended abruptly.

Daddy had an unlimited reservoir of stories locked inside his memory bank. Some were sad stories about the people he met along the way that couldn't fend for themselves. He told about the hoboes he'd met early on, then learned later they'd died from disease or drank themselves to death and even about his first encounter with a drug addict in New York who was "shaking like a fig on a tree for a dope fix." He'd shake his head, sometimes, almost as if he couldn't believe his life himself. "God had to been watching over me all that time. I came in contact with just about anything you can think of, and people always trying to get me to try something they were doing. I was blessed I had my own values, even if I didn't go to anybody's church."

Daddy, with Mama's gentle urgings, joined church and became a full-fledged Christian in 1945, and like everything he ever did, he took his religion seriously. He became adult teacher for the Sunday school within months. Shortly after, he became a deacon of the church and later superintendent of Sunday school. He was elected to head up the laymen's organization a few years into his membership and traveled to nearby districts teaching church leaders the Bible and the ethics of church stewardship.

Daddy's faith in God, however, did not take away his realism or blur his observations of what was happening around him. He was convinced that his plight and the plight of other impoverished blacks had much to do with the still—active racial problems in the South.

He was always active in local politics, and we listened and learned about the yellow-dog Democrat philosophy from his frequent oratories. He volunteered to pick up residents and take them to vote, and we might hear him ranting later that night about something he called "pole taxes." The sharecropping trap that many black farmers experienced during the Jim Crow era frustrated Daddy, mostly because as much as he tried there never seemed a way out. To help mollify his anger sometimes he would simply say, "God got a plan. I just don't know what it is, yet."

I sometimes overheard snippets of conversation between my parents—my father's voice tinged with anger and bitterness behind their bedroom door. The conversations sometimes continued until late into the night. Sometimes, they whispered over their coffee mugs as they sat in front of the living room heater.

Daddy's complaints about how hard it was to pay off the land and catch up on their credit placed an unusually harsh edge to his voice. "That man lying to me, Ethel. I know I paid twice for this little piece of no-count land!" More than once, it was clear Daddy's anger was focused on specific white men, those who rented us the land he never could finish paying for, the ones who refused to sell us a small patch of land to raise cotton or the one who failed to give us a loan to purchase our own land or equipment to tend our crops. Daddy, like many black southerners whose livelihoods depended on the land, believed white landowners were intent on keeping him poor and as near enslavement as possible.

Mama's religion didn't blind her to the ongoing racial problems that plagued our part of the world, and she understood that her husband's personal pride, in spite of his poverty, caused him problems with whites in Lincoln County. "James, most white folks think 'cause we don't have nothing, we don't have no self-respect." She knew as we did that few people in Lincoln County, black or white, had more pride and self respect than Daddy. ℚ

Ten

Pride and Prejudice
on Varner Road

During the 17 years I lived on Varner Road, Daddy was one of the few Negroes in Gould who still sharecropped. The older I got, the fewer black families were in the business of renting land from white people and working it against credit. As a teen, I was torn between my allegiance and pride in my family and my desire to fit in with my new peers who were all as close to middle class as blacks would get in southeast Arkansas. In some strange way, I had shucked my old, impoverished sharecroppers' daughter image and "arrived." Through these new peers, I learned how shameful other families viewed our way of life.

Most times I avoided the subject of my father's source of income. Sometimes I lied, especially if I was talking to people who didn't know any better. In this made-up existence, my father owned the 45 acres of cotton we worked, rather than leased it from the white landowners.

When I returned to my family and lay in bed at night the anger welled up inside me. It was the need to lie that left me angry at myself, at the people I felt obliged to lie to, and at the white landowners who kept us in the sharecropping trap. Daddy was never the target of that anger. It wasn't like he hadn't tried over the years. He simply wasn't the kind of black man they wanted him to be. And because of that, the opportunities that came within his reach continued to suspiciously slip from his grasp, time and time again.

One night, after learning the piece of buckshot land he had borrowed money to buy was suddenly not for sale anymore, Mama told Daddy, "You just as well stop making yourself sick about that piece of no-good land, James. The white folks already decided how they can get back at you...showing you something, then taking it away. They don't plan for you to ever be a real farmer in this place."

A few weeks later, during a typical summer day on Varner Road, Daddy's pent-up bitterness spilled out in a way I'd never forget. The fact that it was an unusually beautiful, summer day and we were playing in the yard rather than working in Daddy's cotton fields are only parts of the reason that particular day is etched in my brain.

Now when I remember that day, I imagine there were likely chickens clucking or a myriad of birds singing-sounds that become like the air you breathe when you live on a farm. But what was most important to Jo Ann and me and the younger brothers we allowed to play with us was that we were playing, not working in the cotton field. We were immersed in one of our favorite games—racing old oil barrels from one end of the yard to the other.

Jo Ann and I were falling off the huge barrels and scrambling back up to win against younger brothers who were quicker and more adept at the game than the two of us. We were so involved that we didn't pay much attention when Daddy walked out the back door into the yard. One of the most indelible memories of growing up with Daddy was how fast he moved. It hardly mattered whether he was working inside the house or in the fields, no one could ever keep up with him.

That day, he was moving to our amazement faster than usual as he hurried to the edge of Mr. Jones' soybean field that came right up to our back yard. What was most unusual was the fact that the work hand on the tractor was a white man. White farmers almost always hired black boys or men to cultivate their farms and plow their fields. They were usually men we knew from the neighborhood or boys attending high school.

Daddy stood on the end of the row, his straw hat tilted mannishly to the right of his forehead, waiting for the white man on the John Deere tractor to make his way to the end of the row. When the tractor arrived on the edge of the row, Daddy stood right in front of it, waving the white man down.

"Mister, I been watching out my back door, and I see that you been plowing more'n a foot into my back yard." He pointed down at his foot where the freshly plowed dirt had landed as the tractor stopped.

The fat man, sweating under the white straw hat, squinted down at Daddy and swiped a line of sweat from his forehead before pulling the hat further over his forehead. He nodded without looking directly in Daddy's face, then turned his head and spat a wad of tobacco on the other side of the tractor. He changed the gears, then started moving the tractor back down the rows without looking back.

Daddy continued to stand at the end of the row, not moving and not turning his head one way or the other even though we were standing just feet from him. It was as if we weren't even there. Our big, red speckled rooster ran across the yard after one of Mama's hens, and I wanted to hunch Jo Ann to tell her to watch, but I didn't because her mind was on watching the white man's tractor move back toward us. Mr. Jones' tractor was a lot newer and bigger than Daddy's own John Deere tractor that was always needing repairs or new parts. It was louder, too, I decided, as it rumbled its way back down the row.

Mr. Jones' worker didn't look up this time, although Daddy stood in the same place he was standing the last time the man came down the rows. Our eyes went from the big tractor to Daddy as the huge machine moved toward us, slowed for just a moment, then made the same turn it'd made the last time, inside Daddy's yard.

Daddy stood for a minute not saying a word, then walked slowly into the house. He was there for what seemed like a long time, but it must not have been so long. The white man wasn't even halfway back down the row when Daddy walked back out. Daddy's gait was still slower than he walked most times, but maybe it was because he was carrying the shotgun he used to hunt deer cradled in his arms.

Jo Ann, the boys and me all huddled together just feet behind Daddy under the black walnut tree. My heart was beating as fast as it ever had and as much as I wanted to go and get Mama, I knew Daddy wouldn't want me to. Jo Ann was looking straight at Daddy's face and trembling some. Our younger brothers were too much in shock to say a word.

Mostly, we stared at Daddy's big gun that we only saw when he took the older boys out to hunt deer in the winter. Daddy stood in the same spot he stood before and pointed his gun straight at the white man's head. The tractor came to a stop, and a heavy swirl of dust covered the tractor and turned the white man a darker tan.

The tractor driver's face, underneath the dust, was almost as white as the straw hat he wore. Daddy's voice now was loud and clear and sounded like he sometimes did when he spoke with so much passion about one of the Bible stories. "I told you, mister, not to plow up my back yard, and I meant it. Now, if you so much as plow one inch more of my yard I'll blow your devilish brains out, as God is my witness."

The man fumbled with the tractor gears, this time forgetting to spit on the side of his tractor. His clumsiness made the tractor jerk some back and forth before he backed the tractor into the field and turned around, squashing a lot of Mr. Jones' good plants under the tractor wheels. Daddy didn't move from his spot as he watched the man drive to the edge of the next two rows. This time he didn't come near Daddy's back yard. ℚ

ELEVEN

James Kearney's Christmas Story

According to my father, his and Mama's lives began in a dream on Christmas Eve in 1936. This is the story he shared with my mother the first week they met and the story he shared with his children as we came into the world.

It was the winter of 1933 when I finally decided it was time I took myself back home to see how Mama was doing. When I walked up to that door, Mama ran out that house like she was looking in the face of a saint. I never remember seeing Mama that happy all during my childhood. She hugged me and was cryin' like she wouldn't ever stop.

I'd been gone from home for about 15 years—left when I was just 11 years old, and the longer I stayed away, the more I began to think I might never go home again. But God works in mysterious ways and just weeks before I went home, I found myself dreaming about home just about every night. I knew for certain God was trying to tell me something.

I have to say, even after deciding I'd done what God wanted me to do, there was still some itching under my feet to get up and go sometimes. I just kept tellin' myself that God had brought me back home for a reason, and I needed to stay around long enough to find out what it was. I started wondering what Papa would have told me if he was still here. I had had time to think about things a lot and decided Mama just didn't know what to do with a houseful of children after Papa died. Maybe, she just didn't know how to be a mother without Papa there.

I guess I musta' decided I didn't have to be a child no more neither. It was a hard time for all of us. In some ways, I never accepted Papa being gone and thought maybe I'd find him somewhere out there. I started thinkin' 'bout Papa and how much I still missed him. If truth be told, the hurt from his dying was part of the reason I left in the first place. It was just so odd the way one day Papa was up healthy and being like he always was and then to fall sick and die, all in three days' time. That was hard.

For the first few weeks back home, I couldn't hardly sleep for thinking about which way my life needed to go, even though there was still so many things I wanted to do and places I hadn't visited yet. One day, after I was back home for a few weeks, I suddenly remembered I hadn't even told Mama about my predicament. I called her into the kitchen, told her to sit down for a minute, 'cause I had something to tell her.

One thing hadn't changed; Mama still always expected the worse. I hurried up and told her it wasn't nothing bad.

"You got a little granddaughter in Pine Bluff. I married a girl named Tempie three years ago, but we separated a year later," I told her.

Mama looked a little surprised, but not a lot. She just hunched her shoulders and said, "Well...." I think she was a little interested in my little girl and the fact that she had a granddaughter somewhere in Pine Bluff.

Thing was, both me and Tempie knew I wasn't ready to be nobody's husband when we married, but we had the baby coming. God forgive me, but it show wasn't long before I was living about the way I was before we got married. One night, after Tempie had put up with me for as long as she could, she shot at me through our bedroom window with my own pistol. Said her friend told her I was out at the club with another woman. That was all the sign I needed. I went back by the house the next morning when she was visiting her sister, packed up my clothes and moved a few streets over to a friend of mine.

"Tempie was a good woman, and if things had gone differently, you would like having her for a daughter-in-law," I told Mama.

Though I didn't say it to Mama, my daughter Clara Bell was part of the reason I came back home. I needed somewhere to hang my hat, so Clara Bell could come and visit with me sometime. I loved that little girl and knew I needed to settle down to a job that would help me provide for her.

After living at Mama's house for a few months, I went to visit my brother Sam, who had moved to England, just outside Pine Bluff. Sam had got married about a year ago to a little girl named Mary. He sent word that he and Mary could use my help clearing the crops on the farm he'd just rented from old Jessie Corey. I told Mama I was going for a few days to help Sam out, but I'll be dog if I didn't end up staying there for the next couple of years.

By the time I left Sam's home, he and his little wife had a son, Sammie C., and Mary was about to have another one. They were just newlyweds, but Mary was already complaining about some of the tricks Sammie thought up to get to the gambling houses. I wasn't nobody's saint, but I was sure glad I wasn't hooked on drinking or gambling. Poor Sam had gambling in his blood on top of that Kearney restlessness. The boy had a heart of gold, but he loved gambling like it was a pretty woman, and most of his spare time away from home was spent at somebody's gambling table. I swear if he wouldn't rather play cards than eat, and many a nights he did.

I moved back to Mama's house about the middle of 1936. By that time, she'd moved on the Buchanan farm in Pine Bluff and had leased some land from Mr. Roy Hanson, just a few miles down the road. She was glad to see me when I came up 'cause she needed some help with her own few acres of cotton. Mama and me made a pretty good crop that year, and with the end of the year allowance, she started shopping early for Christmas.

I was just about settled back into life in Pine Bluff by December that year and had even met a nice young lady named Erlean Davis that I liked a lot and was spending time with. She had already started bringing up marriage, and after a while I was thinking maybe it was time for me to give marriage another try. I knew her daddy didn't like me and wouldn't consent to the two of us marrying. We started talking about eloping, and I wasn't so sure I wanted that. But I promised Erlean I'd give it some serious thought over the holiday. Like I said, I wasn't a confirmed Christian then, but I already knew marrying was something I would talk over with God.

The night I had the dream I had been half-sleeping and tossing and turning about whether to marry Erlean. I had seen her earlier that night, and just like usual the conversation ended up on marriage—her side of the conversation, anyway. Before I left her, I had started to feel real tired and feverish. I went directly to bed when I got home. Just before I fell into a really deep sleep, I remembered I hadn't told Mama good night like I usually did, but I was too tired and sleepy to get up.

It was that very night that God sent me this vision. That's just the only way I know to explain it. He showed me my future in a dream. I was driving my car to the Pine Bluff train station on Pine Street. I can still remember it as clear as if it happened today. When I got out of my car and walked into the terminal, there was a girl standing there as if she was waiting for me.

I swear, in all my years of traveling, I hadn't never seen a girl as pretty as this one. She was walking toward me from the other side of the station. She wasn't real big, but she had a nice figure and a pretty head of coal black hair that hung down her back. And I'll never forget those eyes, light brown and shiny as cat-eye marbles.

For some reason I knew the girl had just got off the northbound train. She was toting a green suitcase that seemed to be real heavy. I was thinking to myself that I ought to offer to tote the suitcase for her, but I never got around to asking her. Before I knew it, there she was, standing right in front of me and looking straight in my face.

"You come to carry me home, James? I'm your wife." Those are the words that came out of her mouth.

She was smiling a real pretty smile, one of the prettiest I ever saw. When I looked perplexed, she started laughing a little. I guess I must've looked like I'd seen a ghost.

"I'm ready to go home, James," she said again. She was still laughing, but she turned to walk out of the train station.

I was outdone. I'd never seen this girl before in my life, not even nobody who looked like her. I didn't know what to say, couldn't even find my voice to answer her. She turned, waiting for me to catch up, and still she was laughing.

"I'm your wife, James. Let's go home, now," was the last thing she said.

I never had paid much attention to women's clothing, yet, I remembered every detail of what the girl was wearing that night from the green plaid coat to her green suede shoes. I noticed the girl's full head of hair and the dimple in her cheek when she smiled and handed the suitcase to me. She started walking toward my car and all the while I was thinking, 'I don't know this girl. Who is she?' I kept looking over my shoulder where she was walking behind me, still smiling. I remembered that she hadn't told me her name and was just about to ask her when I felt myself losing the dream.

"But, you never told me your name..." I was saying, when I felt somebody shaking me, rousing me from the dream. It was Mama, telling me to wake up.

"You dreaming, James, and I think you comin' down with something. Don't bother to get up right now."

It was already morning. I felt hot and sweaty, and I must've looked something awful for Mama to tell me to stay in bed. When she walked out of the bedroom and back to the kitchen, my mind turned to the girl and I found myself disappointed that I never got her name.

Mama came back in and handed me a big mug of tea to drink. She felt my forehead and shook her head.

"You got a high fever, James. Drink that tea and I'll bring some 666."

I must have been real sick for Mama to say I needed to stay in bed. She never believed in grown people layin' around during the day. And, truth be told, I never liked layin' around during the day, but I stayed in bed for two days straight.

Mama used every remedy she knew to break my fever—alcohol, mint tea, turpentine and sugar, cow chip tea, Black Draught laxative, and some more 666 cold medicine—but nothing seemed to work. That fever was just the beginning of a bad case of the flu that kept me in bed for another five days.

December 1936 is the first and only time I ever completely missed Christmas, though there were quite a few Christmases when our cupboards were so bare I might as well have missed it. The flu and the fever had just about left by the end of December, though, and I'd never been happier in my life to get up out of a bed. I was still weak, but stirred around the house some and soon found out that my appetite had come back, too.

On New Year's Eve, Nap, a good friend of mine, came up to visit. He got tickled when he walked in and saw my face buried in a plate of Mama's blackberry cobbler.

"I thought I would come down here and check on you, James," Nap said. "Miss Cynthia told me you been sick ... but look like you doing just fine, now."

We laughed some more.

"If you feeling up to it, I thought you might want to come down the road to the house and help us with our hog killin'," Nap said.

Though I still wasn't feeling 100 percent, I didn't want to sound like

119

I was whining and didn't want to disappoint Nap.

"All right," I said. "Why don't you go on back and give me a little while to get dressed? I'll come on in a little bit. I need to put some heavier clothes on, so I don't get sick all over again."

Nap smacked me on the back and laughed.

"You show don't, if it's gone make you eat like that," he joked. "Miss Cynthia won't be able to afford you getting sick too many times."

Just before Nap walked through the door, he turned around and hollered back that he almost forgot to tell me something.

"Gracie's cousin is visiting from Magnolia, and she wanted to know if you interested in joining us all for a movie tonight? That new movie called 'Big Foot' is showing at the Pines, and Gracie thought that might be fun."

As much as I liked movies, I didn't think I'd feel up to it tonight.

"I don't know, Nap. I probably need to get myself back home and get to bed after the hog killing. We'll see."

Nap hunched his shoulders and started back through the door.

"OK, Gracie gone be disappointed, and that cousin of hers show is pretty," he hollered back.

Nap laughed and stung my eardrums when he slammed Mama's door closed.

I wasn't a bit interested in meeting no woman today. In fact, Nap would be lucky to get me down there at all. I was already missing my evening nap and my comfortable bed. As second thoughts started setting in on me, somethin' in the back of my mind told me I should keep my word and go on down to Nap's house for this year's hog killing.

When Mama saw that I was dressed and ready to go out, she started fussing.

"James, ain't it too early for you to be going out in this winter weather?"

I walked through the living room toward the coat rack behind the door.

"I'm feeling a lot better, Mama."

She walked over anyway and felt my forehead.

"I still think you could use another day inside before you start getting out there, James." She finally said, "Well, I don't guess it's no need for you to stay 'round here. The worst of your flu is likely over, and the fresh air might do you good."

By the time I made it to Nap's house, it was almost noon and most of the hog killin' was done. Nap said they had five big sows to kill that day, and he'd started soon as he got back home. One was still strung upside down on Nap's pecan tree out back. One of his friends was cleaning the hog's innards, scraping everything out into a big pan to feed to the other hogs later on. Steam was coming up off another fat hog whose head stuck out of a big 100 gallon barrel of scalding water.

There were about 10 neighbors and some of their children in Nap's back yard. I stood around for a while, just watching. I still wasn't so sure my stomach was up to butchering and cleaning any of Nap's fat hogs today.

Hog killin' was a special time for people in our community; more a time for enjoying each other's company and celebrating the New Year than real work. The men mostly enjoyed the chance to get out from under their wives so they could swap stories and lies with other men and catch up on what everybody's been up to over the year.

Company almost always ended up staying long past the hog killing. It wasn't unusual to have more than 25 people at one house during that time and sometimes as many as 10 hogs to kill. Sometimes a hog was so large it took four or five men to handle it. After the hog meat was cleaned, cut up and wrapped in butcher paper, a lot of it was sent home with the men for their families and to other families who could use it. The young folk were simply there to enjoy themselves. They didn't see this as important to their livelihood, just another part of their Christmas celebration. The smallest children even brought their Christmas toys to show off and share with friends and kinfolk.

There weren't many full-grown men in the community who couldn't butcher, scald and scrape a hog clean in less than an hour flat. That is, if they made sure the water was scalding hot once the hog was butchered and the knives plenty sharp enough. Sometimes, it was later down the road that folks found out the knife wasn't sharp enough or the water wasn't hot enough when they found hog bristles in their fried sausages or hog-head souse.

Nap had rounded up just enough men from the community to get the job done. A few had come all the way from little towns like Pastoria and Grady. Some of them had turned down his invitation to Christmas dinner because they knew they'd be coming to hog-killing day.

"Hey, James!" I heard Nap calling my name. He was standing with some other men around the wood fire on the other side of the yard. He walked over and looked me up and down, then declared I wouldn't be much help in hog killing today.

"Tell you what, James, why don't you gone in the house and sit by the fire a while and when you rested up, come on back out and see if there's anything left to do."

I tried to tell Nap that I was just fine and could go straight to work, but he wouldn't hear of it.

"If the truth be told, I told Miss Cynthia I'd make sure you didn't get a setback out here in this weather. I don't think she got enough food to see you through another bout of flu."

We both laughed, and he pushed me toward the house.

"Gone in there and find Gracie. I'll call you out in a little while.

I could never win an argument with Nap, so I turned and started walking toward the back door of his house. I was looking forward to seeing Gracie. It had been a while since I saw her, and I missed joking around with her. She was always such a happy girl with a big smile and pretty as a picture. I always told Nap how lucky he was to have her. Just as I headed to open the back door, I saw a girl's face in the window, looking down at me. She quickly closed the curtains when I looked up.

Then, out popped Gracie's pretty head. She was waving and hollering my name out loud.

"Hey, James! Boy, where in the world you been all this time? We ain't seen you in a month of Sundays!"

She was grinning and motioning me to come inside. I waved and started to speak back to her when I saw the other girl's head peek out again, right beside Gracie's. Though I could only get a glimpse of the girl's face, I had a funny feeling I'd seen that face before.

"Go on in the house and make yourself acquainted with Gracie's cousin, James," Nap hollered over to me.

He must've been watching when the girl looked out 'cause he started grinning again. I was feeling pretty strange and wondering if maybe I really should head back home and lay back down. I knew Nap was up to his old matchmaking tricks, and I sure wasn't in no shape to get pulled into that today.

I walked through the kitchen into Nap's living room and hurried to the pot-bellied wood heater that sat in the middle of the floor. Gracie was sitting in a straight-back chair on the other side of the heater when I walked in. I was about to fall into the comfortable-looking wood rocking chair sitting next to her.

Gracie jumped up off the chair and came over to give me a big hug and kiss. "James, where you been? We expected to see you over the Christmas holiday."

I apologized and told her I'd been in bed with the flu for the last week. She nodded and patted my back without saying much more, and I knew she must've already known.

"Well, James, since you here, I want you to meet my favorite cousin who is also my best friend. Ethel Virginia came up right after Christmas and been with me since then, and don't be spreading your germs on her," she joked.

Ethel Virginia walked slowly into the warm living room and stood behind the tall chair. The girl was holding a comb and brush in her hands, and I figured she must've been combing Gracie's hair before hurrying out of the room. She looked up at me long enough to ask, real quick, "How you doing, Mr. James?"

I swear I'd seen that girl's shy smile somewhere before. Gracie and Nap's fat wood heater sat between us, hiding everything but the girl's head and shoulders. While I was trying to make my mouth move, it seemed like the wood in the heater was crackling something terrible, and the heat was just about more than I could bear. Finally, I mumbled, "It's a pleasure to meet you, Miss Ethel."

Gracie was looking from Ethel to me with that same grin Nap had had when he mentioned her. I walked real slow around to the other side of the stove to shake her hand, but when I reached out my hand she looked shyly up at me. We both started laughing when I realized she had the brush and comb in her hands. I must've been staring at the girl's pretty face, trying to recall where I'd met her before, when I realized she'd laid the comb and brush down and was offering me her hand.

When our hands touched, I swear it was like electric currents went through me. I knew in one instance she was the girl from my dreams. She had the very same eyes and smiling mouth and the very same voice. I stood there shaking her hand with my mouth hanging open. She must've thought I was the biggest fool in Arkansas.

Gracie, standing behind Ethel now, was frowning and shaking her head at me. She slowly walked over close to me and whispered, "James, what in the world is wrong with you?"

I tried to straighten myself and at least look like I had some sense. I was about to go sit down in the rocking chair when I looked down and saw the girl's green suede shoes. The very shoes the girl wore in my dream. I moved toward the bedroom door and mumbled to Gracie, "Excuse me just a minute."

While the two girls giggled and whispered, I walked out of the room, bent on finding the one thing that stood out most from that dream. I walked through Nap's and Gracie's house until I got to the guest bedroom where they had laid the visitors' coats. I rummaged through the pile of winter coats, jackets, gloves and scarves on the bed but didn't find the coat I was looking for. It suddenly struck me that the girl's coat would be hanging in the guest room where she was staying.

I took a deep breath, suddenly realizing I was exhausted and needed to lie down. Just as I sat down on the bed to catch my breath, Gracie hurried through the door.

"James, are you all right?"

The frown on her face told me she was really concerned. Gracie was one of those people always in a good mood and never was one to do a lot of worrying. But I could tell my actions were really scaring her.

"...Sorry, Gracie," I mumbled, half smiling, "I'm fine, just still getting over the flu."

She nodded, accepting my answer, then began pushing the stack of coats to the side. She pointed to the cleared space and ordered, "James, lay down 'fore you get sick again. She threw somebody's heavy coat across my legs, then asked, "Did Nap tell you we wanted to go see that new movie tonight? We was hoping you could come, too. Ethel is coming...but first lay down and see how you feel when you get up."

I just nodded, and Gracie started to leave.

"Before you go...," I said, "I just was thinking that Ethel is just as pretty as Nap told me. She favors you a lot, but she show don't talk too much."

I was beginning to feel a nap coming on and kicked my shoes to the floor. I was hoping Gracie would tell me more about her cousin before she left out.

"I'm glad you like Ethel, James. She is a real nice girl. She comes from a good family in Magnolia. You ever heard of the Curry family? They a pretty big family and own a lot of land up there. Ethel's mama is my mama's sister."

She turned to walk out, then turned back.

"Oh yeah, Ethel said you look pretty good, too."

My heart skipped a beat at this, but I decided not to say anything. Before she left, Gracie told me Ethel had a little boy who was home with her parents.

"Most times, Aunt Mattie won't let Ethel bring him out-almost treats Cecil like he's her child."

But before I could ask if the pretty girl was married, Gracie was already out the door. I tried, but there was no way I could take a nap now. My mind and my heart was going a mile a minute. I finally got up from the bed and hurried through the house to find Gracie. She was there in the living room, sitting in the same place while Ethel combed her hair. They were like two school girls talking and giggling together.

"Ah, Gracie, will you let Nap know I'm going home to get my car, and I'll be back to drive us to the movies?"

I was too embarrassed to look at her cousin but could feel them both looking at me with questions on their face. Gracie didn't say much, just nodded.

"All right, James, we'll be here."

As I hurried down the road, I remembered the sound of the girl's voice in my dreams when she said, "I'm your wife. You coming to take me home?" It was like a light turned on in my head, and I knew...I knew that's what God had been trying to tell me. I knew that was why he'd brought me back home. It wasn't the first time God had talked to me through dreams. I was just glad I listened.

126

The Lord show was at work on me that day. When I went to pick Nap and Gracie and Ethel up, they was standing in the living room with their winter coats already on. Ethel's coat was as I remembered it in my dream, a light and dark green plaid coat, and I wasn't a bit surprised to see her in it.

"Big Foot" was Ethel's very first movie in a real movie house, and she and Gracie spent most of the night either giggling or screaming. We sat down in the "peanut gallery." At least that's what colored folks called it because young white folks sometimes threw their peanut shells down on us as we watched the movie. That wasn't a big concern of mine tonight, though. I was listening to Ethel's every word and enjoying myself. Though Ethel Virginia wasn't a big talker, she said everything that needed to be said, and I made up for the rest.

Over the next two months, I spent most of my time at Nap's house. Ethel had talked her mama into letting her come back to Gracie's just a week or so after she'd gone home. I already knew I wanted to be with her for the rest of my life. When she got back, she told me she felt the same way. We decided right away that we wanted to get married.

In all my excitement about Ethel and wanting to marry her, I'd forgotten two important things. I had to tell Erlean about Ethel, that it was God's will that I marry this girl, not mine. And the other thing was getting a real divorce from Tempie.

After all this time, I was still married to Tempie. I went and told her about Ethel and asked for a legal divorce. Tempie was nicer about giving me a divorce than Erlean was about giving me her blessings to marry Ethel instead of her. But sometime later we became friends again, and she was happy for me. When mine and Tempie's divorce was legal, Ethel and I planned our wedding for March, time enough for her to let her parents know.

Ethel's parents, Mr. Luther and Mrs. Mattie Curry, didn't think much of me marrying their daughter. They told Ethel she had to bring me home to meet them before they would consent to my marrying her. I didn't go and told Ethel it just didn't make sense for me to have to go and ask them for her since she was already past marrying age. Ethel's parents then told her we had to get married at her church in Magnolia. But Ethel didn't want to do that, so we didn't.

We got married at a Justice of the Peace's house in Pine Bluff. Mama, Nap, Gracie and the minister's wife were the guests and witnesses. That was just fine with me, though it took some time for Ethel to get over her parents not being there. Turned out, I never met her parents properly until a few years later.

I always wondered how my life might've turned out if it hadn't been for that Christmas Eve dream in 1936. I know it wouldn't have been what God wanted for me, and it couldn't have brought me the kind of happiness Ethel did. When we said our vows on March 17, 1937, God told me then that Ethel and me would live a very special life together. ◎

TWELVE

Ethel Virginia Curry
Kearney

Dreams would play as important a role in my life as the lessons I learned in church or school or from the wise old women who lived on Varner Road. My dreams escorted me through the darkest of my days on Varner Road, the hills of northwest Arkansas and beyond. And while Daddy was the assigned purveyor of dreams in the Kearney home, Mama was his silent partner, acquiescing to Daddy's vivid imaginations without offering a yea or nay. From the very earliest, we were teethed on Daddy's dream-tinged stories of his childhood and his life. Most memorable would be his and Mama's fairy tale meeting in his dream on Christmas Eve in 1936. It was that dream which encouraged me to value more than the logical truths, but truths based on possibilities as well.

But even in Daddy's fever-induced dream, he saw the miles of differences between him and 18-year-old Ethel Virginia Curry. The girl he met at the bus station, with the beautiful smile and piercing, hazel eyes, represented a different world. Her family was the Negro community's version of middle class-teachers, preachers and owners of livestock and land. They owned hundreds of acres of cotton and even had white sharecroppers and day laborers helping clear that land.

Young Ethel Curry must have also reminded Daddy of his own losses, both familial and material—the land and livestock branded TCK back in Tulsa, Oklahoma, their good standing in the community and the much-beloved father's early death at 47.

She must have made him wonder about the life he might have lived had it not been for the early tragedies forcing their return to southeast Arkansas and a life of itinerant farming. Just maybe, the vacuum left by his father's unexpected death could only be filled by someone so different from him.

Mama's childhood environment protected her from some, but not all, of life's harsh realities. And though her parents, Luther and Mattie Emma Curry, were something above poor, they wouldn't easily forget from whence they came-that they were children of former slaves.

Both of Mama's paternal grandparents, Ned and Priscilla Watson Curry, were said to have been born into slavery—Ned in 1833 and his wife Priscilla around 1843. While Ned died in 1894 at the age of 61, his wife lived to the ripe old age of 83, succumbing to a natural death in 1926. Because there are no marriage records, it is estimated they married shortly before Abraham Lincoln set them free—when slave marriages were still not recognized by white men's laws. And it is because of their first-hand knowledge of slavery, Ned and Priscilla would have raised Luther and his 12 siblings to thank God for their deliverance but also to do everything in their power to collect and hold on to the thing that assured their freedom—land.

Incessant work symbolized the Curry family. They are remembered through oral and documented history as a proud group of people with an almost maniacal devotion to religion and work and desperation to pull themselves up by their own bootstraps. Above all this, however, was this family's insistence on upholding the Curry name. Luther and his twin Luthenia Curry, born in September 1886, were the youngest of Ned and Priscilla's children.

Luther married Mattie Emma Russ, also a native of rural Columbia County, in 1913. The couple would bring 10 children into the world—two would die in infancy and one at the age of 17. From all appearances, this was an unlikely couple, except their values mirrored each other's. In physical stature and personality, however, Mattie Emma was tall, thin and pliant while Luther was short, muscular and stern. Family and neighbors recalled Mattie Emma as a sweet, kind woman with a compassionate heart. Luther was compassionate about his family, while he epitomized the Curry dogma for hard work and a stern hand with his family. They were both strict Christians and protective of what they had created for themselves.

Mama never explained how it was she never completed school given her lifelong love for learning. More than any of the rest of the Curry children, Mama favored Luther Curry with her short athletic build, pleasant round face and piercing stare. While quiet and shy as a young girl, she also inherited her father's stern demeanor and stubborn personality, though it was rarely on display. The pretty daughter would disappoint her father twice. The first time was a premature, out-of-wedlock pregnancy at 17, and the other time, two years later, was a marriage to a 27-year-old man who Luther Curry considered a hobo who had probably seen too much of the world and was far too old for his daughter.

Mama never offered us explanations for how her life evolved—the distance she had to travel from the Curry environment to the man with whom she chose to share the rest of her life. Hers and Daddy's differences likely did as much to draw them together as her parents' vocal disapproval. "I never knew there were people who lived like your daddy before I met him," she once said.

While her parents had taught their children the value of money, land ownership and a good name, Mama fell in love and married—in less than three months—a man who offered her little more than beautiful stories and dreams.

My siblings and I had grown up hearing the ragged edges of conversations about Mama's "good" family in Magnolia, Arkansas—a well-respected colored family with deeply ingrained work ethics and high expectations for their eight children. The five girls and three boys, according to family lore, enjoyed a normal, happy existence that included hard work and strict religion. Their lives appeared normal, except for natural calamities like Mama's youngest sister Helen's falling ill and dying at the age of 17; another sister, Ernestine's crippling accident by scalding when she was just a toddler; and Mama's own delicate accident of an early unwed pregnancy.

The unanswered questions among the Kearney children was how someone like Mama, thought to be one of Luther and Mattie Emma Curry's brightest children, could end up pregnant in a home like the Currys' and how these pillars of the community responded to the shame their daughter must have brought on the family? Finally, we wondered what would precipitate a timid, young woman to abandon—within three months' time—the safety and security of the known for an unknown that was the charismatic but penniless James Kearney?

I n November 1969, two months after I turned 16, I sat with a crowd of sad and somber strangers as a tall, round woman in a dark suit stood beside my grandfather's casket and sang a haunting rendition of an old slave hymn, "The Troubles of the World." Luther Curry, Big Daddy, as we called Mama's father, was presented for viewing and eulogized by Reverend J.P. Story at Macedonia Missionary Baptist Church that day. He'd attended the church all of his life and had served as a deacon for almost 30 years.

The small church set on Highway 98 in McNeil, just a few miles outside Magnolia. The Curry family founded and built the first Macedonia Baptist Church after a white farmer, W.W. Wilson, deeded the original plot of land to Ned Curry for five dollars—with the strict stipulation that the land must only be used to build a missionary Baptist church, a schoolhouse or a graveyard. Mama had attended the church all her life, up until she'd married my father in 1937. Reverend N.S. Coleman from Minden, Louisiana, had been her minister then.

The soloist's deep powerful voice was in honor of Luther Curry's love for Negro spirituals, and-as was expected at this and other rural South funerals—the song appropriately moved my mother, Big Mama and the rest of the Curry family to loud, uncontrollable sobs. Mama's daddy had turned 83 years old just two months before his death, and this belated birthday memorial was overrun with Currys, my grandmother's family, and what seemed like a large community of distant relatives.

What I remember most about that day was how beautiful Mama looked and how sad. She had cried the week before when Big Mama sent word that her father had died that morning of pneumonia. I learned, by listening closely to my parents' whispers, that Big Daddy had walked away from the senior home during an early cold spell and wasn't discovered for hours. When Big Mama and her sons found him, the exposure had taken its toll. The aging man shivered uncontrollably and was clueless as at whom these people were who rescued him. Mama said he came down with pneumonia and never recovered.

Mama's three sisters lived in Indiana. When I was younger, I imagined that Mama was Cinderella and the sisters were wicked and mean, harboring jealousy and resentment to the kind-hearted, benevolent Ethel Virginia. I always had that kind of imagination. But as an adult getting to know these women, I came to like them and to realize they were as much in awe of Mama as I was in awe of them. I never stopped wondering, however, about the severed or nonexistent bond between Mama and the rest of her family.

After Big Daddy's death, the three sisters worried about their aging mother living alone in Magnolia. Though she had a son in Little Rock and Mama lived outside Gould, it wasn't good enough for the sisters. They decided Big Mama would move to Indiana—out of the house she'd lived in all her adult life, raised her eight children in and cared for her husband in until his mind went bad.

By the summer of 1969, my grandmother was all loaded up and on her way to Indiana. She made a hurried stop on Varner Road to say goodbye to Mama. My uncle unloaded pieces of furniture, memorials from the Curry home. There were lots of hugs, some tears. I was stunned how the two women's smiles both filled their faces and made their eyes shine. Mama was grateful for the cherry wood bedroom set and the mix-matched dressers and chairs—one of which I'd claim as my own.

My grandfather Luther's funeral was the first time I witnessed my mother interact with her family—except the handful of times my grandparents and aunts had visited. We had grown up with very loose bonds to either side of my parents' families. While there were Kearney cousins, children of my father's half brother who spent summers with us, my first meeting of Curry cousins was during Big Daddy's funeral.

As I sat quiet, still very shy, in my knee-length black dress that day, I was fascinated by this crowd of family members, by the commonalities between my mother's siblings. I had uncovered some beautiful secret about myself. This sprawling crowd of people in every color, height, size and background were all a part of me—the smiles, the flawless complexions, the soft, fine hair that prematurely grayed and receded, and even the proper carriage and articulate speech. I turned the names that claimed kinship over in my mind—Manley, Russ, Lockhart, McCullough, Lawson, Watson and a long list of others.

I had eavesdropped during my parents' conversation enough to know that Mama was this prominent family's version of a black sheep. She didn't fit the mold. I wondered if it was her decision not to fit. I wondered if Mama would be a different person had she followed the family line of educators, government workers and small business owners. I compared Mama to her three sisters, all beautiful, elegant women. Mama was beautiful, too, but her less-than-elegant dress and the extra 20 pounds made her different from the others. I blamed our sharecropper existence and her annual pregnancies.

My mother, sad and bewildered, sat with Daddy toward the end of the front pew among the sisters and their husbands from Indiana. Big Mama sat with her sons at the other end. This family snapshot was the beginning of my longing to know who Ethel Curry was and how she came to be James Kearney's wife. What was the underlying reason for the strained bond with her family? From all accounts Mattie Emma Curry was a wonderful, loving mother. Luther, though stern and domineering, was the salt of the earth, taking good care of his family and even showing his love once all the chores were done. Was my mother's estrangement from her family a voluntary one, or was it precipitated by her early shame?

The few memories I had of Big Daddy visiting us on Varner Road were fond ones. There were a handful of times the short, round man with the wide smile and pop-bottle glasses had visited his daughter. I can only remember him standing in our yard, his hands tucked together behind his back, in awe of this yard full of grandchildren; asking simple questions, offering shiny coins and smiling, always smiling. He had never stayed long, but long enough for my child's perception to sense a change in the Mama I knew as a softer, shyer Mama evolved with little-girl smiles for this father who came so seldom.

Daddy was never there during these visits and rarely traveled with Mama when she visited her parents in Magnolia. I didn't understand why Daddy, who loved so much to talk and tell stories, chose to disappear during those visits. Neither of my parents ever broached the subject of that odd fact.

In spite of Daddy's reticence in interacting with the Curry family, he loyally donned his black suit and escorted his wife to her father's funeral in 1969.

My own mother's passing in 1982 created the kind of searing pain that allows clarity and the opportunity for me to revisit the question of who Ethel Curry Kearney was. After her death, I could look at our past without the use of rose-tinted glasses and move closer to fitting together the pieces of that puzzle of who she was. For sure, that final picture will have a background palette of summer morning blue and winter grays. I would begin to accept as I moved into adulthood that it was OK that I had two pictures of my mother—one locked inside my heart, never to be marred by reality—the saintlike nurturer who supplied her children with all the love and attention we would ever need in life. She was a woman with a deep reservoir of love but too many children to love as openly and individually as we craved.

My first and only conversation with Mama about sex was when I was 11 during cotton chopping season. I had left with the rest of my siblings that morning to put in a full day of cotton chopping. The day had started fine but like most summer days had become increasingly hot as the day progressed. When we stopped for lunch at noontime, my stomach hurt some but not enough to complain. After a sumptuous lunch of cold sweet potatoes, hot biscuits, pork chops and Kool-Aid, we all pulled our shirts and hats back on for the mile trek up Varner Road to Daddy's cotton field. As always, I groaned thinking I had another five hours of field work in the hot sun.

We were halfway through the evening, at the time of day when the wind stands perfectly still, and the sun beats mercilessly down on our already sweaty heads. My stomach wasn't hurting just a little. By now, I was in excruciating pain. Unable to stave off my tears, I walked to the area where Daddy was working and whined that I was feeling sick. Daddy stopped his chopping, blew smoke from his cigarette out in the still wind and asked, "What's the matter?"

I explained the best way I could. "My stomach's just hurting...it's been hurting all day." Amazingly, Daddy didn't tell me to sit under one of the shade trees for a while until I felt better.

"Go on up to the house and let your mama have a look at you." As he returned to his chopping, I hurried off, toting my hoe and dreading the hot walk home.

I was bent halfway over with pain by the time I arrived in our front yard. What's worse, I thought I'd wet myself accidentally—or was it just sweat dripping down my body? Mama would have a fit if she found out I'd wet myself full awake in the broad daylight. I saw that Mama was hanging clothes in the back yard when I walked to the back door.

"What you doing back home, Faye? What's wrong with you?"

I tried explaining without crying, but the tears came. "My stomach's hurting, and it won't stop. It's been hurting all day." Mama frowned some, and I knew it was because I hadn't mentioned it earlier. She finished hanging her clothes and ushered me into the house.

"You eat anything besides your lunch today?" I shook my head. "Go on into the bedroom and lay down. I'll be there in a little while."

I went immediately to bed still whimpering and, even with the pain, fell immediately to sleep. I awoke to a warm, damp towel caressing my body. As I opened my eyes, Mama was sitting on the side of my bed with a strange look on her face. She looked at me but didn't speak for a while. I spied the red-tinted pan of water on the floor and the towel that was now dark pink. "Ma..." I searched her face to see if I could tell what the matter was.

Mama softly shook her head as she handed me a clean pair of panties. "Put these on...then put this between your legs inside your bloomers."

I took the piece of rag, doing as she said. I was sure now that I must be dying. Why else would I be bleeding and feeling so bad?

"Well, Faye, you got your period. That means you got to start taking care of yourself. It'll come every month, so you'll have to make sure you keep you a supply of clean cloths for these days." She pulled the cover back up around my chest and gave me a sad smile. "You not gone die, don't worry. It's just the curse God gave all women. It happens to every girl some time or another; just means you getting older, that's all."

I let out a long sigh of relief and was already feeling better.

Mama got up to leave then hesitated. Without looking back, she added, "Faye, this mean you can get pregnant, too. So it's important you don't let no boys mess around with you. I know you already know that, but it's more important now."

That was Mama's sex education class, and it actually worked, at least until I left home for college. That day, though, I was ecstatic just to learn I wasn't dying...and I had something to prove my maturity to Jo Ann.

———————

During the early years of my transformation into a teen-ager, Mama's and my unspoken contract as mother and daughter had changed. It seemed it had happened overnight. My mother's role was no longer mere nurturer and provider—she became a Nazi—like home monitor, a nagging parent endlessly worried about a daughter who teetered between shy and quiet and the outer edge of the straight and narrow.

"You need to keep your mind off boys and on your books" was my mother's incessant warning to me. Later, as I settled into this almost adult stage in my life and learned to shield my boy—attraction from her, there was a slow softening of the relationship. She began to treat me as an almost ally in our home, creating a bond that would only expand and grow stronger as I grew older.

The miracle was that my mother—at first begrudgingly—allowed me to see beyond the surface of who she was. Unfortunately, a large part of this transformation had to do with her cancer prognosis during my junior year in high school. I was the chosen one to care for her during her recovery from breast cancer surgery, a badge of honor I wear to this very day. What started out as embarrassing for me and humiliating for Mama eventually brought us closer. I was made privy to her female shame—that a thing that had characterized her existence all of her adult life now had to be taken away. Our silent grieving for her loss made us comrades of a sort. She grew to depend on my sense of duty and responsibility.

This was a sacrifice for my mother who guarded her emotions and her privacy with an iron will. From that point in my life, I would always believe I was special, that I was chosen as Mama's caretaker during this terrible time in her life because of something wonderful she saw in me. Most of the mornings before school, Mama and I spent silent minutes together as I cleaned, bandaged and straightened while she offered sparse conversation. I spent those last few moments before hurrying for the school bus cloistered in the back closet—the only privacy in the Kearney home-wrestling with my fear of losing this suddenly human parent. As I'd rush to her and Daddy's bedroom door to say goodbye, Mama would repeat her mantra, "Keep your mind on your lessons, and don't be studying them boys." How did she know that except for books and writing my interest in boys was nearing uncontrollable? That was likely part of the reason my parents didn't allow me to date in high school.

Beginning my sophomore year in high school, I was allowed to have "boyfriends" visit on Sunday evenings. Their visits, though, were restricted to two hours of sitting on the living room couch watching whatever television show—"Ed Sullivan," "Wild Kingdom," "Jacques Cousteau" or a "Sunday Night Movie"—my younger siblings or parents chose to watch. When the local 10 o'clock news show came on, my father began his traipsing through the living room—a sign for the boy to say goodnight.

By 1971 when I left home for college, the Pine Bluff doctors announced that Mama's cancer was in remission. We all let out a sigh of relief and gratification that God had looked down favorably upon the family—at least for that time. As I prepared to leave home for the first time in my life, she again offered the same admonitions to stay on the straight and narrow.

"Mama," I laughed, "you don't have to worry about me. I know books come first, and boys come second."

"And find you a church to go to every Sunday," she offered, ignoring my promises.

"Yes, Mama, I will," I promised. I did find a church but only went once or twice before I became a bona fide Baptist backslider, not setting foot in a church except during holidays. Unfortunately, the longer I was away from Mama's all-knowing eyes the more of her wise admonitions I began to ignore.

While I had fretted over my two versions of Mama for so many years, my college years could only be described as dichotomous. Mama continued to hear from the good, responsible daughter who had been her rock when she most needed it. On the other hand, I was fast becoming indoctrinated into the party life of college life and enjoying every second of it. Classes were exciting, and I was learning worlds of new things, but you would never know it from my grades. I was learning but not applying. Boys were everywhere, and my mother wasn't there to monitor me any longer. I learned to party in earnest, was attracted to the wrong boys and was caught more than once sneaking into my college dorm well after curfew.

In spite of the personal transformations taking place on the University of Arkansas campus, my relationship with Mama was solid, even burgeoning. We exchanged letters weekly, even more than once a week sometimes. I told her all the things about college life I wanted her to know. I kept her abreast of my two brothers and Jo Ann, as well. Mama and I were friends, something I would never have imagined as a child. By then, I understood that she was as much human being as saint and that she needed fulfillment beyond what a family could supply.

I had seriously dreaded the two weeks Mama was away from us each summer. The yearly trips she took to California to visit her older children living there. Now I realized that time away from her often harsh realities must have fulfilled some of those needs and made worthy her many sacrifices. I would never, however, forget the image of seeing my mother board the train in Pine Bluff, leaving us motherless for those 14 days. It was the few times I saw my parents kiss and embrace, furtively, as if the acts were wrong or unbecoming. Before boarding the train, Mama would hug us, one by one—smiling, happy, saying a uniform, "Be good...help your Daddy with his work." We stood, excited and dejected, waving, crying until she and the train were out of sight. Daddy would take a last look at the train's caboose, take the hand of the youngest and guide us to our car and home. I wondered all the way home how she could leave us with a smile on her face.

But I forgot that question when she returned. No matter how excited Mama was to begin her trip, she was just as happy to return to her home and her family. She brought back stories, pictures, gifts and boxes of my sisters' clothes, making her return that much more rewarding for me. While I saw motherhood as a one-dimensional caricature of domesticity in my child's eyes, I would realize as an adult how much more there was to a woman's fulfillment.

Should one look closely at the snapshots of my mother, peer deeply into the eyes of the woman there, one might come away with the realization that hers hadn't been an easy journey from the structured comfort of her world in Columbia County to the harsh life she led with Daddy and us in Lincoln County. One would also see pride and a steely resolve to make something good out of the cards life dealt her— sometimes extreme difficulties. She had compartmentalized her life of hurts and disappointment that marred the miracles, holding them at bay as she went on with her life exhibiting the kind of grace under distress that only a true Curry could. More than anything, Ethel Curry Kearney was a woman in love with her family in spite of her imperfect marriage, an imperfect husband and less than perfect family.

In my own growth, I would continue discovering the essence of Ethel Curry Kearney and learning something each time that made me proud that she was mine.

Mama's cancer edict in the prime of her life, just as I was falling in love with being a teen-ager hurried the friendship we would forge. Before her illness, a tentative friendship was slowly blooming. She was humored by my self-absorption, was even curious about the person I was becoming. More than a little, I think my mother saw a mirror of herself in me—a girl I didn't expect she was ever able to be. Mama's interest in me propelled my own introspection and the conclusion that I was worthy of other's attention.

It has taken me over half my life to admit that Mama was more than just the soft, warm woman with the illuminating smile and proud bearing. That is the rose-tinted memory I've tucked securely inside my heart, holding on to it for those rainy days when I need to believe in the goodness of the world. Maybe it is these memories that most of us cling to as we become nurturers to our own children, hoping they will see us as flawless human beings whose worlds are centered on them. These rose-tinted snapshots are what we pull out of our mental pocketbooks and share with the world, saying, "See, here is the perfect mother."

Throughout the evolving relationships and images I have of my mother, there was always that one that was blurry, more elusive than real. That is the woman I'm not able to explain to others—her reverberating silence, her refusal or inability to share all of herself with her children whose unconditional love would have surely accepted all of her without judgment. Mama, in her kind but meticulous way, hid away the child part of her from her children and James Kearney for some unknown reason and encouraged the closing of that door, that wall of silence. Thus, the

Ethel Curry we imagined was the picture Daddy shared with us—a picture based on his Christmas Eve dream in 1936.

Over the years, I have regretted the endless times and opportunities I wasted in search of a perfect mother. In the early years I'd believed in her perfection, then in my teen-age years I'd questioned that perfection. Through time and motherhood, I learned the futility of that search. There was no one thing that made me understand, except my own frail humanity, my own imperfect parenthood and the look in my son's innocent eyes that told me he knew my shortcomings but loved me in spite of them.

———

The 10 years between Mama's cancer remission and the next sighting were interesting times. An empty nester for the first time in her life, she and Daddy began traveling together; no more putting Mama on a train as he returned home. Daddy retired, finally, from the grind of sharecropping. The change in cotton farming helped him make that decision. The increasingly small profits from his cotton crops were no longer worth the work he put into it. Besides, his children were no longer there to assure him profits. Now he'd have to depend on paid workers.

My parents, free from the responsibilities of raising children, became a couple again—reacquainting themselves after 40 years of talking to each other over a roomful of raucous teens or squalling babies. For the first time, there was a look of unadulterated enjoyment of life on their faces as they looked forward to what lay ahead.

While my weeks were spent focused on my family and my work, my Sundays were devoted to my parents. The weekend trips to Varner Road never stopped, even when D.K. turned 13 and apologetically suggested to me that he not be included on each trip to Varner Road. D.K. loved his grandparents as if they were secondary parents, and they thought he could do no wrong. I finally decided his decision was as much about severing the apron string to me as it was about tiring of visiting on Varner Road.

Over the years, I sometimes shared tidbits of Darryl's and my ongoing marital problems with my mother when we were alone. Not many, and not often. I never wanted our time together to turn into a pity pot discussion. I was always afraid my problems would mar the relationship I valued so much.

Mama's death left a painful vacuum inside me, and for many months afterward I was hard-pressed to scrounge up gratitude for anything else going on in my life. After a time, I would remember the friendship my mother and I had developed and nurtured over the years. That friendship had carried me through my teen years and into adulthood. At 29, I was grateful for the many lessons that would be with me forever. I was thankful that my son D.K. had the opportunity to not only know my mother but to forge a lasting bond with her from his earliest months when he spent weeks in her care on Varner Road. And finally, I was so very thankful for what she'd shared with me, sometimes knowingly, sometimes not, about being a woman in this often unfriendly world. I thanked God for those gifts and for the lessons I'd learned to pass on to my own son.

Mama's final goodbye lasted 36 months—557 grief stricken days after the Indian-American oncologist's soft pronouncement that her previously diagnosed breast cancer had magically returned and transformed itself to stomach cancer. The doctor's edict decreased my mother's odds for recovery—or spending happy, golden years with her husband and family—to zero. It proscribed my days and nights for the next 36 months.

As the doctor droned on about Mama's death sentence, Daddy turned older and feeble before our eyes. My tears blinded me to anything more the doctor might have said. And though I don't recall his words, I still remember the sadness in the man's eyes and wondering how often his job called for such conversations. I remember the tall, thin man's mocha brown skin and the shiny blackness of his hair. I remember it was 1981 in Arkansas, and Indian-American doctors were still a rarity there. I would forever remember the soft, clipped American accent as he changed all our lives within minutes.

How is it that even when death stares you in the face, you are surprised when it finally knocks? When the nurse called on March 19, 1982, I knew but had let myself believe that it would never really happen.

"You should come, Miss Kearney. Your mother went into a coma at 11 a.m., and we don't..." I didn't let her finish, laying down the phone and rushing to the bathroom for my brief grieving period. At last, I admitted my mother's death was imminent and knew Daddy would need my strength for the next few days.

Daddy arrived, surrounded by two of my brothers, just minutes after Mama was pronounced dead. We must have talked, hugged, exchanged solaces. When they took Mama away, we decided there was no reason for us to stay. Daddy followed me to my car and like a lost child allowed me to lead him home. There were family members to call, burial plans to make. The grieving would come later.

That night, I remembered the words I'd never said, the questions I'd never asked. Who was this woman I was saying goodbye to? Just this past weekend, most of her children had flown into Little Rock to help celebrate her and Daddy's 45th wedding anniversary. No one said the words, that it would be her last. Fifteen of my parents' 19 offspring converged at the hospital, piling into Mama's room on the ninth floor oncology level. The cakes and balloons helped us forget. The laughter—as hollow as it was—helped too. We toasted James and Ethel Kearney's anniversary with cans of punch and soft drinks purchased from the refreshment area on the floor.

Mama was alert but quiet that afternoon, except for her childlike twinkling eyes expressing a resigned happiness. Her smile was there, too, as she looked from one of her children to the next. She and Daddy exchanged looks that had nothing to do with us. The tears standing in the corner of Daddy's eyes would wait until later to fall. Mama squeezed my hand and held it longer than usual at one point in the evening, and I knew she was silently thanking me for being a good daughter. It's amazing how entire families can fool themselves into believing what is real isn't real. We left her room believing anything was possible, even her recovery.

It was only after she left us that I could admit my angst, maybe even anger that Mama's own story went to the grave with her. "It was my story, too. It was who I was you took to your grave," I ranted inside my mind.

On visits home to monitor Daddy's progress once Mama was no longer there to care for him, I divided those hours between being a good daughter and guiltily rifling through letters, half-written notes, photos, Bibles, her beloved recipe books...anything I could get my hands on, in search of Ethel Curry. The house on Varner Road—where I grew up and where Mama gave birth to my younger siblings—held sketchy ghosts of the Ethel Virginia Curry that I knew so little of.

When Daddy's progress began in earnest and he was getting on with his life, I unabashedly started in on him—pumping my aging father's memories for details about my mother's past.

"But you have to remember something, Daddy. What kind of child was she? What were her favorite subjects at school? Who were her best friends? What was her childhood like? And why doesn't her family visit? What about Cecil's father? Were they in love?"

Daddy would sit, working his dinner across his plate, quiet, thinking. I was mystified at a man who could remember the conversations he had with his father when he was five years old but couldn't recall what his wife of 45 years had said about her early life. I could never discern whether Daddy purposely forgot their conversations or simply refused to tell me secrets about the real Ethel Curry. I was reticent to examine either option.

Daddy was a master storyteller with an elephant's memory. All my life, he'd regaled us with stories about his and Mama's early years as man and wife. The stories may have been little more than rose-tinted memories, but they served my need. He remembered Mama's innocence with smiles and blushes. "She was always so happy, smiling, full of life all the time." He was speaking of that other Ethel, not the one I remembered as more content than happy but always committed and loyal. Daddy surely saw what a man would want to see in his bride, and I was convinced his story was true, just not the full, unadulterated truth.

Accepting our loss was something none of us knew how to do. Our grief weighed us down and closed off our emotions when we most needed each other. Mama had always been the strong one, the backbone that held the family upright. Daddy had depended on her to structure his days, to fulfill his life, to be there when no one else was there. There is little of Mama's funeral I have been able to share with others because, in spirit and mind, I was not there—another out-of-body experience brought on by pain. What I vaguely recall is how the tears were like a stream inside me that wouldn't stop and how the migraine headaches began that day and never stopped.

I remember the rows of black-clad Kearney children and Daddy, more somber than I'd ever seen us before; and the small Baptist church—where Mama had spent roughly 1,200 Sundays of her life—overrun with people who knew and loved her and pitied her family's loss. "How sad...?" "What a loss...?" they said. There were hugs as Daddy and the 19 children piled into the line of black hearses for our ride to the graveyard. Finally, there is the memory of dirt covering the box that held Ethel Curry Kearney's body.

Only time and God's refusal to let us die with Mama allowed us delivery from the incomparable pain of losing the woman I've since decided was the best friend I'll ever have. Once the pain began to subside, the dull ache of another kind of loss, of not really knowing her, began. Certainly, I believed I knew my mother as well as most of my siblings; the person I didn't know and wanted so badly to know was Ethel Curry. The blank pages from her childhood haunted me.

"I should have been more intrusive," I thought as I drifted off to sleep those nights shortly after her death. But there was a line you couldn't cross with Mama. Intrusions about her childhood were most times met with one—syllable answers or smile—tinged silences. Even so, at the end of the questions are the memories in black and white, good memories that overshadow the haunting questions of Ethel Curry, good memories of Mama on Varner Road that carry me through my days and follow me into my dream-filled sleep.

———————

Mornings on Varner Road arouse my senses like no other time in my life and no other part of the day. Those were my moments with Mama that are colored by the sounds, smells and activities that were uniquely hers. Even Daddy's jarring march through the dimly lit house and the slamming of the screened back door were mere interruptions of those mornings. So were the echoing duet of Daddy's sledge hammer against wood posts and his perfect, sharp whistle or the sometimes whiny—screech of iron against iron as he sharpened our chopping hoes for our day in his cotton field—all backdrops to my mornings with Mama.

I would tune out Daddy's morning sounds as I listened for Mama's in the one room that was truly hers. Her quiet rustlings and feline quiet steps from one corner of the wide kitchen to the other comforted me as I lay still beside Jo Ann. My sister and I slept together in the wrought-iron bed throughout our childhood. I sometimes wondered if our constant proximity lent validity to neighbor's claims that we were shadows or mirrors of each other. As I looked over at my younger sister and felt her even breathing, I remembered how Daddy laughingly called Jo Ann his colored china doll.

It was the magical mornings on Varner Road that softened the harsh reality of my life as a sharecropper's child. On those mornings, I awoke with a child's excitement about another day. Those memorable smells of home awakened me from my sleep. They drifted from Mama's kitchen and into the hallways, then into our rooms, waking the rest of my siblings and nudging them to tumble out of bed.

Quickly, careful not to wake Jo Ann, I'd lean across the bed to the window and move the lace eyelet curtain to watch the rim of orange-red sun melt into the morning blue. For that moment, an indefinable beauty framed our two acres on Varner Road—painting our fruit orchard and cotton fields a filmy orange and blue. The good part of me wanted to rouse Jo Ann and share this morning with her; the other part knew it wouldn't be the same if I shared it with another pair of eyes. I chose to hold this slice of beauty to myself. My sister remained sound asleep through the morning's miracles, curled on her side toward the window cradling her perfect, dark head in the crook of her arm.

I'd slide from the covers and through our bedroom door wearing the faded gown once owned by an older sister. My toughened, bare feet greeted the cold wood, and I scurried to the kitchen door, peeking around the tall kitchen table to see that all things were as they always were. A quiet sigh of relief escaped me as the smells, the warmth of the wood stove and the sight of Mama—standing, moving, stirring, preparing our breakfast—assured me things were as they were the day before. I slid quietly against the hard wall down to the warm wood floor, craving the dry heat from the stove.

Mama's soft voice carried a church hymn most mornings, usually a song Rankin Chapel Church choir sang the week before or the one song she loved most...

Soon, we'll be done with the troubles of the world,
the troubles of the world, the troubles of the world...
Soon, we'll be done with the troubles of the world...
I'm going home to live with God.

Mama's singing in our kitchen was different from her singing at Rankin Chapel. Her beautiful, clear voice was unharnessed, not a loud voice but not a timid one. I never understood why she chose not to share her voice with Rankin Chapel.

I sat on the warm, wood floor in my hand-me-down nightgown, breathing in the buttery aroma of Mama's perfect biscuits, listening to her soft song. Just as I stood and walked to the kitchen table where Mama worked, she bent, opened the oven door and pulled the tin pan of golden brown biscuits out. She gingerly sat the biscuits atop the stove. I smiled at the perfect, round bread and listened to Mama's thick bacon strips respond to burning iron.

"You already up, Faye?" Mama asked without stopping her work, maybe without thinking about her words. She had asked that very question many mornings. I nodded, without thinking or speaking. She smiled and used her kitchen towel to remove the steaming pan of water from the stove and set it just far enough from the edge of the wood kitchen table.

"You want to go wash up before the others start getting up?" She was already at her stove again, stirring, preparing. "You can come back and eat when you finish."

I picked up the pan of hot water to take to my room, but Mama motioned me to set it down. "Here." She smiled and offered me a pinch of glistening, brown biscuit from the tin pan, slipping the soft, hot bread into my hand. I sucked in air and blushed with the same delight I'd felt the Sunday morning she'd picked me out of the children's Sunday school class to make the collection report. I stood close to her, slowly chewing, savoring the succulent bread. As the last crumbs drifted down my throat, I took up the pan of hot water and thoughts of my school day intruded the sanctity of my morning with Mama.

Though she was never like other mothers, Ethel Curry was traditional by necessity, in the way she let Daddy believe he ran the household and made sure his rules were followed even if he didn't take the time to communicate them to his children. As smart as we all knew she was, she never tried to convince anyone she wore the pants in our house. I never got the feeling she was the least bit interested in running our household. She truly believed Daddy's place was at the helm. Even so, as her daughters grew into adults and either married or talked about marrying, Mama would shrug and half smile, "God wants you to give man his due, let him run the house...but sometimes they just not up to the task, and you need to make sure you pick the right one when you start picking."

Each of her daughters and most of her sons went to her with our marital problems and other personal problems. She was our security blanket, soaking in our hurts, listening to our complaints, letting us use her as our sounding board but never telling us what to do. I never wondered if Mama had such problems of her own. The handful of times I witnessed Mama crying were painful and bewildering moments in my life—like seeing the Statue of Liberty struggling to stay upright. Certainly, I've learned since that crying is as natural as breathing. But growing up in the Kearney household, parents and crying did not compute. Mama's struggle with cancer was the impetus for one of those times.

Another was when Daddy got behind on paying for a deep freezer he had bought her for Christmas. It was by then the middle of summer, and the storeowner had sent a letter earlier in that week announcing they would be picking up the deep freezer if Daddy didn't remit payment immediately. I remember Mama standing that day at the screen door in her sleeveless duster, watching the white delivery truck roll fast down the gravel road, billows of dust trailing behind.

Christmas at the Kearney home epitomized all that was good about our lives on Varner Road. Out of all the rich, wonderful memories of childhood Christmases, the one that remains most vivid is the Christmas of 1963, the year my baby sister, Judy, was born. Maybe it was because, at 46, Mama had finally made this one her very last childbirth. But most likely it was the culmination of Christmas excitement mixed with the excitement of a new baby in the house. She had to be a personal gift to us from Santa Claus. Finally, we had a real and lasting baby of the Kearney family, not to be supplanted by the next one 12 or 14 months later.

After a line of 16 middle children in a family of 17, being the permanent baby was something special. Judy would receive individual attention from Mama, like children in smaller families did. Those first days with her new family, Judy was doted over as if she was more a doll, a plaything, than a real, live child—a beautiful black doll from Santa Claus. She received the attention that none of us had known.

The day she came home, though, was an ugly, dreary day with intermittent smatterings of rain and snowfall covering our yard. My parents had left home around noon that day with a vague announcement that they needed to be away for a while and would be back late. We couldn't understand, given the weather, why my parents would risk getting stuck in the mud and snow, but in those days you didn't question. Mama's other 16 children were born at home with the help of Miss Sasporilla Brown, a longtime family friend who happened to also be a midwife.

Miss Brown's distinction was that she had been the midwife for more Negro women than anyone in southeast Arkansas. She'd even helped Mama come up with some of our names—knowing Mama and Daddy were running out of names that began with "J." Even after the white hospitals had taken away her midwife credentials for some unknown reason, she continued to deliver babies up and down the country roads—and just about every child and adult around could claim her as their own personal deliverer.

What I remember most about December 22, 1963, was how cold and gray the morning was as I lay half curled on Mama's bed, watching her dress. I remember Mama's frowning face as she tried to zip her wide-tail, gathered skirt, and I had no idea at the time that Judy was causing the difficulty. Mama was trying hopelessly to zip the green-and-blue checked skirt up on her waist with no success.

"Shoot! I can't believe this thing won't close. I just wore this skirt last week!" Mama ignored my giggles, continuing in vain.

"Mama, let me try!" I said, hoping I could do it and win one of her grateful smiles. After giving the zipper a few more tries, she allowed me to try. I jumped down excitedly and grabbed hold of the skirt waist. I remember noticing how round mama's waist was. But even with her extra weight, I was successful on my first try.

Mama cocked her head to the side and half smiled and half frowned at my success. "Mmph, mmph, mmph." She looked in the dresser mirror, frowning at her lack of success at pressing the skirt down over her stomach and patted her hair before walking to the living room. Mama carried her coat under one arm and her purse under the other.

Daddy stood impatiently near the door with his own worn coat already on and Mama's overnight case in his hand.

"Daddy, why you got that suitcase?" I asked with a quizzical look on my face.

"I just gotta take it with me. I'll be back," was Daddy's only response as he hurried Mama out to the car.

Daddy's impatience with tardiness was legendary. The joke at our house was that even when Daddy's only reason for going somewhere was to take one of his children, if we weren't on time, he'd drive away without us. Neither Daddy nor Mama told us they were going away to have a baby or that Mama wouldn't be back that night. Knowing the Christmas drill from experience, we all decided they were going out for last-minute Christmas shopping, even with almost 10 inches of snow on the ground. Pine Bluff Regional Hospital, where Judy was born, was 32 miles from our house, and since Varner Road was slushy with mud and snow it must have taken Daddy at least two or three hours to make it there.

When Daddy came home later that night, he was wearing a big grin clear across his face. And our main concern, though, were the packages he'd brought back with him. After examining the few packages, our attention turned to Mama. Where was she? There was a chorus of childish voices asking the same thing at the same time.

"Where's Mama?" For some reason, Daddy found everything funny tonight. "She'll be here tomorrow. She's at the hospital, and she wanted me to tell y'all, you got you a real pretty baby sister."

Our eyes must've been the size of saucers.

"A baby!" we all screamed. "How did we get a baby?" "Where did it come from?" "Can we keep it?" "Why didn't Mama bring it home?"

Daddy just stood there fielding our children's questions until he remembered he was exhausted and finally told us, "All right, it's time to go to bed. Y'all see the baby tomorrow when she and Mama come home."

We were all too excited to go to sleep that night. First, we had the excitement of Christmas coming in three days, and now a new baby! How could Daddy ever expect us to fall asleep this Christmas Eve? ℚ

PART IV

Our Early
Education

(1959-1971)

— THIRTEEN —

Our Lessons
in Life

I was four years old when Daddy introduced the magic of learning into my young world. My lessons were almost always at the end of the day as the melancholy sun in its bright redness drifted down behind our back yard. After a long day in the cotton field, Daddy would sit patiently, calmly, as I sat at his knee repeating and remembering words and colors and numbers I could see in my mind.

This raggedly handsome pied piper spent hours bent over a book, lulling me into learning as I breathed in the sharp fragrance of his Pall Mall cigarette and watched it bleed ashes onto the dark wood porch slats. His deep, gravelly voice mesmerized me, making his words that much more important. His pause, as he took a deep draw from the dwindling cigarette, invited my childish questions.

James Kearney had his own ways and theories about teaching his children. He was convinced that his own love for learning could be transferred to his children. One by one, he taught us the rudiments of counting, identifying our alphabets, our colors and how to pronounce the simplest of words. "C-A-T spells what? Come on, you remember...it sounds like hat." He responded to our correct answers with giant smiles, as if we'd performed a Shakespearean soliloquy. As the evening turned a reddish hue of grey and the cricket chirps became a part of the dusk, Daddy begrudgingly closed the book or folded the one sheet of paper in half. He stood, patting me on the head before going inside. "Okay...that was a good lesson. Tomorrow, we'll learn some more."

There was never an ounce of rancor in his laughter when I made childish mistakes. His mild caution was, "You got to remember to always

157

do your very best." And because I'd hear this throughout the years I lived on Varner Road, I knew it was something he believed was important. In later years, my mistakes would garner sterner admonishments.

"You gotta work hard now, Faye. Gettin' it almost right or coming up second don't mean a hill of beans in this world."

Lucky, visionary, or both, Daddy caught his children just as our minds and hearts became ripe for the picking. And it was during those early years that he transferred all his love for learning and the written words into our hearts and minds. And it stuck.

James Kearney was a study in contrasts when it came to his cotton crops and our education. We were raised to take his ravenous love for learning and determination to raise children who used their brains as a given. We also realized that he was just as determined not to raise a bunch of "good-for-nothing children" who didn't know the value of hard work. This was the part of Daddy that justified putting his crops before his children's education during the first quarters of school. While our minds depended on all the things he taught us as toddlers, his and our day-to-day existence depended on this latter determination. James and Ethel Kearney's infrequent arguments were centered on this conflict between school and work.

"Children got to learn the importance of work or they grow up to be useless," Daddy fussed back when Mama begged him to send their children to school. In Daddy's mind, his children helping with the cotton crop was just plain common sense, and the only way the Kearney family could survive.

"James, don't it matter to you that this gone put our children behind the others in school? They already make fun of us and call our children church mice." It was more than that tearing at Mama's heart. Her bitter memories of the education that eluded her as a child were still fresh in her mind. She wouldn't let up. Her children's education was more important than anything she could think of and just as important as their embracing Christianity.

"James, I'm already helping you in the fields all day. The children can help out after they come from school. I just don't want none of them to fall behind in their classes. I'm scared they may not be able to catch back up."

While Ethel Curry Kearney hated asking for favors, she was unbendable when it came to her children's education. My parents made an unwritten pact. Daddy would keep his children out of school to help harvest his cotton crop, but he'd make up for it by making sure that none of us fell behind in school.

"Ain't none of these children gone fall behind, Ethel. You'll see."

Those first three months for all of my older siblings were spent helping Daddy get his bales of cotton out before the weather turned. While other children might have loved such freedom from the drudgery of books and the structure of a classroom, we craved books and learning.

James Kearney made good on his promise. We were even allowed to attend the first week of school before cotton picking season had fully begun. During those days, we collected our books and the instructors' guidance sheets to serve as our maps for the rest of the semester, whether we were sitting in the school classroom or not.

The Kearney children's education was a family affair. During fall evenings after we'd eaten Mama's dinner and cleared the table of dishes, we gathered there for our daily study sessions. My father's attentiveness to us, I learned later in life, had a lot to do with the loss of his own father when he was just nine years old. He had left his home and his mother at the very early age of 11 years old to find his own way in the world. Much of our awe of our father had to do with the numerous tales of his travel and the people he'd met during his vagabondlike childhood.

Priority No. 1 during our autumn days was Daddy's 50 acres of rented cotton fields. The number of bales of cotton we helped Daddy produce had direct correlations to how well we lived and ate that winter. The soft, white stuff subsidized our existence—the food we ate and the clothing we wore for the rest of the year.

It was the nights, however, that the Kearney children loved most. Our nights were dedicated to feeding our minds. While Daddy was convinced the combination of hard work and strong intellect would serve us well for years to come, for us those evenings around the dinner table with our books and paper were simply wonderful respites from our harsh, everyday realities. Beyond the inherent joy we gained from learning was the realization that using our mind meant we were more than just another field hand in Daddy's and the white farmers' cotton fields.

In spite of everything, our home was always filled with laughter. Now, I know it was a kind of balm to soothe the parts of our existence we refused to look at. We had strong, hearty laughs that came from somewhere deep in our cores. Both our parents joined with jokes, stories and games, though my mother tried hard to keep a straight face. Sometimes, we laughed derisively at each other, in spite of our parents' promised punishments.

Though Daddy had gone no further than the 10th grade, he told us proudly that he never stopped learning. "Anywhere I ended up, I found me a library or somewhere that had books I could borrow." My parents each had good reasons to make sure they didn't raise a houseful of illiterate children. Besides the regrets that they had missed out on a completed education, they were convinced that education was their children's key out of the poverty that restricted their own freedom.

To James and Ethel Kearney's credit, we took to learning like tadpoles to muddy bayou water. It seemed that each successive child learned earlier than the one before. We scoured Daddy's well-worn Bibles, milk cartons, oatmeal boxes, the few precious books in the house or the four-page *Lincoln Ledger* newspaper that Daddy picked up in Star City.

We settled down to our nightly homework sessions shortly after dinner—the only time the Kearney household experienced complete quiet, except when we slept. The only sounds in the house at those times were the scraping of our pencils on the thin, lined sheets of paper and quiet mumbling as we read the night's lessons to ourselves or some child asking Daddy a question about something he might know the answer to. ᶜ

Fourteen

Miss
Jessie Freeman

Fields Schools had the dubious distinction of having a number of teachers with amazingly long tenure. My first grade teacher, Jessie Freeman, was one of those teachers who had taught for 20 years when I arrived in 1959. She would continue teaching there after I graduated 12 years later.

Miss Freeman is memorable for a number of reasons but mainly because there were two distinct sides to her personality. On my first day of school, I was comforted by the fact that the small, round woman reminded me of the middle-age housewives that attended Rankin Chapel. These women adored me and brought me penny candy and pennies to put into Sunday school collections. My first impression of Miss Freeman was that she was like these sweet women I smiled at on Sunday mornings. I was at least half wrong.

Jessie Freeman was a sweet and caring teacher, most times. And seeing her smiling round face as I walked into class those first mornings comforted me. Thanks to Jesse Freeman that transformation was easier than either Mama or I believed it would be. The next week, however, the inevitable happened; we discovered that Jessie Freeman had another side.

On these other days Miss Freeman made nervous wrecks out of six-year-old children. Her loud, high-pitched voice would sting our ears as she made us know she was disgusted with our spelling, our adding, our coloring and the way we stood in line for recess. She walked the aisles of our neatly rowed seats and wracked knuckles with her ruler, pulled hair or clapped hands loudly in our ears. She railed on and on about our "sloppy, sloppy work" as she stood over one or another of her trembling wards, spittle spraying and resting on children in her range.

On her worst days, Jessie Freeman produced the dreaded thick black strap that my older brothers and sisters said had sat in her desk drawer since Jamie, my oldest sister, sat in her class. Those were the days I wished with all my heart that Mama had never sent me off to school. One evening after one of these harrowing days with the not-so-nice Miss Freeman, I begged Mama to let me stay home and learn. "But...Daddy can teach me. He know how to learn me to read and write," I pleaded, genuine tears welling up in my eyes as I remembered the sting of Miss Freeman's strap. Unfortunately, Mama didn't agree, and that was the end of that. She also never miraculously walked through that classroom door, as I hoped she would, at Miss Freeman's worst moments.

Shiny, salt-and-pepper curls framed Miss Freeman's face, and she wore colorful, sleeveless dresses that accented her round body. The 50-year-old woman had a little girl's smile when she was pleased or tickled and even when she wasn't. We became cunning six-year-olds and learned early that we couldn't read her mood based on that little-girl smile. The braver students snickered behind their hands at her Tweety Bird voice, knowing also that the tiny voice had nothing to do with the woman's state of mind.

I turned six on September 29, 1959, three weeks after school began. All through the night before, I practiced how I would announce to Miss Freeman that I was now officially six years old. The next day, wearing my new dress Mama had sewn to celebrate my new age, I raised my hand, indicating to my teacher I had something to say.

Miss Freeman was grading papers at the time but looked up at me and smiled, "Yes, Janis?"

I stood up beside my desk, nervous but still proud and said, "Miss Freeman, I'm six today!"

Miss Freeman offered me a vacant smile, "That's nice...Janis."

I sat back down, proud of my bravery and satisfied that the rest of the class knew I had a birthday. I didn't give it a second thought when Miss Freeman was scribbling something on her enrollment book. But before I left her class that day, she called me to her desk and handed me a note to take home to my mother.

"Why did you tell Miss Freeman you was six?" Mama asked me after dinner that evening. There was that small wrinkle in Mama's forehead, so I knew I'd done something wrong. I shrugged my shoulders and looked down.

"Did Miss Freeman ask you how old you were, Faye?"

I shook my head, bewildered, now.

"Well...if the woman didn't ask you...go on in there and start doing your lessons, Faye."

My parents and siblings called me by my middle name instead of my first name. I hardly remembered my first name was Janis until I went off to school. I also didn't know that my parents had told a white lie about my age since the legal age for first grade was six years old by the first week in September. I had missed the deadline by a mere 20 days, but my parents refused to allow me to miss a year out of school because I was born 20 days late.

Jessie Freeman believed in teaching children one way or another. She would not tolerate children to leave her classroom without knowing their basics. Some of us were lucky; we got it the first or second time. Other children needed a lot more drilling. Those were the times when the smiles looked pasted onto the woman's face as she pounded the small students with her hard words or pulled out the ruler to make her point clear. The black leather strap was always her last resort, used as an incentive or a deterrent depending on the time of day.

I would learn another side to Jessie Freeman that year. The woman felt a deep responsibility for her students' well being. She must have known what people said about the Kearney family being "poorer than church mice" when they learned we rarely brought prepared lunches or money for lunch to school. Mrs. Freeman never said anything, but she noticed. I sometimes felt her small eyes behind the wire-framed glasses sneak a glance over at me as I sat and read my book or scribbled on paper when the other students collected their lunch pails or brown paper sacks from their desks or the back window ledge where they sometimes sat them.

She never questioned me when I walked quietly to her desk and asked to go outside and play or visit my brother's classroom to carry him "some clean paper 'cause he didn't have none this morning." She would nod her head, then say, "You may, Janis." Jessie Freeman was proper in her speech that way. After visiting my younger brothers' class, I hurried outside to play alone at the swings until my classmates finished their lunch. When I saw them run to the playground, I waited for just a few seconds before joining them as if there were no differences between us.

Most days, Miss Freeman took orders for milk and cookies before morning recess. I was never one of the students who raised their hands. After a few weeks into the school term, Miss Freeman gave me the task of emptying the Sunshine Cookie box during the lunch period. "Take it out there to the trash room, Janis," she said, nonchalantly. "Make sure everything's out of it before you leave the box in the trash room, Janis...."

What began with childish happiness to be picked by the teacher for a special chore ended in another kind of excitement as I nonchalantly peeked into the box before leaving it in the trash room. I smelled the sweet, buttery aroma before I saw the bottom of the box still filled with lemon, Jackson and Washboard coconut cookies. I felt as if I must be the luckiest girl in the world. After stuffing my face with as many of the cookies as I could and unhappily leaving the rest in the box, I hurried back to class satiated and excited.

For the rest of the afternoon I was fidgety, anxious to get home and share my good news with Jo Ann and the others. Miss Freeman went through her lessons that afternoon just as she always did. As she stood at the door saying "Good Evening" to us as we walked to the bus stop, she touched my shoulder ever so lightly as she said, "Good Evening, Janis." Her smile, this time, was just slightly different from the others. It was like Jo Ann sometimes smiled at me when we shared a secret no one else knew.

These surprises continued throughout my first year in school, including the times Miss Freeman exclaimed to the class that she had accidentally ordered an extra bottle of milk. "Goodness...I over-ordered again. Would anyone like this extra bottle?" Too shy to raise my hands, I looked down at my desk. Without a word, the woman walked over and sat the cold bottle on the desk, just inches from my hand.

Was Jessie Freeman a good woman and a not-so-good teacher or an effective teacher who made up the rules as she went along? She had her good days and her bad days. And, more than once, I was the target of that long, black leather strap she kept in her desk drawer. Even knowing that, I won't forget her kindness, her attending to my needs without letting me know. ℚ

FIFTEEN

Miss
Katie Jackson

I learned to expect the unexpected from adults during my year with Katie Jackson. It was from my front-row seat in her small, second-grade class that I realized that people change from what you first think they are...without even an inkling of a warning. I learned I might be deceived by teachers who reminded me of the sweet and adoring women at Rankin Chapel from Miss Freeman the year before.

There were no contradictions, however, in Katie Jackson, my second-grade teacher. A thin woman in her 30s, Miss Jackson remained for the rest of the year exactly what she presented to us that first day. There was no sweet smile, no childish giggle and no shiny, salt-and-pepper curls. She wore long, thick bangs and a ponytail that reminded me of the movie "National Velvet."

She was a pecan-shell colored woman with Caucasian features, an aquiline nose and a ramrod straight, perfect posture. Though she wasn't a tall woman, she seemed a giant in my eyes. She was a well-put-together woman who dressed in straight, flared or pleated skirts most days. They always matched perfectly the tailored shirts or jackets she wore. To say she seemed out of place in Fields Elementary School with young students who mostly came from poor or rural homes is an understatement.

I have no memory of Miss Jackson's voice. She rarely spoke. When she did, it was to direct us to "Sit down" or "Be quiet!" or to inform us which pages we should read or which problems to work as homework for the next day. If the woman had a kind teacher's voice or a warm smile, she saved it for other people in her life. As we marched into her classroom each morning, she stood with folded arms and an air of impatience marring her pretty face. "G'morning, Miss Jackson" was all we dared say. She responded with a curt nod.

Other Fields teachers whispered that Miss Jackson "thought she was more than" the other teachers or that she was "stuck up." Most everyone, though, thought she was a very good teacher. Even parents believed their children learned a great deal in the woman's class. Certainly, I wasn't objective, given the fact that she scared the living daylights out of me. To a seven-year-old not long out from under my mother's dress tail, Katie Jackson was more like the scary witch who devoured children for dinner than a woman who taught because she loved children and cared about our education.

Corporal punishment was as much a part of the black South as church, and Katie Jackson's whippings were legendary, even for a typically southern black school. It was normal procedure for the woman to call at least one child up to her desk during the week and allot a public beating. Sometimes it was punishment for a recent infraction, but more often, it was for some perceived misdemeanor that had happened weeks ago. As ward over 30 students for that year, she was free to decide when she would mete out her students' punishment. There was no question that young children strained Miss Jackson's delicate nerves.

She rose from her desk as if it was a bother, tugging the child's arm as they moved to the front of the classroom as if they were embarking on a stage play. With strap in hand and without warning, she laid into the child. It was an unspoken warning to those of us watching. Tomorrow, it might be one of us.

The irony of the very public humiliations was Katie Jackson's extreme secretiveness. Unlike Jessie Freeman who had brought her entire family in to visit with us before my first year was up, Miss Jackson brought her one daughter in once or twice and then didn't bother to make formal introductions. She never mentioned a husband, and we never saw a man who might be her husband. The students whispered about this and made up funny jokes.

Staged whippings were not the only mode of punishment Katie Jackson had up her sleeve, of course. At least one child peed on themselves while she barked directions to them as they attempted to work a problem at the blackboard. Sammy, the only child to befriend me during my second year, soiled his pants as we all sat watching Miss Jackson's brutal humiliation. The seven-year-old child had forgotten the lines to a lengthy poem assigned to him. Miss Jackson abhorred "dumb children" in her class. The child and his parents left Gould just weeks after that episode. I was sure his public humiliation had something to do with the move.

After all of this, Katie Jackson proved she had a soft spot. She decided just weeks after I came to her class to adopt me as a charity case. Even at my age, I understood this was not simply an altruistic gesture on her part. Like others at the school, including my classmates, I was convinced the woman had a cold, hard dislike of children. The fact that she was said to spoil her own child was unexplainable.

Whatever her reasoning might be, it was no blessing to be mentored by such a disliked teacher as Katie Jackson. None of my classmates would have jumped at the chance to change places with me, and there wasn't the least bit of envy in their eyes when the woman called me up to her desk to remind me of the box of shoes or clothes she'd brought from home. They did wonder and whispered questions to me during recess and lunch periods, "Why she acting so nice to you?" They made up more stories. One caused me to even laugh. They giggled that the witch-woman had left me out in the woods when I was born because she didn't want to be bothered with me, and the Kearneys had found me.

I found out by accident why Katie Jackson chose me as her young charity case. The one person she genuinely liked was my older sister, Janeva, who was a senior at Fields High School. Teacher-student friendships weren't unusual at that time, given the fact that many teachers were quite young. Even students who had already graduated would return to the school sometimes to visit their favorite teachers.

Since Fields High was more than a mile away from my school, Janeva brought her lunch and sat at Miss Jackson's desk to eat and talk with her. Janeva's visits were the only times I heard the woman's laughter or experienced a smile directed at me. After lunch, Janeva stopped briefly by my desk to ask how I was, pat my shoulder and return to her high school class. Those visits meant a lot to me. I was always happy to see my older sister, but more importantly, the recognition from Miss Jackson meant even more.

Later, I decided it was my sister's fair complexion and her sophisticated personality that drew Miss Jackson to her. Janeva was also a very bright student that the woman simply enjoyed conversing with. I was always baffled, however, as to what Janeva and the woman might talk about.

Just one of the boxes of shoes Miss Jackson gave me cost more than my whole wardrobe of second-hand, thrift store clothing. They were rich people's beautiful shoes that corroborated my belief that Katie Jackson didn't belong with us. Janeva and my parents looked through the box of shoes with me. Daddy grew bored, but Janeva and Mama stayed on, gently turning the shoes over in their hands. Mama went on and on about how an elementary teacher could afford such shoes. Janeva rolled her eyes as if to say Mama didn't know everything. There was a strange smile on Mama's face as she half whispered, "I use to have shoes like this...." I guessed she meant before she became our Mama or Daddy's wife.

I didn't want to like Miss Jackson's gifts, but I fell in love with one pair of black, patent leather shoes with satin bows. "Jo Ann can wear the others, Mama," I told her, after I found the special ones at the bottom of the box. Because patent leather shoes were foreign to me, I imagined they held magical powers, maybe could change me from a poor church mouse to someone more special and worthy of the shiny shoes. At night, I set the shoes just far away from my bed to see their beautiful gleam before I fell asleep.

When I wore the shoes to school for a school event, I bumped into other students on the school sidewalk because I needed to make sure the shine remained on my shoes. After the bus ride home, I took the shoes and my socks off to walk barefoot down the mile-long dirt road to our home. I didn't want the red clay dust to dull the shine on my beautiful black shoes. When I wore the shoes to church, my chest swelled when the smiling women would say how pretty the shoes were and other children looked sideways at them without saying anything. As soon as our yellow station wagon stopped in our yard after church, I would pull my shoes and socks off, go directly to my bedroom and place the shoes in their allocated spot across from mine and Jo Ann's bed.

The only problem with those and other shoes Miss Jackson gave me was their size. They were always two sizes too big. But Mama stuffed the toes with sheets from the *JCPenney Catalog*, and by the next week I had forgotten the pain of the paper pressing against my toes.

My classmates rarely commented on my shoes, though I often saw them sneaking a look. I imagined they snickered about the "good" shoes and my second-hand, often tattered clothing. I would try to resolve this problem before the open taunts began. I hurried into the kitchen one morning after I heard Mama singing in the kitchen.

"What you doing up so early, Faye? It's not six o'clock, yet."

I shrugged my shoulders and smiled, then sat down in one of her table chairs, watching her knead the dough for our morning biscuits. When Mama was busy in the kitchen, you couldn't tell whether she was paying attention to you or not. She didn't pay much attention to anything except the bowl or skillet or pot sitting in front of her. I let out a little sigh.

"Mama, I need some good clothes to wear with my shoes," I started.

"It look funny to wear my good shoes with the raggedy clothes I got." I swallowed, waiting for her to answer.

Mama was busy now stirring rice in the steaming hot pot. When she finished she put the spoon down on the stove and frowned over at me.

"Faye, where you think I'm gone get money to buy you some new clothes to go with your shoes? Everybody in this house need some new clothes." She shook her head in consternation.

"But..." I tried again, feeling the tears welling up in the corners of my eyes. "I just need like one dress, Mama. That's all."

She was laying the thick strips of bacon on the iron skillet now, and I already imagined that sweet-salty smell that woke me up in the mornings as the bacon fried. Mama set the skillet squarely on the stove, then looked down into my face. I was surprised this time to see that her face was softer and there was no anger there.

"I already sewed all the holes up in your clothes, Faye...I put buttons on your winter coat. So what raggedy clothes you talking about?"

I shrugged my shoulders now, for some reason not able to think of anything more to offer.

"Go on back to bed, Faye, or take your hot water and start washing up..." she said, kindly, before turning her mind back to her breakfast. As I walked back to my room, I knew I had asked the impossible and that I'd just have to bear the children's taunts when the time came.

After a few weeks, Miss Jackson called me up to her desk just before recess and told me she had another box for me. "Thank you, Miss Jackson," I responded with less anticipation than before. "Another box of shoes!" Mama said, shaking her head. When she opened it, Jo Ann and I screamed with excitement at the box of almost-new clothes. Mama looked over at me with a strange smile on her face. A few of the dresses had missing buttons or an unraveling hem.

"Mama, will you sew this up for me?" I asked.

"I sure will, and it'll be good as new again." I knew it would. Mama had that strange smile again. ℚ

SIXTEEN

Miss
Rosie Jones

Had it not been for Rosie Jones, Jo Ann's double promotion would have been the most memorable event of 1964. Though she would, indeed, join me in Miss Berba Jones' fifth-grade class, I had Miss Rosie Jones and my fourth-grade class all to myself.

The joy of my fourth-grade class had everything in the world to do with getting the right teacher at the right time. Rosie Jones was a young, pretty teacher just recently into her 20s. I thought, "Bewitched," that September morning as I walked into her classroom. She stood with softly folded arms and a bemused smile at the children who would be her students for the next year. She wore a dark brown skirt and blouse, sheer stockings and dark pumps. "Samantha," I thought, returning her smile.

Except for her color, my new teacher was the spitting image of Samantha Stephens, the good witch on the TV show "Bewitched" I sometimes watched on Thursday nights. I wondered if she ever tried twinkling her small, pointy nose. By the time I scooted into my front-row desk, I was already feeling lucky to be in this woman's class.

My classroom was adjacent to the school gymnasium and, though I was excited about being housed in Fields' new annex, I was more than a little anxious about what kind of teacher I'd get this year. I didn't know then that this would be a pivotal year in my education. It was a special year with a very special teacher. Rosie Jones would change my perception of myself and spark my love for books in a magnificent way.

It was in Rosie Jones' fourth-grade class that I experienced for the first and only time the phenomenon of being a teacher's pet. I had no idea what I was missing during my three earlier years of school. Each of my younger siblings—Jo Ann, Jerome, and Jude—had all been "chosen" by their teachers as special. I never had. Being chosen as a charity case by Katie Jackson didn't count since the woman didn't even like me. I hadn't known what it was like to have a teacher actually like you and show confidence in your abilities. Years later, when I happened upon "Bewitched" reruns, I would smile, remembering that special time in my life.

Carl Ray Lewis was the other student in my class who was viewed by Miss Jones as special. I remember him most because we were fierce competitors. He made a point of challenging my place with our beloved teacher on a daily basis. That wouldn't have been a problem, except Miss Jones genuinely liked the horrible boy.

The only way to describe Carl Ray is a delinquent-in-waiting, a child bad to the bones and whose favorite classroom past-times were thumping boys in the back of their heads, throwing spitballs at girls and playing the dozens whether he knew the culprit's parents or not. He taught me and others in class curse words we might never have learned otherwise. We all held Carl Ray in awe for his courage. He talked back and argued with Miss Jones as if he was her equal.

There were many days when Carl Ray wasn't there to answer when Miss Jones called his name. I imagined he had overslept or spent the morning watching cartoons, just deciding against walking the few blocks to school that morning. And in spite of all that, Miss Jones saw something in the boy and continuously implored him to "please work hard and reach your potential" as if he was her only child. And in spite of the many times he pulled my ponytails and threw spitballs across my back, I daydreamed about Carl Ray when we weren't in class together. It was my terrible luck that my first crush targeted a boy who never looked at me twice, except to call me dirty names.

Carl Ray hated me. "That raggedy-ass girl gets on my nerves" were the only words I remember him directing toward me. When we were the last two standing for the infamous spelling bees, he looked at me with such dark dislike that more than once I misspelled a word, leaving him to gloat over victory. I spent the rest of those days regretting my loss but also hoping against hope that Carl Ray's winning would soften his heart toward me. It was innocent but futile hope.

While Katie Jackson had tolerated her students, Rosie Jones nurtured our small psyches and pushed us to excel. She learned as much about her students as she could in the time allotted. "How's your mama doing?" she'd ask sometimes as we left for recess. "Say hello to your parents for me and tell them you're doing well," she'd say as we left to catch the evening bus.

Rosie Jones challenged me in a way I hadn't been challenged before, and the more I achieved the more she would push me to move beyond that. Because of her, I learned that I was better at some things than others. I soared in the areas that meant most to me during that year, discovering by pure accident my love for writing.

In the late spring, we took an all-day aptitude test. None of us knew what exactly an aptitude test was, but because I usually did well I viewed it as another challenge. It was a month later that Miss Jones announced the results from the tests had come back. After telling us how important the test was to see how we measured up with students across the state and the country, she scheduled conferences with each child to share our individual grades.

"Janis Kearney, can you come up here?" She had scheduled the meetings alphabetically, and by the time she got to my name I had forgotten about conference day. As I walked slowly up to her desk, she smiled and nodded toward the seat facing her. The butterflies were awaking inside my stomach the way they always did when I didn't know what was coming. She held the folder with my name written on the tab sideways so I could see the test results and went down the list of scores. "English, 98; Math, 90; Reading, 99...." The butterflies suddenly fell

175

dead asleep again. Her smile solidified what I couldn't believe. I had done better than I could ever have imagined.

"You did exceptionally well, Janis...exceptionally well!" I smiled a little, looking in her eyes to see what that meant. "I've already talked to the principal and put your name on the list for a double promotion. Not only did you score at the top of the class, Janis, but your reading aptitude is higher than most students' in the whole school." She laughed as she saw my eyes widen and the disbelief appear on my face. "I'm sending a note home to Mrs. Kearney so she'll know how well you did."

She laughed and patted my shoulder before ushering me back to my seat. I couldn't talk for the rest of the evening, I was so filled with excitement and self-pride. I prayed Miss Jones wouldn't call me back up there and say she got my test mixed up with somebody else's—not before I got home this evening.

One of the hardest truths I had to swallow early on was that I wasn't as brilliant as Jo Ann. Most adults in our community couldn't tell my sister and me apart. The only differences between the two of us were my lighter shade and Jo Ann's height. My hair was coarse and thick, Jo Ann's was soft and curly. Most of our neighbors wouldn't have a reason to know that Jo Ann was smarter. While I tried hard not to show my jealousy over the years, I never succeeded. My younger sister excelled in everything without the least bit of effort. I did well in most things and excelled in a few.

Miss Jones had no idea what this news meant for my self-esteem. But with a lot of effort I was able to contain my excitement. As I left, Miss Jones slipped the note in my hand, "Give it to your mama...I'm so proud of you, Janis." I nodded and looked down. In my mind I was already practicing how to relay the good information to my parents and especially to Jo Ann.

That year was full of exciting news for me. In December, Miss Jones announced the cast for the "Christmas Messiah," the most important school play of the year. She announced the roles for the shepherds, the three wise men, the angels, Mary and the extras. After all the excitement, she looked from Carl Ray to me. "I'm still deciding on the narrator role. Right now, it will likely be Carl Ray or Janis, but I haven't made a final decision...I'll let you know soon."

I believed Miss Jones would choose Carl Ray. She was always finding reasons to do things for him even though he showed no appreciation for her efforts. For the rest of the day, I wore a pleasant face that wasn't real. I wanted so bad to be the narrator, to show everyone how well I read. But I was sure Carl Ray would get the part. I didn't mention the role to my parents. I only shared good news, not my desires or goals. I didn't want to experience their disappointment when I fell short of my expectations.

I had hardly slept the night before and had kept Jo Ann awake most of the night with my worrying. By the time I walked into class I'd decided to ask Miss Jones if I could just read a Christmas poem. I'd chosen the longest one I knew, " 'Twas the Night Before Christmas." I knew the poem would play up my reading voice almost as much as the Messiah narrator's role. I wanted more than anything to see that rare gleam of pride in my parents' eyes when I did well or stood out. I already knew Miss Jones wanted to give the narrator role to Carl Ray as an incentive for him to "live up to his abilities" and to give him a reason to straighten up and fly right.

Carl Ray had told everyone in class he was sure he had the role, even though Miss Jones had asked us both to read over the narrative and practice so we'd be ready when she made her decision. Just weeks before the program, Miss Jones called me to her desk. "Tell your mama you need to stay after school to practice the Christmas play. You'll be the narrator for the play." There wasn't a smile on her face as she told me this. Instead she was more impatient than she usually was. I walked back to my desk wondering why she'd decided to give the role to me, after all.

Carl Ray wasn't in class that day, and Miss Jones didn't mention the boy. She also didn't bother announcing my selection to the class. While I left class that evening still wondering about the decision, that didn't dampen my excitement about getting the part or my anticipation of sharing my wonderful news with my parents and family.

I rushed home to tell Mama and Daddy my good news. They were proud of me, though Mama laughingly said I was going a little overboard. "All this excitement just 'cause the teacher chose you to read out loud at a play? My goodness, girl...." I frowned, knowing Mama was proud. "But I'm the narrator, Mama. It's the most important part, and Miss Jones picked me 'cause I'm the best reader in the whole class!" Mama looked at me with her head tilted, and her face lit up with a half smile, half frown. More than getting the part, I was so happy to have Mama proud of me.

A very small part of me was sorry that Carl Ray had missed out. I knew this was something he really wanted. I promised myself I wouldn't rub his face in it the next day. But the next day Carl Ray was absent again. Miss Jones announced that morning that he wouldn't be returning to school until after the holidays. Miss Jones hadn't chosen him for the role because he was suspended from school for fighting.

While I didn't have to be afraid of his glares the next day, I knew he'd remember when he returned. My feelings were confusing. I felt guilty but at the same time was ecstatic to be the chosen one. Besides, Carl Ray wouldn't be back until January.

On the night of the program, I walked with my parents into the gymnasium as it filled with families and school staff. The voices of young children excited to be out past their bedtimes echoed through the large open space. "I gotta go, Mama. I'll see you after the play." I gave them a shy wave before turning and walking to the stage.

I hurried up the stairs, then backstage where the three wise men were studying their parts. The butterflies were stirring. My face was warmer than usual, and I thought I might throw up any minute. "I think I'm getting sick," I whispered to my friend, Linda, one of the wise men. She looked at me, concerned. "You want me to tell Miss Jones?" I shook my head, "No!" Not only wouldn't I let her down, but this was too important to me, as well. I knew my parents were sitting out there waiting to hear me speak and Miss Jones sitting right down front depending on me.

"Janis, you ready?" It was Miss Jones' smiling voice as she walked up the stairs. I tried to smile. "Yes, ma'am, I'm ready." She looked at me and was about to say something more when another student called out to her. I patted down my black pleated skirt I had talked mama into buying for the event, along with my good white blouse she'd starched and ironed. I still smelled the starch on my collar. I walked to the podium and placed my handwritten narrative there. I was grateful the parents and teachers in the audience wouldn't see me behind the heavy stage curtains.

Before long, Miss Jones was hurrying across the stage half whispering, "Get ready now...places everyone. The curtains are about to come up." She looked over at me one last time and smiled. As I paused between readings to allow the cast to speak their lines, I became calmer and the butterflies flew away. I knew the story by heart now. We presented the same play at Rankin Chapel each Christmas, but we'd never had a narrator. By the end of the first intermission, I was feeling fine, reading my narration with a lot more enthusiasm.

Miss Jones walked back stage during intermission and gave me a warm smile. "You're doing real good, Janis...you feeling okay?" I smiled back and said with truthfulness this time, "Yes, ma'am, I'm feeling fine." She went back to talk for a minute with the other students, then hurried back down to sit in the front row for the rest of the play. That night, I felt the closest to the actress I admired most, Loretta Young, than ever before.

I most certainly would be a different person had I not ended up in Miss Rosie Jones' class that year. Her perception of me as a "special" and "gifted" student made a world of difference in how I'd view myself from then on. Her confidence in my intelligence helped offset some of the other teachers' views of me and the rest of the Kearney clan. It also allowed me to feel differently about Jo Ann. With the realization that I had my own special gifts, I didn't feel so resentful of her brilliance. That lasted at least until the end of the year when I learned Jo Ann had been given a double promotion, and I hadn't.

Fields School teachers over the years had been both repulsed and in awe of the Kearney family. They were never able to understand how a family of sharecroppers could produce children who missed a quarter of the school year and returned to school at the top of their classes. Being sharecroppers and overachievers didn't add up in their consciousness.

The key ingredient that they all seemed to miss was James and Ethel Kearney who lived and breathed education. They wrote the book on home schooling and preschool education before it became a federal policy. They expected the best from us and took responsibility for nurturing that excellence with their late-night drilling and sitting with us at the kitchen table until our lessons were finished and all our questions answered.

It wasn't just our poverty but the sheer magnitude of our family that riled blacks in the community and made us the target of vocal and whispered derisive taunts. Many whites and blacks were certain that James and Ethel Kearney were responsible for their own poverty "having babies year after year." Time would toughen our hide and help make us immune to the humiliation from some in the community. As children, the humiliation was less about the shame of being poor than about our peers' reaction to our being poor. ℚ

James and Ethel Curry Kearney at family gathering (circa 1975)

James Kearney, 45 year old

Ethel Curry Kearney, 25 years old

James and Ethel Kearney with
photo collage of Kearney children

Ethel's parents, Luther and
Mattie Emma Curry

Varner Road

Daddy's chicken coop

Daddy and the Black Walnut tree
A shell of the Kearney station wagon in the background

Daddy at Rankin Chapel Church

Jo Ann (left) and Janis (right) with visitors at the University of Arkansas, 1972

My brother, John "the Black Elvis"

Kearney family reunion

Arkansas State Press
founder, Daisy Bates and
her protégé, Janis Kearney

Kearney men: (front) Joseph (stooping) Dad
(l to r) John, James, Jesse, Jude, Jerome, Jack
(back) Julius, Cecil

Kearney family: (front) Janis, Janeva, Joyce, Daddy, Jamie, Judy, Janetta
(standing) Joseph, James, Jude, Julius, Jack, Jesse, Jerome, John

Photography by Tony Baker

185

Jo Ann's high school graduation photo, 1971

Janis' razorback beauty photo, 1973

— S E V E N T E E N —

A Time for All Things

I n the spring of 1964, I learned a painful lesson about the proximity of happiness and hurt—how there's sometimes not a second's difference. All throughout my childhood I depended on the seasons to direct my happiness and unhappiness with my world. Spring was a crescendo of bright pastels and sounds that encouraged a smile on my face and a sweet taste in my mouth that stayed with me, even into my dreams.

The wondrous fall—a potpourri of rich silence—cloaked me like Mama's seldom embraces while the warm-cool breezes and darkly lit sunsets responded to my hunger for a world of quiet and beauty.

There was in my world the numbing cold of winter, as well. Surprising appearances that came like clockwork, taunting me with thoughts and remembrances of the parts of my world I least wanted to remember. The inevitable days of picking cotton with cold, bleeding hands left me dreaming at night of other families, those I read about in our school books who traveled to England and visited grandmothers on Thanksgiving Day. Later, it would be during the cold of winter I would learn the painful truth of Mama's chronic, sweet sadness. Each night after learning, my dreams encompassed giant letters floating, floating through the air. C...A...N...C...E...R...wafting higher
and higher in the blue sky, reminding me of lost birthday balloons.

The punishing heat of July was there during my first, painful period. I was 11 then—a very innocent 11-year-old who had just found the Lord and was convinced he was punishing me for a promise not kept.

Then it was the spring of 1964 and I learned that for all my believing differently, good things and bad things have no special season. The

187

perfume of new Easter lilies and the arias of birds stealing across the sky precipitated a hard lesson that day.

Jo Ann was my classmate and sometime friend. I had almost stopped remembering the day my younger sister had hurried home to announce she'd "caught up" with me. My blood would boil each time I remembered how she had smiled and announced, "I'm skipping and going to fifth grade with Faye next year, Mama!" That day, I'd walked slowly through the kitchen door, watching Mama's eyes brim with pride. "Go tell your daddy!" she half whispered to the pretty, chocolate girl. Mama's smile said what she never found it easy to say, just how proud she was of her daughter.

Jo Ann would be my classmate now—not me skipping to the sixth grade as I'd dreamed would happen. As my sister walked pass me on her way to fill Daddy's eyes with the same pride Mama's held, I looked down and away. I felt the sting of tears trying to drop but swallowed hard and willed them to stay. Mama looked over my way, gave me a small smile before returning to the simmering pots on the stove. "Go on and change your clothes before dinner, Faye," she said, over her shoulder.

Jo Ann never rubbed her good fortune in my face after that day as if we were meant to share our classroom. And then the wonders of childhood summers smoothed the hard edges of my jealousy and self-pity. Over the summer, Jo Ann and I became more than classmates. We resolved, without speaking it out loud, that we would be best friends. When school started in September, students were seated alphabetically. I sat one seat ahead of Jo Ann. We sat together during most recess and lunch periods and spent our evenings after dinner going over the day's events. At night in bed in the room we shared with our younger brothers, we whispered secrets.

On a beautiful spring day I remember more than any other, Miss Jeanie Morgan announced recess and walked to the door to monitor our departure from the classroom. Jo Ann and I liked our fifth-grade teacher a lot. Her voice was soft, full of warmth and concern, especially for the students who needed it most. She always seemed to know. She was a tall woman whose curves fell perfectly in place. We all whispered about the older boys and young male teachers finding excuses to come around and stare at her. But she was full of love and caring and never seemed to notice their more-than-friendly looks.

She stood on the porch of our classroom, smiling out at the large flock of children and waving at some from other classes who sought her attention as well. Jo Ann and I drifted out to the middle of the large school ground that separated our classrooms from the bathrooms. It was an exceptionally riotous day. The day's warmth and the smells energized us. "You all play safe and be careful out there near the street," she said kindly before turning and walking back into the room. Our schoolyard backed all the way up to an active street in the all-black community, and we often found ourselves running across that street to get balls we'd thrown too far.

"Tag...I say, Tag!" That was Bell having the final say about what the class game would be today. No one bothered to argue since Bell was usually so nice and seldom got her way. For the next five minutes, teams were chosen. For the first time, I was chosen before the very end. Jake, the cutest boy in class, chose me.

Bell had gained captainship of the other team, just because it was her idea. The girl had a transparent but unreciprocated crush on Jake. Bell was a smart girl but skinny at that period in our lives when skinny wasn't the same as pretty. Most everyone in the class secretly called her mosquito—even Jake. And Jake, the object of her affections, had chosen me.

Bell and Jo Ann and I were constant competitors. Though she was usually a nice girl, she wasn't too pleased that she was ever being pitted against the Kearney girls. So she sometimes sniggered with her friends that she couldn't stand the Kearney bumpkins. Bell and Jo Ann topped everyone in the class when it came to math and science. My love for reading put me a little ahead of them in reading and spelling, and Bell took it pretty bad when I beat her out during Miss Morgan's spelling bees.

I forgot our competition, though, as I ran and laughed with the other chosen girls and boys across the schoolyard. Bell ran too, her long, thin legs streaking across the yard as she valiantly tried to catch her "it" for the morning. I was happy, probably as happy as I'd ever been at school. I was happy that I was chosen and happy that I was viewed as simply one of the classmates for this moment. I was most happy that Jake had chosen me before the very last.

In my childish delirium that morning, I overdid the running and had to slow my pace. I was panting, trying to catch my breath as I looked over my shoulder and stumbled. The stumble sent me tumbling down, sprawled across a giant rubber tire we sometimes used for other racing games.

I was up again, straightening myself, ready to start all over. But the tumble had given Bell time to catch up, and there she was. During my quick look back, I saw the evil glee in the girl's eyes and heard the childish but dark laughter. As I tried to increase my speed, I realized it was useless. Bell had caught up with me. I laughed, remembering it was just a game. But Bell had crushed my dress tail between her thin fingers, slowing me almost to a stop. I tried half-heartedly to wrench away from her hands when I felt the coolness and the whoosh of my dress   flying above my head. Bell's laughter turned louder and darker as she held the tail of my dress up from my body.

Her laughter was contagious, for only seconds passed before the other children on the playground stopped, turned and began laughing too. Some were embarrassed snickers. Some were kind enough to turn away, pretending they hadn't seen. These were the boys and girls I'd been so proud to be apart of just moments ago. Bell's laughter, though, grew louder. "I told you! I told you!" The children's faces told me all. Their eyes were locked on my bare behind. "I told you Janis Kearney's parents can't afford to buy her no underwear!"

There were students I didn't know, older and younger. They all had seen. After what seemed like an eternity, Bell let my dress fall and cover my shame. Her laughter followed me across the schoolyard as I ran blinded by tears into the classroom.

The room was quiet and empty except for Miss Morgan who sat at her desk reading and looking over our test papers. A very small question of how I did on my test crossed my mind. I hurriedly chose a desk other than my own, one further back, away from Miss Morgan. I folded my arms across my face and lay upon the desk. Hiding my shame and my tears and praying the woman wouldn't speak to me.

Just moments later Miss Morgan's soft voice startled me. "Janis...Janis, are you all right?" She stood nearby, almost touching me. Quietly, she continued to stand. "Janis, why did you come in early...? What happened?"

"I don't feel good." It was half a lie.

"Tell me what's wrong, Janis...sit up and talk to me."

I straightened myself but turned my head away. She was a kind and caring teacher, yet I wouldn't say the words. All the students and even the other teachers admired her kindness. Still. She stood, looking at the side of my wet face. While she looked, the tears started again and wouldn't stop. She touched my shoulder and wiped the tears from my face. "Here." She handed me a handkerchief, then walked out the classroom door.

The rest of the day is lost to memory. I learned that Bell was punished in front of the other students. The girl didn't look or speak to me for a very long time. Her ignoring me was due to anger; my ignoring her was out of shame and humiliation. I didn't run home and whine. The "tag" game was yet another lesson in life for Jo Ann and me to dissect as we fought sleep that night. ℚ

Eighteen

Mama
and Miss Bailey

In 1964, I was in sixth grade and my younger brother Jerome was in fourth grade. This story is pretty much about Jerome, who was a student in Miss Pearl Bailey's fourth-grade class. But I'll get around to that. Jo Ann should have been just one grade above Jerome, in fifth grade, except that my older brother Jerrel, who everyone said was the spitting image of Mama, dated Jo Ann's fourth-grade teacher, the good-looking Miss Tommie Bradley who everyone said was the spitting image of Mary Wilson, one of the Supremes.

As likeable as Jerrel was, he was the only Kearney child who absolutely cared nothing about school. Teachers and students at Fields High described him as the Kearney boy that's not a good student. By the time he was in the 11th grade, he told friends—before he announced to my parents—that he was wasting his time in classes. He dropped out that same year.

Jerrel was charismatic and handsome, and the fact that he wasn't cerebral didn't seem to phase women. He was what most people described as a smooth talker who knew how to have a good time and make girls laugh. Jo Ann's good-looking teacher was one young woman who found Jerrel irresistible, and it was the very year that Miss Bradley and Jerrel dated that she gave Jo Ann a double promotion.

As smart as Jo Ann was—and Daddy convinced us all that she would outshine the rest of us one day—I made myself feel better about the whole thing by believing the woman's interest in Jerrel had more to do with the double promotion than Jo Ann's good grades. Having her in my class meant having to compete with her eight hours a day. I had enough problems with her at home competing for one thing or another—mostly Daddy's attention. Jo Ann usually won because Daddy realized early on that she was as near a genius as any of his children. Daddy had a special place in his heart for people who turned out to be more than what the world expected them to be...and he was sure that Jo Ann, a beautiful girl who was the color of smooth chocolate, would amaze people with her brilliance one day.

Since he was sure this would happen, he made it his business to encourage it in every way he could, blowing Jo Ann's head up five times the size it should have been. Daddy was impressed with intelligence and abhorred stupidity. How many times did I hear him say, "Keep your mouths shut as long as you can when people talking to you...that way they don't find out how big a fool you are."

There were Kearney children in just about every elementary class most years I went to school. That year, Julius and Jack shared seventh grade but that was because Miss Mary Baldwin flunked Jack in the sixth grade, and Julius caught up with him. Jack's crime, even though he was a straight A student, was that he failed to return a book on the last day of school.

In 1964, Miss Bailey had taught at Fields High for over 20 years and was showing no signs of packing up. After being demoted from the high school to the elementary school, it seemed she didn't demonstrate one whit more compassion for the younger children than she'd shown the older students. To many students' chagrin, there was no mandatory retirement age at Fields schools in those days, so the woman could end up teaching their grandchildren.

Jerome was one of Miss Bailey's students that year. The one thing in the world Miss Bailey had in common with my father was her attraction to excellent students. Jerome was an excellent student, and from all reports he and Miss Bailey got along quite nicely. Jerome would breeze home with canarylike smiles on his face to report all the little niceties involved in being a teacher's pet.

193

"Miss Bailey let me clean the chalk board, today." "Miss Bailey let me go buy the milk for the class today." "Miss Bailey said I was the best student she had this year."

The self-congratulations went on and on. It was about halfway through the school year that Jerome's reports seemed to stagnate, then end altogether. The teacher-pet romance seemed to have fizzled for some strange reason. Jerome still brought home straight A's on his tests and his report cards. But there were no proud announcements about how much Miss Bailey liked him.

One day, Jerome came home with a note from Miss Bailey. "Mama, Miss Bailey told me to give you this," Jerome said, as if he had no idea what it was. When Mama asked, Jerome shrugged his little shoulders, "I don't know," and skipped back to his room to change his school clothes and put his books away until homework time. We all called Jerome by his nickname, Ron, and mercilessly taunted him about his small stature and voracious appetite. No one could figure out how he could eat the largest Kearney boy under the table but never seem to add one pound to his small frame. "Ron got tape worms! Ron got tape worms!" we'd sing when we most wanted to see him swell up with rage. It was a well-known fact that Jerome dreamed about food and made up songs centered around his favorite meals. The boy honestly seemed to think about food in his sleep.

Many evenings as Mama cooked dinner she had to shoo Jerome out of her way as she cooked. "Go on out of this kitchen and play outside, Ron!" she'd say, still stirring her corn bread or turning a chicken breast over to brown. Jerome obviously didn't want to be far from the center of things when dinnertime rolled around. Even when he left the immediate area of the kitchen, he didn't go far, telling us later that he had mealtime down to a science and knew almost exactly when Mama would walk out of the kitchen to tell Daddy, "Dinner's ready!"

Other than his almost paranoiac preoccupation with food, Jerome rarely gave our parents or his teachers much trouble. He was a fairly docile child who was innately happy and funny but just had a bottomless pit in his stomach. So, Mama was puzzled about the note from Miss Bailey. She quickly opened and read it:

Mrs. Kearney,

I would really appreciate it if you will visit my classroom tonight after the PTA meeting and your visits with your other children's teachers. I need to speak with you about a matter.

Sincerely,
Miss Pearl Bailey

Mama looked at Jerome and asked if he knew what it was Miss Bailey wanted to talk to her about. Jerome's young, innocent face was blank. "No...I don't know, Mama. She just gave me the note and said give it to you." Mama took the note to her bedroom, and Jerome skipped outside to play.

Miss Bailey had sent notes home with Jerome before but most times they were extolling the boy's virtues and his superior work in class. Mama had known the teacher for most of the 20-plus years she'd taught at Fields schools, and most of her older children had taken classes from her. If Mama totaled up all the notes she'd received from Miss Bailey about one Kearney child or another, they'd probably fill up a 10-gallon bucket.

Pearl Bailey was a well-preserved woman in her late 50s and was what black folks in those days called "high yellow." She was straight and almost six feet tall. Her conservative, tailored way of dressing played up her handsome physique. It was likely she was a pretty woman in her earlier years, but the stresses of teaching children for so many years had taken its toll. Besides that, Miss Bailey didn't seem a bit interested in presenting an attractive front to Gould's children or parents.

The teacher wore her wire-rimmed glasses perched on the tip of her nose, reminding students of a studious owl. She wore her long, dark hair pinned in a bun at the nape of her neck. She had what black folks called "good hair." It was fine and wavy and required little hot—combing when it rained or if she sweated from the heat. Given her light complexion and the texture of her hair, Gould's gossipers giggled and whispered that "somebody did some muddy-water dipping back in the day."

Though we lived eight miles outside town, my parents had a handful of friends in town who passed on rumors about their children's teachers. Rumors had long circulated that Pearl Bailey beat children for the smallest misdemeanors. "That woman don't play around with the students in her class," one parent told Mama.

Jerome came home one day and said Miss Bailey had turned red when she walked to the back of the room and found out one student came to school "smelling like he peed to bed." After having a good laugh at his classmate's expense, Jerome said the teacher sent the boy home. He went on, humorously imitating his teacher's proper enunciation, "Young man, you will go directly home and wash yourself...and you will tell your mother you are not to return until that smell cannot be detected in this classroom!" The rest of us bent over laughing, as much at Jerome's imitation as at the boy's plight.

Miss Bailey's reputation for demeaning her students and for corporal punishment continued for as long as she remained at Fields school. Rumors flew that she slapped children for "talking back" in a disrespectful tone or that she hit girls in the back of their heads when they were caught cheating. One student, according to rumor, wore a wad of chewing gum on her forehead for hours after Miss Bailey saw her blowing bubbles in the back of the classroom.

None of the rumors bothered my parents in the least. They were strong proponents of corporal punishment. They were staunch believers in the verse: "Spare the rod, spoil the child." They were not the type of parents to visit our school incessantly or call on a teacher because their child complained of unfair punishment. Though we all came home whining at one time or another, it didn't take us long to learn the futility of that. In fact, our parents were more likely to administer additional punishment, rather than take our sides against a teacher. More than once, I was sent to bed with a fresh whipping after my parents learned I'd been punished by a teacher at school.

"Don't let me find out the teacher had to whip you," one or the other of my parents would admonish us on the first day of each school year-mostly for the benefit of the first-graders in the bunch. "I can tell you now, it'll be worse when I learn about it." This taught us to either behave or, if we chose not to, to take our punishment at school and never mention it out on Varner Road.

Jerome was a good boy, an unlikely candidate for "acting up" in Miss Bailey's class. But because he was such a good student and because Miss Bailey had forged a close relationship with her stellar student, Jerome fell prey to feeling too comfortable with his teacher, sharing information about his family life that would lead to a most discomfiting scenario.

My parents were regular attendees of Fields' PTA meeting all of the years they had children there-more than 30 years. That night in 1965, they attended, as well. Though they weren't daytime or regular visitors in our classrooms or at the school, James and Ethel Kearney made it a point to be at every PTA meeting to participate fully in the decisions being made about their children's schooling. That night after the PTA meeting, my parents must have hurried through their visits with the rest of our teachers, happy but expectant of the good reports about each of their children's school work.

What was surely at the top of their list for that night was the meeting with Miss Bailey. After their last teacher visit, Mama looked around at her cluster of children and said, "Y'all go out in the hall and wait for us there." She looked at Jerome, though, and nodded. "You, come with us...we're going to talk to Miss Bailey." If Jerome was any way worried, he didn't show it.

Though it was a few days before Jerome would breathe a word to us about that meeting, we never let up begging him to tell. Finally, he gave in one night after our parents had gone off to bed and shooed us to bed. The three of us—Jo Ann, Jude and I—lay quietly listening to Jerome's story about Mama's meeting with Miss Bailey. Jerome prefaced his story by spewing his distaste for the teacher he used to adore.

"That woman is the meanest woman in the whole world, and I can't wait to be out of her class." Jerome's story picked up where we left off, sitting in the hallway watching Mama, Daddy and Jerome hurry down to Miss Bailey's classroom.

Jerome walked with our parents down the hallway to his fourth-grade classroom. When they arrived at the room, Jerome said there were still other parents there. Mama and Daddy gently pushed him to the back of the room ahead of them and sat quietly in the child-size desks while Miss Bailey finished talking with the parents up front. As the last couple said good night to the teacher and walked out the door, Daddy and Mama rose and moved to the front of the room. "Come on, Ron," Mama prodded Jerome from his desk and up to the front of the class with them.

Miss Bailey stood with her hands folded in front of her, watching Jerome and my parents make their way to the front of the classroom. She offered my parents a small smile, greeting them in her signature high-pitched voice that sounded as if it belonged to someone else. She held out her hand to Mama and Daddy and asked them to "Please sit down, Mr. and Mrs. Kearney."

Miss Bailey looked over at Jerome and smiled. "How are you doing tonight, Jerome? You do your homework already?"

Jerome nodded, embarrassed, "Yes, ma'am."

For the rest of the meeting, Miss Bailey acted as if the boy wasn't sitting there.

"Lord, Mrs. Kearney, if your children aren't the spittin' image of you and Mr. Kearney!" She chuckled and continued, "I swear...." Adults often said they found it hard to tell one Kearney child from the next. My parents sat quietly without much to say as the teacher continued her small talk.

Finally, Miss Bailey pulled her desk chair near my parents, smoothing down the skirt of her dress. "I'm sorry to have you waiting like this, Mr. and Mrs. Kearney. I swear it seems like every parent decided to come out tonight." She chuckled lightly. "I thank you for waiting for me, and I know you want to get the children home before it's too late.

"I guess y'all got my note?" the teacher asked. My parents nodded and continued to wait for the woman to tell them why they were there. Though a few of their children had gotten into trouble with teachers over the years, my parents had never received anything but good news about Jerome from his teachers.

Miss Bailey cleared her throat before she began. "Mrs. Kearney, Mr. Kearney...Jerome is doing really good in my class. In fact, he's about at the top of the class and is reading better than most of the children in the ninth and 10th grades." The woman seemed a little nervous talking to my parents that night. She stood up and got Jerome's class file, handed it to Mama, then settled down on the edge of her desk.

"As you all see, Jerome is a really smart boy...but I have to tell you that lately he's been acting a little strange; coming to me during lunch period and asking for food for lunch. Mrs. Kearney, he tells me that you wanted him to ask me for food because you don't have money to give him for his lunch. Now, Mrs. Kearney, it's not that...."

While the woman continued to talk, Mama's body was turning harder and straighter. As Jerome looked from Miss Bailey to Mama, he saw Mama's eyes glaze over the way they did when she was at her angriest with her children. She didn't take her eyes off Miss Bailey as the woman told her how bad she felt about having to give Jerome food because his family couldn't afford to feed him

"Mrs. Kearney, Mr. Kearney, I been giving Jerome lunch money pretty much every day for the last couple of weeks. But you know, it's just not proper for me to continue to do this. The other children watch this, and they start talking and calling Jerome names.

"I just don't know how to handle this. I was hoping you all could talk to Jerome, and we can nip this in the bud right now. Mrs. Kearney, do you think there is some way...anything you can do to make sure Jerome and the other children get fed so they won't be so hungry while they're in school? You know students learn a lot better when they eat three good meals. Besides that...the other students...it's just not a good situation."

Jerome said the woman finally stopped talking and looked over at him, while he looked down and away.

"Mama was so mad she wanted to cry. I could tell the way her mouth was so straight and her face had turned hard the way it do when she's so mad," Jerome said.

"Mama said, 'Miss Bailey, I don't rightly know what to say, except to apologize for my son's foolishness. I don't know what my son told you, but I do feed my children. And I do hope you know I would never tell my son, or none of my children, to ask their teacher to feed'em. Fact is, Miss Bailey, I'd be much obliged if you not feed my son or give him any more money for lunch. We can guarantee you he won't be asking you for no more lunch money.' "

Jerome said Daddy was quiet the whole time, letting Mama talk.

"When Mama got up from the chair to leave, she stood there for a while looking at the teacher, and Miss Bailey finally stood up, too.

'Miss Kearney, I didn't mean to...I just....'

"Mama was crying...for real, and she was still mad because the rest of her face didn't change," Jerome said. "You couldn't hardly hear her when she asked Miss Bailey if I needed to do any extra work or did I have all my homework up to date.

"Miss Bailey said, 'Miss Kearney, Jerome is one of the nicest boys in class and he's my top student, always gets his work done before anybody else in the class. It's just that....' "

Mama didn't let the woman finish, cutting her off. "Thank ya', Miss Bailey. Now, we need to be gittin' the children home."

Jerome walked slowly behind his parents out the door and down the hall where the rest of us joined them for the quiet ride home. Daddy talked a little, peaking the rest of our interest by asking Jerome why he'd been lying to the teacher. Mama didn't say a word and neither did Jerome.

I vividly remember the rest of that night's story, how we had all gone straight to bed after returning from school. My parents were still talking quietly as we went to bed that night. Jerome was still quiet while we joked that he must've gotten in trouble with Miss Bailey.

Just as I was falling asleep, I heard our bedroom door open and close and saw Mama's outline in the moonlit room. I sensed my other siblings also stirring to see who had come in. Jerome, a ferocious snorer, must have been the only one of us already asleep. Without a sound, Mama-wielding a skinny switch-walked directly to the bed Jerome shared with Jude. She snatched the boy up by his bony shoulders-ending his sleep and the snoring. Without any explanation, Mama began what she must have anticipated all the way home.

"You little liar, you had the nerve to lie to that teacher about me wanting her to feed you, making me look like I ain't no good parent-like I can't take care of my own children."

Mama didn't let up for the next five minutes with the switch lashing out across poor Jerome's almost bare bottom. I'm sure now, Mama must have been taking years of frustration—the anguish, self-pity and hopelessness she'd borne—out on her son. Ron's loud wails awoke the rest of the house and surely the chickens, the dogs and the livestock out in the fields.

"You go to that woman tomorrow n' you beg her pardon for your foolishness, and I mean you better do it 'cause I'm gone ask next week if you did!"

The rest of us all feigned sleep as Mama whipped and talked to Ron. And even when she finished and Ron crawled back into bed crying and whimpering, we remained silent.

"She didn't have to do that," Jo Ann offered quietly. I imagined the pain my brother must be in and was confused as to why my mother was so angry. None of us moved to comfort our brother. We had all been there before and expected that by tomorrow night he would hardly remember it happened.

Though I listened to my parents' whispered voices and my mother's muffled anger that night, I was too young to understand where the depth of Mama's anger had come from. I wouldn't know until Jerome was ready to tell us that Miss Bailey had ignited the anger, accusing Mama of negligence.

Unwittingly, the teacher had shone a light on my family's impoverishment that my parents never referred to in public. Pearl Bailey had crossed the line of forgiveness by questioning my mother's ability to love and care for her children. The children's star performances at school were the Kearneys' entrée into something beyond our poverty and the ugliness of our lives. It was through our superior grades that we measured up to everyone else and was able to forget who we were. It would take years for Mama to forgive Miss Bailey for taking away what had been so hard to create.

For all the years Miss Bailey remained at the Gould schools, Mama never visited her class again, even when she taught a Kearney child. While the revelation that Jerome would use such tricks to satisfy his physical hunger didn't surprise Mama, Miss Bailey's shoving it under her nose was more humiliation than Mama was willing to forgive. ℚ

PART V

The
White School

(1965-1967)

NINETEEN

Our Colored Education:
Gould's Freedom of Choice

Gould's black schools mirrored so many others in Arkansas' Delta region—sparse population with no industry to speak of and endless acres of almost blinding white cotton fields. Though we never used the word and wasn't aware of its presence, Jim Crow was an incipient part of everything we experienced in the Arkansas Delta. Years later, though, we would all agree that for young, poor children, there might have been an ironic blessing in that terrible law.

In spite of our needs, black children in towns like Gould were blessed to have teachers and school administrators who believed their mission was to lay a foundation for our future. Both history and personal experiences made them understand the obstacles before us, and the majority of them worked hard to prepare us for the mountains and molehills that might obstruct our paths.

The school boards were made up of both good and not so good white citizens who were all, like us, victims of the times and their environment. Black children's education was not a priority. The most that was expected of even our best and brightest were future careers in teaching, clerking or entry-level state government jobs.

Many black children—including the Kearney children—grew up believing our tomorrows could be something more than what we saw in front of us. Our parents and teachers with vision helped us see those possibilities. They took the sour lemons life gave them and made the best lemonade money could buy.

I attended the all-black Fields Elementary School from 1959 to 1965. When my teacher would distribute my text books in class, the first thing

I did was peer inside the front cover. There on the dark lines were   hand-written names scrawled, often haphazardly. I knew they were the white students' names because my father had railed about the used books his and other black children received from the white school.

The worn, sometimes tattered books were one more symbol of our second-classed citizenship. When I was able to read well enough, I read the white children's names out loud, "...Laura, Michael, Susan, Debbie, Sarah...," I tried imagining the white faces and how these children's lives differed from mine. I wondered if Laura or Susan had little brothers or sisters as I did. Did they fight? What did they talk about at night when they lay in bed, and did they all share beds, too?

I would turn over in my mind that the girl or boy had held this very book, took it home and copied homework from its pages. I knew they would be given new books with shiny, unmarred covers and a new book smell. Their books would have blank lines inside, awaiting their own fresh scrawl. No Laura or Michael or Sarah owned the books before them.

When desegregation finally forced its way into Gould in 1967, the white leaders offered black families the South's version of experimental school integration called "Freedom of Choice." Mine and other black parents may have understood that they and their children were on trial, but that didn't stop them from hurriedly signing us up and shuttling us off to the domain of the white school system. They had dreams of their children acquiring a quality education, something that would take us further than a job teaching or clerking.

The white children's names in the cover of our texts had haunted me all those years. Those last summer days before we entered the white school, I dreamed of finally meeting the Laura, Sarah or Michael I had imagined the years before. I wanted to match those names from the books, with the faces they belonged to. I found Michael by the second week I was at the school. Sarah took me longer to find. The second-hand books had afforded me a glimpse of these students while they knew nothing about me.

In spite of what I may have missed in quality during my years at the segregated black school, it was years later and my continuous analysis of the white school experience that I realized just how invaluable those early school years had been. I would treasure even more the black teachers who cared and made a difference in my life. Those women and men not only identified with us but also believed in our capabilities.

In many ways, black schools did offer second-rate education. We received hand-me-down books, little funding for extracurricular programs or activities and sparse physical maintenance or repairs of our schools. Our education was secondhand, just as the clothing I wore most days to school was secondhand. Both were previously used or throw-away but still functional...still in good enough shape to serve my purpose and others' purposes. Great minds were nurtured and expanded in the midst of that secondhand education.

Most teachers who came to our schools came with a mission—to prove the world wrong about black children's inability to learn. They didn't come armed with pre-conceived notions about black children's worth or their abilities based on the color of their skin. Because they didn't have a long list of options in what schools they would work, they were primed to work against the tide—to transcend their physical environments to give us the best education they knew how.

Many of our teachers were not much older than the high school students they taught. They already were feeling the wind of change, however, and their efforts were toward preparing us for those changes. For black communities, our academic successes represented success for the race. Our teachers toiled in the often bare schoolrooms to transform the rough diamonds we were into smooth, sparkling gems that would one day make the world sit up and take notice. They were nurturers of our young minds and spirits and the foundation upon which we would begin our lives.

All during the pre-civil rights era, a quality education for black children was never a priority of Gould's all-white school board. In my twelve years at Gould's public schools, I was blessed to have many gifted teachers and only a handful of those who were teachers in name only. My first six years were at Fields-memorable years that would stay with me through the best and worst of times. My two years in the experimental freedom of choice program at the all-white Gould Public Schools would leave scars and create questions about what "quality" education truly meant.

In 1967, after two years of Gould's practicing integration, the school board agreed to the federal government's desegregation plan. The former all-black Fields High School took the name of the former all-white Gould High School. The former Gould High School became Gould Elementary. Like most southern towns, the black institutions lost a great deal in the process. In spite of the fact that less than 10 percent of the 500-student population was white, neither of the formerly all-black institutions existed after September 1967.

My experiences at this new high school were greatly different from my earlier experiences at either Fields Elementary or the white Gould School. It was as if Jo Ann's and my time at the white schools had magically transformed us in the eyes of our former classmates and schoolmates.

Suddenly teachers and students saw something more than the poor, ragged Kearney girls who had left the black school in 1965. In the four years I would remain at Gould High, my self-esteem soared. My popularity quadrupled, and I was actively involved in extracurricular actitives—serving as captain of the cheerleader squad for three years. Without the transformation, this would never have happened to the Janis Kearney from Fields Elementary School. That real Janis Kearney, though, was still there, watching the miraculous transformation with awe and some wariness.

90 percent of Gould's white parents, even those teaching at Gould High, attempted to stay one step ahead of the school desegregation law by shuttling their children off to the new private academies popping up along highway 65 and in other areas of the state. These parents, some well-to-do and others barely making ends meet, used their savings accounts and changed their addresses to assure their children continued learning in a segregated environment.

The late 1960s and early 1970s meant dramatic changes in every day life for small southern towns such as ours. The old comfortable relationships between whites who accepted their first-class citizenship and blacks who had pretended to accept their second-class citizenship suddenly changed before our eyes. The court's desegregation laws meant we were suddenly equal in every way and the relationships would never be as comfortable again.

The country's well-intentioned integration effort took its toll on our small town. While black residents were valiantly trying to catch up with the rest of the world, white residents were valiantly trying to hang on to the past. The funding of their children's private educations was ruining many of the rich white families who mortgaged homes, sold off hundreds of acres of land and traded their wealth and standing in the community for a trailer house classroom that guaranteed no black faces.

Whether it was part of this tragic tumble or an incidental sidebar of the times, cotton was fast losing its luster and its value in the South, and white students whose parents had gone broke educating them in segregated schools were deciding in droves that education wasn't such a big deal after all. An amazingly small number went on to college after their private academy education. ℚ

TWENTY

Walking on the Other Side
of the Track

It is more than myth that throughout America's South and many northern cities as well, the races are separated by railroad tracks. Ironically, our small town of Gould, Arkansas, was named for railroad baron Jay Gould whose view of America never included having little black children cross his track to interact with little white children, not unless they were there for work or to deliver a message.

The town's white citizens, its few grocery stores, the one laundromat, the cotton gin and certainly the school for white children were well-situated, almost perfectly, on the white folks' side of the track. As for us, that is those of us who lived "in town," there was one grocer—minus the few "candy stores." Ah, the wonderful corner candy stores! I remember so fondly the noontime jaunts to Mrs. Tucker's candy store.

Mrs. Tucker was a tall, broad almost-white woman with curly but fine hair. She'd sit in the middle of her small store in an easy chair, sometimes nibbling on some of her own candy watching our comings and goings. She counted our few pennies and nickels with a smile and a cheery word to take back with us to school.

Fields Elementary and Fields High, named for one of southeast Arkansas' early black educators, were separated by three miles. While both were smack in the middle of the black community, the high school was located near the local highway and included sixth through 12th grades. The elementary school was built in the early 1950s and was adjoined by the high school gym. Graduating from elementary to junior high school was not only a guarantee that you would move to another area but also that you would now be joining the high school students on campus. What a rite of passage!

While the high school was a sprawling five acres that included three wood-frame buildings that separated and housed the high school and junior high students, it was not impressive physically. The rooms were drafty, and the windows often were in disrepair. The bathrooms, used by all 500 students, were situated in a large building with two large rooms separated by a wall. One room was for boys, and the other for girls...and, oh, the things we learned in that huge gloomy space!

Though it was equipped with indoor plumbing, the plumbing rarely worked. If there was a plumber employed by the school, he was rarely if ever in evidence. The bathrooms were simply unfit, let alone for young children. Our outdoor toilets at home were in better shape—even without the luxury of a wash basin and flushing mechanism.

I have two distinct memories of those days. There were some teachers who bruised our fragile self-esteem. But I believed most of my teachers cared about me and my well-being, and it was important to work as hard as I could to please those teachers to assure they wouldn't stop smiling with approval. I also remember with nostalgia the freedom I felt exploring the school grounds, sometimes with friends and often alone.

I would never forget the childhood games we played on the schoolyard. The games were one way my siblings and I were able to forget, temporarily, the realities of our station in life. The hand games, which called for amazing hand-eye coordination and ambidexterity, lasted throughout our lunch breaks some days.

"The sailor went to sea, sea, sea...to see what he could see, see, see...but all that he could see, see, see...was the bottom of the deep blue sea...sea...sea."

I remember the ball games, softball, volleyball, "box"; the running games such as "It" and "Tag"; "Simon Says," which tested our ability to freeze all movement on the drop of a dime; and my very favorite game "Jacks." How I loved to sit in that circle of three or four girls and wait my turn to throw that small, soft ball into the air as I scrambled to pick up all the jacks. I was good at it because I loved it so.

I also remember the thrill and fear as one friend or another pushed me in the schoolyard swings, higher and higher into the air...and how I was one of the few children who were never brave enough to jump out of the swing in midair. Those memories of my days at the black school can still bring tears of nostalgia to my eyes.

Still, there are the bitter-sweet memories of that same childhood, those same years at the black school. Even with the childish games and fun, there were the reminders for me and my siblings, even before the white school experiences, that we were "different," "less" than others, simply because we had less. There were days clouded by the humiliation of not being accepted wholly by our peers and being starkly reminded of our place.

The richness of our everyday lives, in spite of our poverty, was something that only my family understood. We weren't adept enough at that time to make the rest know. What they knew from gossip and hearsay was that my father, a sharecropper who "worked" 45 acres of cotton and soybeans on a white man's land, always ended the year with just enough to buy seeds for the next year; just enough to buy the staples that would—in the best of times—get us through the winter without going hungry; and just enough to buy his children a round of second-hand coats and boots to get through the winter.

Just getting by was our existence at home, and it carried over into the schools. Everyone knew of our dire predicament because we wore it, or failed to wear it, on our sleeves. We were the "Jed Clampetts" of the black community without anything close to an oil find. I think we all must have spent nights dreaming of what it would be like for that Hollywood creation like "The Beverly Hillbillies" to become reality for us.

While James and Ethel were desperately poor, their every working day was filled with prayers and admonitions that their children do well in this world that was so un-accepting of them. In 1965, they wanted their children to gain the education that had been wrested from them, one way or another, at an early age. Their vision had more to do with erasing the myth that black children couldn't excel in a white world.

Together, with their hopes and dreams for their children, James and Ethel took a stand and stuck to it. They refused to stand by and see their smarter-than-average children repeat the lives they now experienced. This experiment in integrating the races, as one local paper described it, was James and Ethel's chance to give their children an education equal to the town's white students.

It was beyond even the most understanding of black teachers and students to get their minds around this. Most found it aberrant, strange, even humorous that the Kearney children, saddled with abject poverty and nonacceptance by even the black community, would dare leave the quasi comfort of the black school and venture into the white world with our ragged, pulled-together wardrobes and wounded self-esteem.

And yes, we were traveling across the tracks with a barrage of fears and feelings about our shortcomings. Our only shield, our ammunition, was that offered by a few sensitive, early teachers and our parents who made us know that we could excel and that no one could take our love for learning away from us. And, thanks to our youth, there was an innocent curiosity, an open willingness to seek that something better that our parents believed awaited us.

———

I have beautiful, but painful memories of my first day at the white school. The sky was a clear blue, and fall was right around the corner. The smell of ripened cotton was mixed with the fresh smell of Juniper trees. It was 1965, and I was experiencing one of my otherworldly feelings as I stepped off the school bus that morning. I turned and looked back at the bus driver and found that he was looking down at me with a strange smile on his face. This was the same driver who, for the last six years, had picked me and my siblings up in front of our home out on Varner Road and dropped us off in front of Fields Elementary School on the other side of the track. Today, he was leaving me in foreign territory, and I'm sure he silently wished me well.

The four of us, minus my three brothers who had morning football practice, stood together for the first time speechless with each other. Our eyes were wide, dilated from fear of the unknown, as we waited for the morning school bell to ring. I saw no one I knew, only a sea of white faces. More white people than I'd seen in my life, including the few television shows Daddy let me watch after work in the summers.

Jo Ann and I walked my younger brothers to their classrooms then hurried to ours before the second bell. While some of the students pretended to ignore us, as if they could, others peered brazenly and curiously at us. None smiled or pretended they were glad we were there. Not one. In fact, it would be near the end of the two-year "experiment" before we'd feel any real human kindness in the voice of a white person at Gould High School.

My first days were filled with awe at the contrasts between "our" school and the pristine school we had now entered—the wide linoleum hallways, the large classroom space, the always—working bathrooms and water fountains and the smell of brand new text books. In contrast to the impoverished black school, the wealthy white school had robes for its choir students who took regular trips outside the city; a cheerleader squad who traveled on the well-maintained buses to football games; a football team with all the trimmings; and even a well-equipped gym with exercise equipment that included a trampoline and tumbling mats.

Outside of the awe, however, I was painfully aware that neither the students nor the teachers were "prepared" for our infiltration into their world. In fact, their anger at our presence was etched across more faces than I could possibly count as I stepped onto the luscious grass adorning the school each morning. While the first week was a rude awakening for our fragile sensibilities, the next two years would be filled with open rudeness and hostility. It seemed as if, once they saw we were indeed there to stay, their internalized anger turned outward.

The two years at the white school was a traumatic change for both Jo Ann and me. Yet, in some strange way, it was also an exciting time. I felt as if I was watching and existing in a live movie each day I set foot on the schoolyard. Even then, I knew I was a part of the changes being made around the country—not just for Gould.

Though Daddy seldom allowed us to watch "foolish" cartoons or comedies, he was happy to have us sit with him and watch the more serious programs, such as "Wild Kingdom" and the TV networks' evening news. It was because of this avid newsgathering that we knew integration was the buzzword nationwide. We knew we were not the only ones going through this strange dance of nonacceptance at white schools, but knowing that didn't make experiencing it any better or easier.

Jo Ann and I talked about those two years many, many times during our adult life. We always wondered how things could have been different; whether we could have been different. Some of the blame for the bad experience at the white school might have, in fact, been averted if we'd tried harder to fit in. But our parents never taught us to fit in except at home. Though Jo Ann was the courageous one, we both were young and scared and, most of all, we were our parents' children—poor but proud and believing in our own intelligence. All of this, at that time in American history, hurt our chances of being accepted there.

Jo Ann and I forged a friendship during those two years that would last a lifetime. It wasn't perfect, and we would experience some bumps over the years. However, we learned it was okay to need each other and to lean on each other's strengths. For the first time, I thanked my lucky stars for the double promotion Jo Ann had received in fourth grade. For years I had resented her being in the same grade with me. We became inseparable and spent our nights after the lights were out rehashing our days, calming each other's concerns and fears.

———

This freedom of choice wasn't as smooth a transition for Jo Ann and me as it was for our three older brothers—Jesse, Jack and Julius—who won the hearts of the coaches and teachers by being star athletes. They, in fact, excelled in football, basketball and track during their years at Gould High, breaking every school record.

While they were welcomed at the school with opened arms, Jo Ann and I were reminded daily that we had nothing to offer the school, except another black body to take up space. Like most of the other black students given this "opportunity," we were viewed as a distraction and a craw in the throats of many of the white teachers and their students.

Jo Ann and I had been A and B students at Fields Elementary. However, our grades quickly deteriorated at the white school. We began to question whether we had really been as smart as everyone, including our parents, had thought we were all those years. Maybe, we thought, it was true that white students were really brighter, even though our everyday experience was proving that a myth.

We didn't run home happy and eager to show our parents our perfect cards anymore. Instead, we hid them away hoping they'd forget to ask about them, so we wouldn't have to internalize the hurt and embarrassment at their displeasure.

Though my parents knew racism in the schools was real, they refused to accept that as an excuse when it came to our grades. They expected our grades to reflect what they knew we could do, no matter what else was going on in the school or the classroom.

They didn't listen when we complained that our teachers wouldn't take the time to explain things we didn't understand, or that some graded us unfairly simply because they could get away with it.

"So, why is it that your brothers still doing good? If you can make A's in the black school, why can't you make 'em in the white school?" Mama would ask, exasperated. "You just going over there and letting the white folks laugh at how dumb you are."

Though Mama's words stung us, we didn't see how we could change the directions our grades were going. We studied. We did our homework. Nothing seemed to work. One day, in exasperation, we decided we just couldn't compete at the white school. We missed our friends and wanted to go back to our old school, the black school.

When our report cards began to reflect more C's and D's than A's and B's, my parents' disappointment changed to anger and no explanation or excuse appeased that anger. For the first time, we were punished because of our grades or, probably, because they knew the grades we were capable of bringing home.

"You won't ever be able to compete with them if you can't even compete with them in junior high school," Mama said with both anger and sadness in her voice.

My parents were embarrassed and hurt by our mediocre grades, but they finally gave up punishing us after realizing that nothing would help change our grades. If we had been "middle class," my parents would have been able to take away things we valued like a radio or television or telephone or car. As it was, we had nothing to take away. Daddy already dictated when we watched television and what we watched. Making us go to our rooms and read would have been more like a Christmas gift than punishment.

Jo Ann and I decided, at that point, that we wouldn't tell our parents about the insults and racial slurs from schoolmates, or about the teachers who treated us like second-class citizens. One teacher went so far as to throw my books to the floor after declaring I wasn't paying attention. Neither would they want to hear how a number of teachers completely ignored our presence in their classes, refused to speak to us and obviously didn't care whether we learned or not.

In those two years of hell, Jo Ann and I lucked up on one kind teacher—Mr. Pat Craig, our English and choral instructor. It wasn't that Mr. Craig was extraordinarily kind or warm toward us, but that he treated us like any other student—praising us when we did well and urging us to do better when we didn't. Our grades soared in his class.

Jo Ann, the more outspoken of the two of us, became known by the administration as a "troublemaker," after being sent to the principal's office a couple of times for "talking back" to a teacher or defending herself against a racist student.

The fact was, the white teachers just didn't know what to think of Jo Ann, which translated into not liking her. That dislike helped bring us closer together. We probably wouldn't have made it at that school any other way. The teachers' and students' resentments came out in a number of different ways, but the most lasting effect was the drastic drop in our grades.

Amazingly, the three classes Jo Ann and I excelled in—English, civics and choral—were all taught by Mr. Craig.

Both Jo Ann and I sang in the Gould High School Choir. While my voice was average, Jo Ann had maybe the most beautiful voice in the school choir. Like most things, Jo Ann learned quickly and always excelled in the class.

I was happy to find a class I enjoyed attending. I discovered that in Pat Craig's class, the voice was a natural equalizer. The most beautiful voices were the ones he prodded and nurtured most, and it didn't matter who they belonged to. He was drawn to Jo Ann's beautiful contralto voice and made sure she put it to good use during our public events.

It was through the high school choral class that Jo Ann and I got the opportunity to travel to different parts of the state, singing at college and school concerts. Our parents were able to see us perform during one of Mr. Craig's Christmas concerts. This was always a big event for the school, and choir members worked hard to make it a success.

Though Mama fussed when we told her we needed choir uniforms— a black skirt and a white blouse—for the concert, she scraped up the money, somehow, to buy our outfits for the event. We were especially proud that Mama and Daddy were able to attend the concert, hoping it made up some for our academic performance in other classes.

If smiles and nods were any indication, our parents were proud of us that night, especially of Jo Ann. Though we all sang little tunes around the house from time to time, no one except me had heard Jo Ann belt out a song the way she did "What Child is This" that night.

Among other things, I gained a real appreciation for Christmas classics under Mr. Craig and never forgot them over the years. At the end of the year, to show his appreciation, he treated the choir to a field trip to Arkansas A&M College in Monticello where "South Pacific" was being performed. We were surprised and pleased when our parents said we could go and gave us spending money to take with us. The play itself, though, was the real excitement. I felt as if I'd died and gone to heaven. Jo Ann and I couldn't stop talking about the play on the way back home and for weeks afterward. ℚ

— TWENTY-ONE —

Our Good
Brothers

Our three brothers were athletic heroes at Gould High School, and all through our two years at the school, Jo Ann and I believed their lives were made easier by that fact. I would understand, much later, that their lives were no more perfect than ours. Their worth was measured by the white students' and coaches' estimation of their performances on the football field or the basketball court or the track field.

But, with my parents' early drilling that we were "as good as anybody...white or black," the boys held onto a sense of themselves outside the adulation of the white colleagues and school coaches. I would understand later that my brothers wrestled with personal conflicts as they became the center of attention at the white school.

Like the rest of us, their years on Varner Road had merited few warm greetings from whites, except the fat county man who drove his car into our front yard and told one of the boys, "Go tell your daddy to come out here...I need to talk to him," or the white men who drove into our yards before dawn to haul us to their cotton fields. Their sun-burned faces, peeked out from under the straw hats and their arms usually dangled loosely outside their windows as they waited for us to crawl into the back of their mud-riddled pickup. "Y'all set down in the back of that truck 'fore you fall out...."

Now, my three brothers had white coaches chauffeuring them to and from football, basketball and track practice and making sure they had enough money when they traveled with the team. Their nightly whispers before Daddy threatened them with a "whipping" if they didn't go to sleep, must've been about how strange life was for them and how you never knew what tomorrow might bring.

Julius, the youngest of the three, seemed least affected by this newfound adulation. Though he was a superior athlete and cared as much about winning as his brothers, he saw himself first and foremost as an intellectual—preferring recognition for his brains rather than his athletic prowess. Julius was cocky about how smart he was, especially since he learned just shortly after coming to the white school that he could compete with any of the white students in his class and out-perform most of the boys on the football field.

Jo Ann and I were both envious and proud of our brothers. We never missed the opportunity to attend the Friday night football games with our parents, whose pride lay quiet inside them but bursting out periodically during the games they attended. Mama sat quietly through the games, her face expressionless except for a small smile when her sons' names were thrown up in cheers.

"Go bring me some popcorn and Coke and get yourselves something...James, you want anything?" That was Mama, after watching the white families walk back and forth along the bleachers with arms full of goodies.

Daddy would vaguely shake his head, not taking his eyes off the football field. Mama would shake her head and smile at how engrossed her husband was in their sons' game. She pushed the change into our hands and snapped her purse closed, "Hurry back."

Our anticipated trip to the concession stand was a small and temporary freedom , and we made the most of it. We traipsed along the sideline, peering over the rope at the game and listening for Jesse's or Jack's or Julius' name from the blaring announcer's box. When their names finally moved through the airwaves, I exchanged smiles with Jo Ann, fighting the warm blush of pride that swept over me.

We were always amazed to hear the white students and their parents call out my brothers' names in their south Arkansas twang, cheering when they made touchdowns or when their scores won the game. We smiled and clapped with Mama, without shouting or standing, to see our brothers outshine every other boy on the team.

Daddy sometimes stood and watched as one of his sons took the ball all the way to the end zone, but he never yelled out his sons' names. Our excitement was all wrapped up inside our chests and expressed through our smiles that night at nothing in particular.

Because the white students and teachers treated my brothers different from other blacks, we couldn't help but begin to see them differently, too. Mama and Daddy, who never bragged about their children doing what they were expected to do, found it difficult to treat my brothers the same. They were self-consciously pulled into conversations about their sons' athletic prowess by men on the street. "Your boys are something else, Mr. Kearney."

As my parents shopped at Failla's Grocery or sat waiting for church service to start, they'd be stopped in the aisle of the store, interrupted from their thoughts by a smiling admirer. "I saw one of your boys in the paper yesterday...how many touchdowns did he make?"

Without saying a word, my parents would clip the newspapers, fold the articles neatly and tuck them between the Bible pages. We would later find faded newspaper clippings, articles and pictures of the Kearney boys making touchdowns, catching a ball in the air or making the winning play on the field. They had succeeded in drilling the importance of education into us, now they could take credit for raising outstanding athletes as well.

When the young, white coaches drove out to our home that July in 1965, my parents were taken completely off guard. They had never considered their children putting their minds to anything except their books. And maybe because the black schools had never had a football team, my parents had never heard of high schools courting students to play the game.

After the coaches made their pitch, Daddy cleared his throat and offered them his usual response. "Well, I don't rightly know...I can't give you an answer right this minute." Daddy's first concern, he told the men, was whether playing football would interfere with his sons' education.

Secondly, he said, "I might as well tell you, I need my boys to help me with my cotton crop this fall."

The white coaches cleared their throats then, before the taller, more aggressive one placed his hand on Daddy's shoulder and said, "Mr. Kearney, I promise you we'll make sure we don't interfere with your cotton crop or the boys' education." They would personally see to it, the young coach said.

Finally, the coaches ran out of conversation with Daddy. When they got up to leave, they repeated their promises to make sure the boys didn't fall down in their grades and that they could practice whenever they weren't helping Daddy out in the fields.

"Well, I'll thank about it...I'll let y'all know," Daddy said as he walked the men to the front door.

"We'll come back out tomorrow, Mr. Kearney, if that's all right...see if you've made your mind up."

Daddy hardly nodded, but waved and closed the door behind the men. Daddy and Mama discussed the dilemma that night in bed, the place where they always discussed, then solved their problems. As an afterthought, Daddy asked his sons the next morning before they left for the cotton fields, if they might be interested in playing football at the white school.

The boys, overcome with excitement, laughed and yelled, "Yeah, Daddy...can we?" The next day, as promised, the white coaches returned to our house. Daddy met them out in the front yard, saving them the effort of coming in.

"Well, I guess we gone try it out...see how it works out." The three boys, almost identical in size, stood on the porch, peering at the white coaches. The two men looked askance at Daddy before easing out of their truck doors and anxiously greeting their new athletes.

For the next few weeks before school started and cotton-chopping season ended, the boys left the fields every evening by five o'clock and walked eight miles to the school to practice football with the white players.

I never saw three boys so excited in my life. Football was all they talked about night and day. They would've walked twenty miles to the school to practice if they had to. By the time school started in late August, the coaches had dug up an old ugly army truck they loaned to my brothers to get back and forth to practice and home every day.

Sports brought my brothers even closer. They spent every day and night together, sharing experiences and feelings. Many a night, Daddy would have to holler into their room to quiet them. "Y'all need to cut off that light and go to sleep, now!"

Julius was the one most likely to question authority. He'd started that at home but had gotten punished so many times for "talking back" and asking "disrespectful questions" that he started doing all his back talking under his breath.

Julius' fearless pride scared Mama and Daddy. They'd lived through such terrible experiences when a Negro's questioning of white folks' authority was punishable by unmentionable crimes. While Julius' constant questioning of right and wrong was no less than what Daddy had taught us all our lives, that fact failed to calm their fears.

It was 1966, a time ripe for a child such as Julius to ask the right questions and test the waters. It was the middle of the civil rights era when Afros and dashikis were worn as a source of pride and rebellion against the past.

Because the white folks in the city and at school treated my brothers like "special" Negroes, we began to feel differently about them as well. Even Mama and Daddy talked about their popularity in school and saved the newspaper clippings. They now had more than just their sons' brains to be proud of; their boys also excelled on the football field.

Jesse was the oldest of the three boys and served as mentor to the other two. Though he was only in the ninth grade, he was one of the most popular boys in high school. His most memorable time at the white school was getting into a fight with a fellow football player and being suspended for two weeks.

Jack was a year younger than Jesse but was the star athlete. Considered the all-time best athlete ever at Gould, he won just about every athletic award known to high school football and track. Like his other brothers, he also kept up his superior grades. In 1970, Jack won a football scholarship to the University of Arkansas. He played only one semester before injuring his knee and ending his football career.

Though Julius was a superior athlete like his older brothers, his heart and soul was in being a star academic. He told Mama when he was 10 that he wanted to be the first black president of the United States. Given a choice, Julius would always choose academics over sports, and the touchdowns he made wouldn't be half as sweet as graduating valedictorian of his class and gaining a scholarship to Harvard. ℚ

TWENTY-TWO

Julius and Sheriff Pearson

The story of Julius's altercation with Sheriff Harold Pearson is another Kearney legend that was passed on and tweaked to fit the teller over the years. The younger Kearney children still find humor and awe in my brother's courage, missing the levity of such a situation during the pre-civil rights South. The version passed on from Julius and other family members helped define the environment and times in which we lived.

In the fall of 1966 during the middle of that year's football season, one of my parents' deepest fears for their children was realized. My brothers—Julius, Jesse and Jack—had finished their after-school practice session that day. Wildly hungry, the boys decided they couldn't wait to get home and eat dinner but would eat before they began their 30-minute ride home.

After some discussion, they agreed on burgers at the Tastee-Freez, the only real diner in town. They would order at the takeout window, eat their food outside on the bench, then drive home. When they arrived at the Tastee-Freez, the line was unusually long, and they argued again about whether it made sense to wait in line or just drive home and eat.

Julius piped up that they should wait. An avid reader, Julius told his older brothers that he'd read an article in the *Pine Bluff Commercial* newspaper that said integration was the law of the land and that Negroes now had the right to eat at any public place—including public restaurants—they wanted to. "I don't see why that law don't include us," he offered.

While the other brothers were aware of the integration law, neither was interested in testing that law in Gould that particular night. Maybe they simply weren't as hungry as Julius was. Whatever the reason, Julius couldn't be talked out of his decision to test the law in Gould's Tastee-Freez diner. Jesse and Jack looked at each other and shook their heads, "Aw right, if you insist, Julius. But be ready to get our asses kicked out of there."

Just as the three black teens prepared to walk through the diner door, a burly white man stood and blocked their entrance. "Wait a minute, now boys... you know you can't come in here. We don't want no trouble here tonight. Why don't y'all jest gone 'round to the window there, and we'll be glad to take your order 'round there."

The three brothers nervously but courageously stood their ground. Julius, again, piped up defiantly, "There is a new law that says we can eat in this restaurant, Mister, and it's illegal for you to try to keep us out'a here,"

The white man's face turned red as he shook his head. "Son, I don't know 'bout no law, but you can't eat in here."

When the boys didn't budge, the white man began shoving the boy who seemed to be the leader toward the door. Instinctively, the boys shoved back.

Just about that time Sheriff Pearson, Gould's chief of police, showed up-likely in response to a call. Harold Pearson was tall and skinny and had a reputation of being a tough cop. He chewed tobacco and wore glasses and a cowboy hat. The small-town sheriff walked into the small diner and stood for a while before finally speaking. "Boys, what's goin' on here?" When Julius spoke up before the proprietor could, the illiterate sheriff looked over at the white man, waiting for another explanation. "Don't y'all know y'all don't eat in this restaurant?" Sheriff Pearson asked patiently.

My brothers were well aware of Sheriff Pearson's reported treatment of blacks in his jail. There were rumors of strange accidents happening in the jail that could never be fully explained. It almost always involved black men who had been arrested for innocuous crimes like disorderly conduct.

Rumor had it that the sheriff could not read or write and signed his tickets with an X. He also was known for doling out more traffic tickets than any other law enforcement officer in Lincoln County, including the nearby town of Grady that which was notorious for what travelers called "speed traps."

By the time the sheriff finished his warnings, Julius was hungry, angry and belligerent. "Sheriff Pearson, didn't you read about the new law that says Negroes can eat at any restaurant they want to now?"

Harold Pearson ignored the boy for a while. "Boys, I know y'all oughta be tired after finishing up your practicing over at the school. Y'all jest need to gone get yourselves home 'fore your parents get worried 'bout you."

While Jack and Jesse started to shift from one foot to another, Julius didn't budge. "We are being discriminated against. We got a right to eat here," Julius demanded, even louder this time.

Sheriff Pearson walked toward the boy, placing his hands on his shoulders and shoving him toward the door. "Come on, son, let's go..." The other white man pushed the other two boys at the same time. The people in the restaurant had stopped eating to watch the commotion.

Moments later, before the few diners could sit back down in their seats, a loud exchange was heard outside. The black boy and Sheriff Pearson were going at it. The sheriff had used the bottom of his foot to help Julius out the door, and Julius had turned and spat in the white man's face. The sheriff had turned purple, hauled off and slapped Julius hard across his face. Julius punched the white sheriff, who was at least a foot taller, knocking him to the ground.

By the time the melee had ended, Julius was handcuffed, pushed out to the sheriff's car and taken to the jail. The other two boys were left at the Tastee-Freez with a stern threat to "Get home, now!" They hurried home, coming back an hour later with Daddy. In spite of Daddy's pleading, Sheriff Pearson refused to release Julius, explaining how Julius had disrupted the diner's business, hit an officer and cursed at him. "The least this boy gone get is a night in jail."

Daddy left the jail house and drove the 35 miles to Pine Bluff to retain one of the few Negro lawyers in Pine Bluff. The one lawyer he was able to find, however, told Daddy he didn't have the time that night but would get to it the next day.

Daddy couldn't wait until the next day. He left Pine Bluff and went to the school superintendent's house late that night, waking him from his sleep. The next morning, my parents returned to the jail and met the school superintendent there. The tall, older white man walked over to Daddy, put his arm around his shoulder and motioned him over away from Mama and the other boys.

Daddy never said what they talked about, but he always said the white man was a good man to "stick his neck out" on Julius' behalf. We all believed my brother's football prowess surely had something to do with the white man's help.

Daddy rarely got angry, and we all knew when he was. He was plenty angry during this ordeal. We never talked when he got that way, and he didn't have much to say to us. Later, he said, "I swear, if it hadn't been for Ethel and my children, I probably would be in somebody's prison myself." None of us doubted he meant every word of it.

Like thousands of black parents in the South, he had kept his thoughts and feelings to himself out of fear for his son. His relief at his son's freedom, though, was dampened by the knowledge that such a thing could so easily happen.

The sheriff had reluctantly unlocked the cell that morning, but not before he told Julius, "Get out of my jailhouse...and I don't want to see your face around here no time soon." The white policeman's face was almost as red as it had been the night before. He told Daddy, "Mr. Kearney, y'all better keep that boy away from that diner. He need to learn how to treat white folks and respect the law or he got some bad days in front of him."

Daddy didn't say a word but kept moving toward the door. Mama's face was like stone—no sign of tears or apology in her eyes. She just kept her eyes in front of her. Julius's face had turned to stone, too, in just that one night in the sheriff's jail. This was likely a wake-up call, a stark reminder that he was still a Negro in America's South. That realization seemed to have suddenly dawned on my parents, too, as they walked out the jailhouse doors. Daddy believed that Harold Pearson was a lot better to Julius than he would have been if the white people hadn't thought so highly of him and my two other brothers.

Nobody talked on the way home. Mama and Daddy didn't begin to say what they really felt, the horror they'd lived through in less than 24 hours. Daddy would say, later, that he likely would have done the same thing as his son. But he didn't dare say a thing on our way back home. Nobody felt much like talking anyway.

Mama walked ahead into the house, and Daddy turned to Julius. "They kill colored folks for half what you did last night, son. Do you know what that would'a done to your mama?" Julius nodded before walking quietly into the house and to his bed.

In 1967, after our second year at the white school, the education leaders agreed to full integration for Gould's public schools. Amazingly, this meant that all the black students and less than ten percent of the whites would go to the former Fields High School. The rest of the whites attended the newly built private academies that had popped up throughout the county over the last two years. Most were in surrounding towns with a much smaller population of blacks.

Jo Ann and I were ecstatic. We were returning to our old "stomping grounds," to friends and teachers who cared whether we showed up every day or not. ℚ

PART VI

Goodbye
Yesterday
(1971-1973)

Twenty-Three

A Change
of Seasons

Jo Ann was a beautiful child who had grown even more so in her adult years. Because Jo Ann was darker than most of the Kearney children, Daddy believed she would need more to get by in the environment of racial inequity in which we lived. During our childhood, he took special pains to instill the self-confidence that Jo Ann would use as a cloak throughout life.

We were on the cusp of the civil rights struggle years before the maxim "I'm Black and I'm Proud" would be drummed into our consciousness. Negro children of a darker hue simply endured more humiliation than Negro children with a lighter complexion. This came not only from whites, but also from   fellow Negroes, as well.

James Kearney, proud as any man of his African heritage, refused to allow his 17 children—whose skin color ranged from "high yellow" to paper-sack brown to dark chocolate—to denigrate each other about something so inconsequential when there were much more important things going on around us.

"All us colored as far as white folks concerned. None of us got nothin' on the next one. You all wasting your time deciding who one speck lighter than the other."   Daddy would shake his head in consternation as he broke up our arguments and threatened deathly punishment if we repeated the self-denigrating sayings we'd picked up over the years.

"You so black we have to turn the light on to even see you during the day!"

"Tar baby, Tar baby...black as tar, slick as snot! You'll never get to heaven on a slop jar top!"

These words drew jeers and laughter and perpetuated the myth that color had something to do with our worth. They were hurtful words that sometimes stung whether we showed it or not and were often internalized by children on the receiving end.

Daddy's face would turn hard as he looked at the perpetrator. "I don't want to hear another word about anybody's color," he'd say. "It's just plain crazy for you to be thinking you better than somebody else 'cause you one shade lighter!"

Jo Ann was often the butt of our terrible barbs, and when Daddy was there, he was at her defense. He must have sensed the invisible harm the words might cause. As a child, I simply saw my younger sister's color as another thing to garner my father's attention. Daddy said Jo Ann was a beautiful, black kewpie doll. Her bouncing black curls never kinked like mine did and her smooth, creamy skin was flawless.

By the time we journeyed through elementary school and then through high school together, Jo Ann and I had experienced a myriad of transformations in our relationship—more than most friends experience over a lifetime. We simply couldn't decide whether we wanted to be friends or enemies. No matter which, there was always a bond that held us together. It was only with each other that we could ignore those who snickered and called us "just one of them raggedy-ass Kearney children." Throughout our lives, though, and in spite of that bond, we could never completely let go of our childhood jealousies and competitiveness.

We were best friends in 1971 when we graduated from Gould High School. We had forged that friendship after our first day at the white school in 1967 and held on to it. That friendship had been invaluable during those years, and the experience had miraculously invalidated most of the small wrinkles in our friendship.

Our graduation night, however, was not the joyous occasion we had hoped it would be. While our parents and family sat in the audience, proud to see the two of us marching down Gould High's gymnasium, we were pretending happiness. We congratulated our close friends and the rest of the 35 classmates, even as our hearts were breaking. Neither of us was acknowledged as honor students. Two of our best friends had been selected as valedictorian and salutatorian, and the other three friends who made up our senior class clique were all honor students. Our friends were kind enough not to mention that Jo Ann and I weren't on that list.

"Can you believe they gypped us like this?" Jo Ann asked, with a childish pout on her face as we sat in the back seat of Daddy's station wagon on our way home. "We know why...so there's no use wasting our breath talking about it," I whispered under my breath. The last thing I wanted was to get my parents involved in the conversation. We didn't need to hear, again, about how bad it was that we could go from A students to C and D students within two years...and how those two years had ruined our grades.

We had redeemed ourselves after our first two years at the white school. We'd both excelled in most of our classes during our four years at the new Gould High School. Yet, the white school experience had followed us back and done its damage in more ways than one. The thought incensed me, as it would over the years. We wouldn't receive scholarships and would have to get through college on loans and grants.

Jo Ann and I had decided earlier in the spring to join our two older brothers at the University of Arkansas at Fayetteville. Our white chemistry and English teachers had chaperoned a weekend tour of the university earlier that year. What a sight that must have been for the folks up in mostly white northwest Arkansas—five black teen-age girls traveling the hills and dales of Arkansas chauffeured by our white instructors.

Our van drew strange looks and probably stranger conversations. While I joined in the laughter when Jo Ann joked that the onlookers probably thought we were our teachers' adopted children, I was overwhelmed with excitement and wonder about this part of the state that seemed like another world. I'd never traveled this far from home. Pine Bluff was the closest thing to a metropolis I'd visited, and it was only thirty-five miles from Gould.

Each summer, my parents drove us to Pine Bluff where we would spend most of what we had earned that summer—making three or four dollars a day chopping cotton for white farmers. This one-day trip was the highlight of my summers most of my years on Varner Road. Daddy always parked near the Pine Bluff bus depot. As he parked, he would turn and admonish us, "I want you all back here in two hours...if you not here, you get left." Too excited to think of how long two hours were, we quickly paired off and began our two-hour journey.

Our vision of Pine Bluff's bustling streets and interesting people populating those streets must have been like more experienced travelers' views of the streets of New York or San Francisco. I could never decide which was the best part of the Saturday trip, watching the people or shopping in the stores on Main Street. Jo Ann, who was more focused, kept us on track, reminding me that we had just two hours to go down our list and return to the car.

My shopping list changed over the years. By the time I became a teenager, I was frequenting the United Dollar Store's cosmetic area for lipstick, Noxema skin care and feminine hygiene products. Staples such as writing tablets, loose-leaf paper, pencils and notebooks never changed. I never graduated from our basic choice of stores, mainly because these were the stores we could afford. It was an exciting two hours as we went from one store down Main Street to another.

When our time was up, we all drifted back to the station wagon. My younger brothers, J.D. and Ron, overly excited about their freedom to roam this big city, continuously arrived late to Daddy's consternation. They cowered quietly in the back seat of the station wagon, awaiting

Daddy's tongue-lashing. The rest of us were too busy comparing our bulging shopping bags to pay attention to my brothers.

Lerner, Keds, the Dollar Store, Kress or Sterling were most often the brand names scrolled across our shopping bags. We also frequented Pine Bluff's Good Will store, but they didn't have their own printed bags. We had no sense of shame about the stores we shopped in or the second-hand clothing my mother helped us choose for the school year. My siblings and I felt as rich and blessed that one day as any wealthy child. Our ignorance was indeed bliss; and those Saturdays were joyful excursions for the Kearney children.

The Saturday shopping sprees were incomparable to any other trips during those early years. They couldn't, however, compare to my senior weekend trip to northwest Arkansas when we spent two nights on the university campus. The topography of southeast Arkansas was flat surfaces covered with cotton and soybean crops and surrounded by wooded areas for as far as you could see. In contrast, northwest Arkansas was majestic mountains, dales, beautiful bodies of water and dense, gray fog escaping into the mountains. It gave the area an otherworldly effect.

After the weekend trip, Jo Ann and I returned home even more excited about going to the university. We knew we would need to apply for full financial aid packages as well. As much as our parents pushed us to go on to college, we all knew theirs was moral support only; they were in no position to help financially. It was nearing the end of the school year before we realized that the applications should have been in much earlier. Jo Ann and I wrote to our brothers on campus asking for their help in getting the necessary paperwork.

We received the two packets the next week. After dinner that evening, we hurriedly finished the dishes, then sat for hours completing the forms...at the very table we had spent years doing homework and studying with my parents. To be safe, we put the envelopes in the mailbox that night. As we walked back into the house—by then tired and sleepy—we both crossed our fingers for good luck. The next day, we sat on the porch and watched as the white mailman drove up to our oversized mailbox, took our envelopes and drove off with them. We again crossed our fingers as we walked back into the house.

Less than two weeks later, two packets arrived in the mail—one with my name on it and the other with Jo Ann's. We had been accepted to the school and because of our poverty received full financial aid—grants and work-study stipends that only required my parents' signatures. We were official university students. Our parents smiled and told us they were proud of us taking responsibility the way we had. Mostly, though, they were happy we would be going to school where our two older brothers could watch over us.

Though Jo Ann was mature for her age, my parents didn't forget that she was still just 16 years old. Even so, when she asked if she could spend the first month of summer in Ohio with an older sister, they acquiesced. "I want to make some money babysitting to buy clothes before I start summer school in July," she told Mama, killing two birds with one stone.

Jo Ann had struck gold, figuring out a way not to spend more than a few days at home that summer before going off to Ohio, then on to the university. My parents had always been strict and inflexible about most things during our childhood, but at some point we learned their soft spot. As long as we could connect our interests to our education, we could get around their rules.

I had no interest in either summer school or leaving home before September but resented Jo Ann's decision to leave me home all summer while she went off to Cleveland, then to Fayetteville for summer school. To make matters worse, in spite of the weeks I spent dogging Daddy into driving me to Dumas and Star City to fill out employment applications, no one was hiring high school graduates for factory jobs in 1971.

When Jo Ann wrote asking Daddy to pick her up from the bus station just a few days before going on to the university, I was both excited and nervous that she was coming home. More than anything, I was embarrassed that my summer had been so lackluster compared to hers. I sat on the porch eating peaches from the basketful that Mama would can later that evening. When Daddy drove into the yard, I had already decided I wouldn't act happy or excited to see my sister.

The girl who stepped out of Daddy's station wagon was not the girl who had left home just a month ago. Jo Ann had grown taller and lost every inch of fat she took with her. When my eyes moved up to her face, I saw that she was smiling over at me and my mouth was open with half-chewed peaches inside. "Hey, girl!" Jo Ann laughed, as she walked up to the porch. I stood up. "Hey..." We hugged briefly, lightly. I offered her a small smile and a willingness to help with her bags.

My younger sister had changed. I couldn't put my finger on it, but I knew it was more than the fact that she was now a beautiful young woman with poise and grace and amazing self-confidence. She wore an air of worldliness and sophistication. Once she had settled her bags into the room that had been ours for so many years, I sat on the bed and began nonchalantly asking about her summer. Jo Ann laughed a lot, grinned and answered very few of my questions.

"What have you been doing all summer?" she asked, to stop my questions. "Daddy said you couldn't find a job..."

I looked down and barely answered. "No, nobody's hiring anywhere." She shrugged and left it there.

I could tell by the way Mama watched Jo Ann walk through the house and how she sat at the dinner table that she saw something different, as well. Jo Ann had changed into a beautiful stranger within a matter of weeks, into someone who didn't fit on Varner Road. When she left that next week for summer school at the university, hugging us and hurrying to the car, we were still very much in awe of this new girl. ℚ

TWENTY-FOUR

Goodbye
Varner Road

I was excited and completely horrified to be leaving Varner Road in August 1971. By the end of the day, my new home would be up in the Ozark Mountains of Fayetteville, Arkansas—light years from what I'd known all my life. I was on my way to becoming someone I'd spent most of my childhood dreaming about. Yet, I still wasn't sure who that person might end up being.

What I remember most about that day in August was the sweltering heat and my mother's sad eyes. "The whole world is waiting out there for you," Pat Failla, my chemistry teacher had told us during the field trip to Fayetteville. I still wasn't prepared to leave the people who gave us such comfort.

As I finished my packing, I glanced through the window at the old walnut tree that held so many of my secret dreams. I would be losing that along with all the other parts of my childhood. The snap of the lock on my suitcase told me it was already too late to turn back to wonder what it might be like to stay right here with Mama and Daddy.

I dragged the stuffed suitcase from the bed and stood it upright beside the door. I smiled, pleased with my purchase at Pine Bluff's Salvation Army. The clerk had asked for seven dollars for it but gave me a discount when I bought a skirt and top, too. The curly-headed white man had winked and said, "You're a good customer. I think I'll let you have that suitcase for five dollars flat." It was part of my savings from chopping cotton and soybeans that summer.

That summer was also the first time I was allowed to keep all I made. It was traditional in the Kearney household to contribute whatever money we made to the family. If I made six dollars a day chopping cotton, I would give three dollars to my parents. This meant, for sure, that my parents saw me differently now, and I wasn't so sure how happy I was about that fact.

I felt Mama standing in the doorway and pushed away the thought that I would be losing the bedroom Jo Ann and I had shared—as friends and enemies—so many years. Mama looked almost as lost as I felt. As we offered each other conspiratorial smiles of sadness, I remembered how our relationship had evolved into something as close to friendship as any mother and child could have in the Kearney home.

We were both losing something in my leaving today, I suspected. "You need to make sure you got everything. You never know how long it'll take mail to get there, if we have to send it." I smiled and nodded, as I stuffed smaller items into Mama's gray overnight case.

After a few minutes of uncomfortable standing, Mama sat on the side of the bed, quiet and still smiling. I tried to smile back, but found I couldn't look in her eyes without tears welling up in my own. I sat down beside her, swallowing the lump in my throat and looking down at the brown, plump hands so much like Mama's.

I prayed my fear wasn't showing. "You know, your daddy and me gone really miss you a lot. I don't know how we gone get along without you here to help out like you do..." Mama's voice was hardly audible as she searched for words. She looked down at her apron, straightening imaginary wrinkles.

I knew how difficult this was for my mother who seldom expressed her feelings to her children. I knew she was proud of me and at the same time was sad I was leaving. I knew she loved me unconditionally and would be there for me no matter what. I knew...that Varner Road would never be the same.

I half smiled, realizing that Mama had gone through this at least eleven times before. She had been sad and happy to see her children sprout their wings and fly or fail. She and Daddy had done their part, preached the importance of a college education from the day we started looking in books. But when it became reality, I wondered if it was any easier because this is what they wanted for us?

Mama cleared her throat. "I hope you'll remember the things we tried to teach you, while you're up there." I looked briefly in her face, then past her—pretending to ignore the wavering voice. "I will, Mama. Besides, I'll be coming home every chance I get. I won't be able to forget, even if I wanted to." I tried laughing.

I remembered how Mama would lay awake, unable to fall asleep until all of her children arrived safely home. She was always in bed, but never asleep when my brothers and I made it home from football and basketball games. After asking who had won, she would look over at me in my cheerleading uniform and-as if she hadn't remembered what they looked like-say, "My goodness, do all the schools have cheerleader skirts that short?" I always laughed and nodded, "This is what they all look like, Mama," as I headed to the kitchen to grab a piece of cold chicken, a peach or a cold biscuit before going off to bed.

I would stand in their bedroom door talking for a while as I ate whatever it was I had found. Mama would tell me which of my older siblings had written, who was visiting during the summer or coming home for Christmas and how her children in the various colleges were doing. Daddy would sometimes pipe up, and I was always surprised he was awake and listening in. Finally, I'd yawn, a prelude to my departure. "Oh well, I'd better get to bed so I can get up in the morning." Then, all three of us would say our "good nights" at the same time.

I was already half asleep by the time I took off my uniform and dressed for bed. Jo Ann's even breathing helped lull me further into that unclouded sleep that would never be replicated outside Varner Road.

I walked slowly through the room trying to make sure I wasn't leaving something I meant to take with me. Mama stood and looked with me. "Did you mean to take this?" or "Didn't you overlook this dress?" I would miss so much about Mama—the mornings I awoke to her soft voice sending some familiar song into our sleep, the smells that were inextricably "hers" like baked sweet potatoes in the fall, squashed butter beans in the summer and freshly ground sausage on Christmas mornings.

Mama had begrudgingly let her guard down two years earlier after being diagnosed with breast cancer. The evolution of my role from daughter to caretaker to friend began after the doctors took away her breast. For many years after that, I carried the assignation as a badge. She had chosen me to care for her after she'd lost such an important part of her womanhood.

Yet, while I maintained a stoic face, the tears flowed endlessly when I left her and found a quiet place. The cancer's invasion of this beautiful woman's body angered me; and the fact that she was not indomitable scared me and made me privy to the frailty of life.

"Keep your mind on your lessons, and don't be studyin' about no boys up there." Mama half smiled over at me before looking away. She believed boys were my Achilles' heel. I had had only one real date in all my 17 years and that was after my high school graduation.

They had conceded to my "keeping company" with the boy I had "dated" for almost four years. Fred was nice as far as they could see—which wasn't far since no more than ten words had passed between them that entire four years. He came on Sunday nights around eight o'clock, sat with me in the living room where we watched television and mumbled small nothings for two hours, and he left when the 10 o'clock news came on. When he didn't leave at 10 on the dot, Daddy would walk through the room as a signal that the boy's visit was over.

"Mama," I laughed, "you don't have to worry about me. I know books come first, and boys come second." She rolled her eyes and shook her head. "And don't stop goin' to church...you gone need the Lord more'n ever, now." I promised her I wouldn't.

Daddy was calling us, and I grabbed up Mama's gray overnight case she'd offered for my trip to school. She had used the case during most of her summer vacations to California to see her children. I took a deep breath and took a few steps toward the door. Mama stood awkwardly for a moment before I saw the tears at the edges of her eyes. Without saying a word, she pulled me to her, holding me tightly. I couldn't hug her back because of the heavy suitcase and overnight case I still held in my hands, and I couldn't see because the tears flooded my vision.

In all the 17 years I had lived with her, Mama had only hugged me when she left on the train rides to California and when she returned as happy to be back in Arkansas as she had been to leave for California. I had never seen her openly cry or freely show her affection like she did that day. I put the suitcase on the floor and held Mama as she sobbed. "I'm gonna be fine, Mama. You'll see. I'll write you every week to let you know how I'm doin'." I patted her back, like a child's, as she dabbed at her wet face with her apron. Finally, smiling, we walked through the living room and out into the yard where Daddy was waiting. ☺

Twenty-Five

Woo...Pig...
Sooie!

It was three in the afternoon when the Greyhound bus pulled into Fayetteville's only bus station. I followed the few passengers off the bus, nervously scanning the station for sight of my sister, Jo Ann. It was late August, and while the bus driver had nearly frozen us all with the air conditioner, I was missing it now as I stood in the hot bus station.

I retraced my last few days at home and was sure I had written Jo Ann to let her know what time I was arriving. I sighed, disappointed that she wasn't there but still too excited about this new environment to spend the afternoon pouting about Jo Ann not showing up. A cab driver stood inside the cracked door of his taxi and called out, "Needing a ride, ma'am?" I nodded, and he asked if I was going to the campus. I nodded again and began carrying my suitcase and bag to his car.

"Woo...Pig...Sooie, you're in Razorback country, ma'am!" the cab driver's dirty blonde ponytail flicked onto his shoulder as he laughed and stared at me in his mirror. He stopped in front of the brown, fourteen-story building. "Pomfret Hall...I guess this'll be home sweet home for a while, huh, young lady?" I smiled and nodded. "Well, enjoy college life...and that'll be three dollars and twenty-five cents." I pulled the dollar bills and coins from my wallet that held my small stash of summer savings. As I walked toward the building, I felt the butterflies awake inside my stomach.

The perky white residence aides smiled as I walked up. They motioned for me to come to the counter, "New student...freshman checking in?" I smiled back and nodded. She quickly found my admission card and checked me into Pomfret Hall. "You can sit over there for a while...we'll see if another group of students come in before we take you up on the floor.

While I waited, she asked a young intern to show me the mailroom where I would mail my letters, the television room, the laundry room and an entrance door for late nights or weekends. When we returned to the desk, she gave me a key to my room on the fourth floor. I was struck by the huge lobby that was easily the size of our entire house on Varner Road. A   couple sat at the cherry wood piano, playing lively tunes; guys strolled from one side of the dorm to the other, talking loudly and laughing; and another couple sat on one of the oversized couches, smooching in broad daylight!

"Hey, Faye!" It was my brothers hurrying across the lobby. "What time did you get here? Why didn't you let us know when you were coming?" I told them I asked Jo Ann to tell them. They frowned, saying they hadn't seen or talked to Jo Ann more than once or twice since she had arrived on campus.

We chatted until the resident aide or RA gave me a look, and I hurried off with the other new students. "I'll find you guys, later," I said, waving. Later that evening after I was settled into my dorm room, Jo Ann came by. She stood nonchalantly in the door, before walking over and offering me a brief hug. "Sorry I didn't make it to the station...but, I did want to make sure you made it in okay." That was Jo Ann's only explanation for not meeting me at the station.

The bus station was the furthest thing from my mind at that moment. I was taking in this young woman standing in the dorm room. It was Jo Ann, all right, but she was also someone completely different from the girl who'd left home less than two months ago. There was a cigarette in her hand, and she wore a huge Afro. I had decided weeks ago that I would replace my bobbed permanent with the new "hip" hairstyle as soon as I got to school, but as usual Jo Ann had was a step ahead of me.

When I realized how silly I must look staring at my sister as if she was a stranger, I laughed and hurried to give her another hug. She moved away, disconcerted by my open show of affection. "I see you already have all your stuff put away." I nodded, and we both moved to the bed and sat opposite one another. "I haven't seen my roommate yet; I see she is already here, though.

We talked until the ease of our relationship reasserted itself. She told me about the summer session, the friends she had made and the classes she was signing up to take this term. Before we knew it, it was dark, and Jo Ann said she had to get back. "I'll walk you up to your dorm," I offered. She nodded, and we left the room together, as if nothing had changed.

There were stretches of time when Jo Ann was just Jo Ann, her old self. Those were the best times of my college days when we spent time together, joking, laughing and whispering about guys like we used to do. We went to parties together and scoped out who we thought was cute and gave each other the eye when we ended up dancing with them or sometimes leaving the party with them.

It was times like these when I pushed the darker thoughts about Jo Ann's changes to the back of my mind. She was still my beautiful, smart, fun-loving sister; and I couldn't have been happier that she was here with me at the university.

My life began to change during my second semester in college. Though I was intent on holding on to my sister, I began spending much of my spare time with a fellow student I had met during a weekend party. In spite of his compact build, Darryl had been a football star at North Little Rock's Ole Main High School. Though I would never have admitted it then, my attraction to Darryl was a statement of rebellion. He was so different from any of the guys I considered "boyfriends" in high school. He was confident and cocky and had been raised in the big city of Little Rock, rather than the rural towns in southeast Arkansas.

247

Jo Ann was unimpressed. She thought I was making a mistake when I told her how crazy I was about him, asking me "What in the world do you see in that little boy?" Later, she complained that I was so "hung up" on Darryl that I'd forgotten I had a sister at the university.

Other than the idiosyncrasies of Jo Ann's and my relationship, college life was exciting and enjoyable. My grades were far from what they should have been, and I shuffled from one major to another for the first few years on campus. Yet, I loved the idea of being a college girl, meeting new friends from different parts of Arkansas and the country and learning new things about myself. The icing on the cake was falling in love.

By my second semester, Darryl and I were inseparable. He took me home to meet his widower father in Little Rock. I was a little afraid of the gruff, but jovial man who enjoyed music, dancing and having a good time-nothing like my own parents. At the end of the spring term, we drove to Gould where Darryl met my parents.

I spent the summer of 1972 in California and found that I actually enjoyed not having a boyfriend around all the time. When I returned to school in the fall, I told Darryl I wanted to devote more time to improving my grades and that we should take a breather from each other. We did for a couple of months, but by December of that year, Darryl and I were together again...and making up for lost time.

In January 1973, I discovered I was pregnant. It started with morning sickness that I had no idea was morning sickness. I forced myself to my classes those mornings and by the afternoon the queasiness had subsided. I hadn't thrown up more than three times in my entire life and got a little concerned when it became a daily thing. At that time, I decided something was wrong but passed it off as a virus I'd caught. I drowned myself in orange juice for vitamin C and tried getting more rest.

It wasn't until I missed my period that I figured out what the problem was. Now I knew without a doubt. I was pregnant! All my life I had wanted to control the who, when and what of that part of my life but had let my guard down when I fell in love. I was disappointed with myself, but more than that I knew I had let my parents down.

I had been naive to believe Darryl when he said he would make sure I wouldn't get pregnant. I was furious at myself, furious at him and scared out of my mind about my parents. I didn't tell Darryl until I went to a doctor to make it one-hundred percent for real. It was. When I told him, I was surprised that Darryl didn't hit the roof. I was the one crazy with fear and anxiety.

We fought for weeks about the pregnancy. I was bent on having an abortion yelling, "I can't have a baby, now!" He was bent on just the opposite, saying, "You're not getting rid of any child of mine!" I was convinced it was more my child than his. The most important part of my consternation was how to keep my parents from finding out what I had done.

Confused and scared, I gave in to Darryl's ego and my own fear and decided to have the child. We finally agreed that the best option was to get married...just like that. I wrote Mama, telling her Darryl and I would marry in June. They knew we were seriously involved, yet I imagined the shock this announcement would cause. The fact that I was pregnant would be a P.S., an afterthought. ℚ

Twenty-Six

The Wedding on Varner Road

I found the nerve to write the dreaded letter to Mama just weeks after learning the pregnancy was real. The first thing on the page was the announcement of Darryl's and my decision to marry in June and that we were extremely happy. "By the way," I'd added, "Darryl and I are expecting a child in October." There were tear stains on the first letter. I balled up three drafts before I was able to finish one without the stains. As I placed the stamp on the sealed envelope, a heaviness overcame me and a taunting voice reminding me how terribly I had let my parents down.

A week later, in the middle of February, I received Mama's letter. The bulky envelope forewarned me that it wasn't her usual bright, chirpy, brief letters to her college girl. The first thing I noticed was how tiny the cursive was written, unlike Mama's neat, but expansive handwriting. I took a deep breath and sat at my small desk, before beginning to read Mama's letter.

"Dear Faye,

I got your letter today, and I won't tell you how it made me feel. I never been so surprised and disappointed at the same time. You were the last one of my girls I expected to get pregnant and end up marrying this soon. I wish to God I could say I'm happy about this marriage, but all I can say is I will pray that things work out.

I always prayed that all of you would wait until you were out of school before you began having babies or married. But, I never thought I had to worry much that you would mess up.

I believe it was God's will that your Daddy and me have so many children, but it wasn't something I'd wish on my children. It's not that I don't love all of you, it's just that having babies and being responsible for somebody else all your life just not the way to live if you have a choice.

There was many a day I wondered how my life could a been if it hadn't been for me having a house full of children. I always dreamed of working at a real job and getting more involved in some of the things I liked to do like the home extension office, and missionary work. I just hope this baby and marriage don't put an end to everything you want in life.

I always said you was a lot like me, and I guess that is truer than I thought. I was 19 when I married your Daddy, and I was pregnant when we married, too. Even though I loved him, there was lots of other things I wanted in my life. If I'd got the education others in my family did, I believe God would have directed my life differently.

I pray to God your life will be full of things other than having babies and taking care of a family. If you can promise me that, I'll be real happy for you, and I'll love that baby like it was my own.

Love,

Your Mama

The second letter from Mama two days later finally stopped the tears and eased the depression that had sat in after reading her first letter. She wanted us to start planning for the wedding as soon as possible. "Do you realize you just got about four months left before June 30 comes around?" she had written, and I knew then she had accepted the inevitable.

She had already begun making lists of what had to be done before the wedding. Rankin Chapel needed a thorough cleaning—something that hadn't happened since Reverend Shaw was our pastor more than 20 years ago. Mama would go shopping for cloth for my wedding dress and for the bridesmaids' dresses. I would look through catalogues and patterns over the next week to get some ideas.

Mama had completely taken responsibility for my wedding. "Don't you be worrying about this, right now. You finish up your classes and by the time you leave school in May, we'll have most of the planning already done." She used the rest of the letter to tell me how the few Kearney siblings still at home were doing. Since 1971, every Kearney child had left home in tenth grade to attend college preparatory schools... either Andover in Massachusetts or Western Reserve in Ohio.

The schools had discovered the Kearney family back in 1971, when Andover first recruited my brother Julius. His success brought them back to Varner Road the next year and every year after that—plucking up Jerome, Jude, Jeffrey and finally my baby sister, Judy, who left in 1979. I wondered, sometimes, how Mama felt having her children leave home so early. I knew too well how home was never the same once you left. Even the weekend visits and holiday vacations made you realize you couldn't go back where you were as a child.

The more I thought about it and remembered the letter she had written, I knew the answer already. Emotionally, she had to let us go to assure a real life for ourselves. Though she knew what she wanted for us, it was our own dreams and work that would make those dreams come true. It was a bitter-sweet thought that Mama's lifelong dreams became a reality through us, and when we stumbled her dream was stumbling too.

Mama was looking forward to the wedding...finally. I had successfully convinced her I wouldn't abandon my education for marriage and a child. I would return to school in September until my child was born and resume shortly after the birth. After that commitment, she thought marriage was the most wonderful thing in the world for Darryl and me.

When the spring term ended in late May I went directly home, and Mama and I spent the next couple of weeks discussing my wedding plans. Of course, I would be married at Rankin Chapel, Mama said. She would make my wedding dress. Jo Ann would be my maid of honor and my friend Beverly would be my other bridesmaid. We would have a reception for all the guests back at the house. She had decided at some point over the last weeks that there was nothing she could do to change what was already done, and as she always did...she would make the best of what life offered her.

I returned to Little Rock the next week to work through the summer. Darryl was already working for the city transportation department. My job would be the start of a nest egg to go toward our new home at the university. As I lay, some nights, in my future father-in-law's home, I wondered that neither of my parents—strict Christians that they were— never broached the subject of my living in sin with Darryl under his father's roof. They never asked if I was, indeed, living in sin during that summer, either.

Darryl's father told friends that summer he was convinced that we had probably already gotten married. That must have eased his discomfort with our arrangement. Darryl thought my concerns were silly and assured me his father loved having us there with him. "He gets lonely in this house all by himself all the time. Besides, he needs to have someone to complain to about the rest of the family." I still wasn't so sure "enjoying our company" meant knowing we were brazenly sleeping together under his roof.

I worked all summer at the Arkansas Employment Security Division as a file clerk...filing employment applications into a new filing system. The work was monotonous, but I had no room to complain. I needed the work, and the summer wasn't forever. When the Friday before my wedding date rolled around, my supervisor and colleagues gave me a nice wedding/baby shower. I'd worked there all of two months and was both surprised and touched by the kindness they showed me.

After loading my car with the gifts and saying goodbye to the office, I went home and packed—including the new black negligee I had bought for my wedding night and the green, polka dot minidress I would wear at my wedding reception. I packed enough to last until we returned from a two-day honeymoon in Memphis, Tennessee.

As I set out for the drive to Gould, my emotions fluctuated between nervousness and a feeling of awe that tomorrow I would be a married woman. Darryl would remain in Little Rock and arrive in Gould in time to dress for the wedding and say "I do." His friends had boasted all week about the bachelor party they had planned for Darryl. "I suggest you have yourself a stand-in, just in case," K.P. said, with his usual loud laughter. K.P. and his brother Tommy were Darryl's best man and groomsman. They were also members of a local soul band called Ebony and were just as "wild" offstage as they were onstage. I shuddered to think what kind of bachelor party they would throw.

I gave Darryl a worried look, and he giggled like a kid caught already doing something wrong before he actually did it. He pecked my cheek and promised nothing could keep him away from his wedding. "I'm not worried about you making it...it's what shape you'll be in when you get there," I joked. We made a final checklist together before I began my 90-minute journey.

———

Varner Road. These five miles of red clay dirt and gravel had been a sturdy thread in the tapestry of my life for all of my nineteen years. More than a decade of sweet and bitter memories lay beneath the surface of the road, embedded in the pits and crevices of this unpaved country route. Mostly, they were sweet memories, except for the handful of dark, youthful moments I had buried away.

The rocks grinding beneath Daddy's truck tires all those years on Varner Road had been comforting reminders that I was headed home. Today, exactly 90 days before I turned 20 and the day Mama dubbed as my "wedding eve," the road was anything but comforting. "You'll remember the day before as much as you do your wedding day," Mama promised during one of our late-night conversations. I wondered.

The shallow creek ran along one side of the road just as it always had, and the anemic willow trees still stood knee-deep in its cloudy water. I remembered the families of turtles who once lazed atop the rotting limbs, multiplying before our innocent eyes. I had breathlessly ran in from the bus to tell Mama of the thousands of turtles we had seen sleeping on the logs.

Cummins Prison Farm, with its luminously green vegetable field, sat on the other side of Varner Road, and as we passed each morning I would sit quietly, clutching my books to my chest and pressing my face against the cool window. The sea of black men in white uniforms mesmerized me.

The school bus had stalled one Tuesday morning in 1961, as we started to cross the railroad tracks. The men stood clutching their hoe handles and watching the bus pass. One boy had stood slightly apart, nearer the bus than the others and directly outside my window. His cloudy eyes searched the row of windows and settled on mine. My round eyes, it seemed, stared endlessly into his almond-shaped ones, and the dark, granite face melted into a boy's smile, as white and innocent as the gleaming uniform he wore.

I wondered all day about the world the boy had left behind and grieved his lost freedom. Ghosts of the young man visited me as I fell asleep many nights.

I turned the wooded bend where Fred Lack, our tall, white neighbor, had lived and died a sudden, strange death. I was almost home but slowed the small car to watch the scarlet tint of evening sun become one with the giant trees. In just two short years, I had forgotten such simple beauty. But so much had changed since I had left Varner Road, and I wondered if tomorrow would make it all right.

I was late, and Mama would be less than happy. She wouldn't know I hardly drove the speed limit or that I dreaded approaching that bend in the road that brought me home. As I walked through the living room door, Daddy's blaring evening news accosted me as it always did; and as always, I headed for the oversized television set to adjust the volume.

Daddy continued sitting, focused on the evening news, but a tiny smile flickered on his lips and when the Mr. Clean song began, he raised his straight, unbending frame from the chair and moved toward me. For the first time, I realized Daddy was closer to sixty-eight inches tall...not seventy-two or more as I had always believed. His hesitation told me my father wasn't sure how to treat a daughter who would be a someone's wife within 24 hours.

"Your mama's been worrying," he half-whispered and gave me a grown-up hug. I shrugged and playfully rolled my eyes. Daddy patted my shoulder and returned to his evening news.

On my way into the sewing room I slowed, leaning gently against the door frame. Mama sat leaning over the sewing machine and her work, tenderly straightening the voluminous fold of lilac across the thread feeder. I stood a moment longer, studying this small woman who had maintained her youthfulness even with the roundness brought on by eighteen pregnancies. At 55, her piercing eyes were still bright and sharp and her smile still soft and knowing.

The guest-room-turned-sewing-room was small with oversized windows that offered Mama the light needed for her work. Big Mama's beautiful poster bed took up most of the room, but only visitors and family traveling from distant places slept here. After most of her children grew up and left home, Mama claimed the space as her sewing room and the only invited guest was her best friend Miss Lizzie Baker, whose company brought with it glimpses of the girl Mama must have been.

"I thought you'd be here a lot earlier, Faye...something wrong?" She gave me a soft once-over and returned to her task. "No...nothing. I got off a little late, and the traffic was..." I couldn't finish the sentence. I had always felt silly lying to Mama.

I stared at the five yards of soft satin that had claimed Mama's attention for the last few months. Every conversation we'd shared before hurrying off to work, every coffee break chat, every lunch spent working on the mounds of files atop my desk while cradling the phone to my ear ...was yet another discussion about the wedding dress.

It had taken me 30 days to make the hard decision to marry Darryl— a boy I'd just met at Christmas time. It took another 14 days to write the dreaded letter, announcing that decision... *"By the way, Mama, Darryl and I decided to marry in June."* The letter had rearranged our lives.

Now, I missed Mama. I missed our easiness together and the light, meaningless chatter and gossip. I missed, most of all, being able to pretend the bond between us wouldn't be changed tomorrow.

Mama sat working, engrossed in the dress but offering a sentence here or there. "You eat something?" "You talk to Jo Ann, today?" "Is she coming tonight?" "What time is Darryl getting here in the morning?"

She hardly looked up to acknowledge my weak responses, biting her lip to help keep the delicate basting on the dress straight. She was hurrying, I knew, so I could test the wedding ensemble-the dress, dyed shoes and veil. "I need to know if something needs to be fixed before I go to bed tonight...I won't have time tomorrow, you know." She was talking mostly to herself as she knotted the last stitch but looked up to check if I had heard. I nodded. "I know, Mama...I know."

Mama had searched every fabric store in the three-county area, Pine

Bluff, Dumas, Star City...even Grady, to find the lilac satin. When she called to say Miss Lane had found the cloth in Monticello, her girlish delight exceeded my own.

Three days later she called breathlessly happy. She had found a pattern in Dumas' fabric shop, "almost exactly like the dress you want!" The commercial patterns had always been mere guides. Mama put her own stamp on every outfit she sewed, and this time it was a mix of Butterick's pattern and Mama's and my own idea of the perfect wedding dress.

"OK, let's see if this fits!" Her smile of contentment was mixed with just a trace of weariness as she unzipped the dress. She guided the weighty coolness down over my body, slowly twirling me around to face her. She gingerly pulled the zipper all the way to the top and snapped the almost-invisible hook. She frowned, pulled and tucked the shiny cloth until it fell to her liking.

"Now, move back a little...let me see. Now, turn around," she ordered, gently. She opened her mouth to speak but for a moment couldn't find her words. Finally, a small voice directed me, "OK...OK, you can look now."

The guest room had the only full-length mirror in the house. As a teen, I made countless morning trips between my bedroom and the room with the mirror assessing my acceptability before leaving for school. Mama had shooed me away, remonstrating that "God don't smile on vanity." Now, Mama was fussing over me, wanting to assure I looked my best...as if God had suddenly given vanity a nod.

The girl looking back from the reflection in the mirror was hardly anyone I recognized. My heart thumped, and this time the cat had my tongue. Mama smiled into the mirror and stepped back. "Well...?" I looked from the image to the corner of the room where Mama now stood, her arms loosely folded. "I...I ...It's so pretty, Mama." Her one lip trembled slightly as she smiled, folding her arms tighter around her breasts.

I turned from one side to the other. "You really outdid yourself, Mama. It fits perfectly." She slowly moved closer and smoothed the dress's front tucks. "I was never this flat carrying any of you all, especially at six months," she half whispered as if it was our secret. Mama had truly worked magic. The bodice tucked in just above my natural waist and the rest hung just so, skimming my body rather than hugging it.

"Mama, I think I'll make a pretty good-looking bride. What you think?" She laughed out loud, embarrassing herself. In my own happiness, I swirled playfully around the room as Mama quietly watched with a faraway look in her eyes. "You haven't finished, yet," she finally remembered. "You still have to try the shoes on, and let's get that veil straight on your head."

I slipped on the shoes, and Mama helped me with the veil. I pranced down the narrow hallway and dramatically turned at my old bedroom door. Her slow nod of approval sent a ribbon of warmth through me as I turned to walk back.

"You look ...pretty, Faye..." she sighed, as if the announcement had pulled something more from her than just words. Before I lost my nerves, I threw my arms around the woman who had nurtured and loved me for 19 years showing little physical affection. I held her and whispered, "Thank you, Mama...for everything."

I stood back, still holding onto the small, plump hands until she wriggled them loose. "Go on, now, and get out of that dress before you mess it up." She sniffled, swiping at the tears she wasn't fast enough to hide. After she helped me remove the dress and the veil "to save from wrinkling," I sat, a little dizzy, on the edge of the bed. I removed the shoes and, looking over at Mama, wondered how my life could change so fast.

She was back at her chores, making sure Jo Ann's and Beverly's bridesmaid dresses were ready for tomorrow. I touched the cool lilac fabric hanging against the wall and thought again of the strangeness of life. "Mama, you should go to bed...we all have a long day tomorrow. Anything that's left to do, I can help you with in the morning."

Mama finished up the last stitch, then took a deep breath. While she made a little fuss, I could see the weariness setting in. "All right, I guess I need to rest, now; but I'll be up bright and early tomorrow." She walked slowly to the door and hesitated before turning, allowing me a glimpse of something in her eyes. "Get a good night's sleep, Faye. Tomorrow is an important day, you know."

I smiled. "I know, Mama, good night."

I caressed the smooth, dark wood of the old sewing machine, remembering the days Jo Ann and I sneaked into the room to play all those years ago. Daddy had bought the Sears machine in 1962, a year he'd proclaimed "the best cotton crop of my life."

By December of that year, his 45 acres had produced 25 bales of cotton. It was an unforgettable Christmas at the Kearney home.

I had adored the beautiful Indian doll I found in my Christmas box that morning, but fell most in love with Jo Ann's Chatty Kathy, a talking doll with the thick body and coarse, blond hair. Mama began putting her sewing machine to good use the very next day and never stopped.

I pulled the cloth string that controlled the electricity in the sewing room and tiptoed through the dark to the back door. I hurried onto the back porch and into the yard where a warm breeze greeted me and the window fans whirred behind me.

The cool dew reminded me that I was still wearing only my slip. I walked out to the walnut tree, my other home for so many years. The worn space in the old tree trunk accepted me easily, unquestioning. This had been my sanctuary during the hundreds of restless nights when the house and my family crowded my thoughts and dreams. The moon-drenched nights had served as emotional balm, a kind of unconditional freedom to dream a world for myself-a different world from Varner Road, something more where neither a husband nor a family played starring roles.

It was during this time that Mama began worrying that my interest in boys was catching up with my love for learning. Out of the clear blue sky one day she declared: "If you not careful, Faye, boys will be the ruin of you." I knew better. I knew what I wanted out of life, and marriage and children were nowhere close to the front end of my wants. I was destined to be a writer of sweet love poems and romantic novels or travel the world as a missionary.

I wanted an education as much as Mama wanted one for me, but I also wanted more—a life experience that came from somewhere other than books. Yet, on this wedding eve, I knew Mama almost always got it right and that there was something brave and selfless about her giving upa daughter she had shaped and formed to a boy she hardly knew.

As I walked lazily back to the house, the distant hoot of an owl sounded through the night, and I wondered if it might be a message about my tomorrows. I had come home needing to hear Mama say I was doing the right thing and needing to know she would grieve what we were losing. Now, I just wanted tomorrow to come and go and to get on with the rest of my life.

The dew and freshly mowed grass had clung to my feet. I towel-dried my feet and changed into my nightgown. I took the one picture of the boy I would marry from my purse and lay it on the pillow beside me. I slid deeper under the light, summer quilt decorated with frames of my yesterdays. Finally, sleep overtook me, and I went gladly, knowing that tomorrow would be Mama's and my wedding. ℚ

TWENTY-SEVEN

D. K.'s Arrival
Signals Change

Darryl and I had settled into the married student housing a week before classes began in the fall of 1973. Though I was almost seven months pregnant, I was hardly showing and was proud that I could walk up the steep hill to the administration building where we completed our registration and enrolled in our classes. I signed up for 16 hours, refusing to take fewer classes than I would any other time. I knew I would be out of classes for a while but would figure that out when the time came.

Darryl Wayne Lunon II chose a muggy, stormy Tuesday night—exactly four months after his father and I were married—to make his entrance into the world. Darryl and I agreed that we would call him D.K. so that Kearney would be somewhere in his name. He weighed seven pounds, seven ounces and was 19 inches long. My new baby was red with tiny eyes, a thin, slick cap of hair and a button nose. I fell in love with him the moment I laid eyes on him and knew the nine hours of pain had been worth it.

The epidural hurried my son's birth and probably had something to do with my descent into a deep sleep after he arrived healthy. When I woke the next morning, Jo Ann was the first visitor at the hospital, even before Darryl. She was a constant visitor during the three days I remained at Washington Regional Hospital and met us at the apartment when our friend James Smedley deposited us there. Our car had chosen the day I was to take D.K. home to call it quits.

Jo Ann had also fallen in love with our small reddish brown son who smiled early and seldom cried. Although this was my first and only child,

I was convinced this one was nothing less than perfect. Jo Ann spoiled D.K. early on with attention and gifts. Even so, I was happy she was there to share him with me. I was most happy to have my sister back in my life, even if it took the birth of my son to get her back.

Before the spring semester of 1974, during one of Jo Ann's weekend visits, she casually announced that she was transferring to Boston University. I was surprised and crestfallen. Just as it seemed we had recaptured the close relationship we almost lost over the years, I was afraid I was about to lose it again. I tried futilely to talk her out of leaving, knowing all along that I never won arguments with my younger sister.

"Well, can't you just finish up this year? There are just a few months left."

Jo Ann shrugged, as if she was making a decision to move across the street. "I just feel it's the right thing to do, right now," she said, ending the conversation.

Even with that disappointment, I refused to accept that there was anything wrong—just Jo Ann being Jo Ann, stubborn and contrary. After she left, we wrote each other regularly. We talked less frequently, but when we did the conversations were always warm and full of jaunts down memory lane. I had returned to my classes just two weeks after D.K.'s birth, and my days had grown increasingly busy with motherhood, married life and college life all wrapped up in one bow. To make matters worse, I resumed working part-time during the day, and Darryl and I switched off being Mr. or Mrs. Mom. I was driven to finish school as early as I could.

The next year, Jo Ann left Boston University and transferred to Arkansas State University. She was just hours away from her degree and, thankfully, was able to graduate that May. ℚ

TWENTY-EIGHT

A Summer
of Changes

An old wives' tale promises that when we lose something precious in our lives, we almost always discover something new. That trade-off played out for me during the summer of 1987. It was during the heat-drenched days of August, just weeks before my 34th birthday. First came the painful loss of my 32-year-old sister, Jo Ann. Following on the heels of that was the beginning of the end for my 15-year marriage. True to the old wives' tale, something new would come into my life just weeks later.

In late July, shortly before my brother Jude's wedding day, my family said our final goodbyes to Jo Ann at a small, solemn ceremony at Dora Bell Church. We laid her to rest at a cemetery five miles from home where we had played together as children, become best friends during high school and at times fiercely resented each other.

To the family's satisfaction, Dora Bell's cemetery was half-hidden from view, tucked inside a grove of unwieldy trees along Varner Road. Our dark, ashen faces were bare and untelling during the 30-minute interment. The minister—a tiny man, neatly put together in his good Sunday suit—spoke softly, endearingly of my sister, Jo Ann. He had known her as a child, had baptized her into the church and taken note of her dark beauty and rebellious nature even before she approached womanhood. He spoke with genuine sadness of her passing, describing my sister as "a good girl with a good foundation...who somehow lost her way and left this world too soon."

The small man's eloquent voice was the only human sound in the church cemetery. Daddy and I and Jo Ann's 17 other siblings stood still and silent, clutching our hands, clenching our jaws and denying our tears as we stared down into the deep well that contained the box that held Jo Ann.

Five days after Jo Ann's goodbye, I traveled the 500 miles from Little Rock to Pittsburgh, Pennsylvania, to our brother's wedding. Along with a small suitcase, I carried the fresh, hard stone of Jo Ann's death. It was a constant companion, even as I took pictures with the wedding party, danced at the joyous reception and celebrated my handsome brother's commitment to his beautiful, new bride.

The plane ride to Pittsburgh was a kind oasis from the reality of Jo Ann's death. I imagined the miles I left behind allowed space to examine the hardness inside me, to forget after a time that it was there. Yet, on the pages of the airline magazine, it was Jo Ann's illuminating smile that I saw, not the manufactured ones of the perfect, airbrushed models. I imagined that Jo Ann was, somehow, nudging me, daring me to move on with my life, to begin living the dreams we had shared all those years ago on Varner Road.

In 1987, I'd celebrated my sixth year as press director at the National Migrant Data Bank in Little Rock. I went to work in 1981 with the mission to "put a face on the country's migrant student population." My new boss said the agency needed to publicize its good work and the success stories of migrant students and their families. More veteran staff did the real work of visiting the schools to make sure migrant children's health and school records kept up with them as they followed seasonal crops.

Though I was sure when I got there in 1981, I would leave after three years; I had actually liked the work and the mission. More than that, I'd become comfortable with the people. Still, August 1987 changed my life and marked the beginning of my introspection. I revisited my decision to stay on at the job. Was this what I was supposed to be doing with my life or what I really wanted to do for another six years? What about my dream of being a serious writer? Was I putting that on hold for the sake of security or because I was afraid to take that leap on faith?

Armed with questions I had not confronted in years, I spent solitary lunch breaks during the next weeks at Little Rock's quiet parks. MacArthur Park, surrounding Little Rock's stately art museum, was my favorite. I spent my lunch breaks debating whether I should make a career change, and if so, what would it mean for my husband Darryl and my son D.K.?

Reluctantly, I admitted my dissatisfaction in writing canned press releases I could now compose in my sleep. It wasn't the writing I had always dreamed of doing. My answers came, finally, during one of those quiet lunch breaks when the only other inhabitants of the park were the dueling songbirds and homeless men rummaging through trash barrels for a quick meal. It was in the midst of such a day that I decided to leave the comfort of my state job and take a giant leap of faith.

I spent part of my days in the next week mentally preparing for that leap from the safety net of state government into...God knows what. I was suddenly on a mission, and though I knew it wasn't logical, it felt right. I imagined Jo Ann's smile, approving my courage and urging me to go after that childhood dream.

I would miss my job, certainly the salary, and most of all the comfort of the friendships and environment. With all that, I might even have put my decision on hold if I had known just how drastic the changes in my life would be.

In early August, Patsy, my best friend at the agency, rang me on my office extension. "Hurry up to my office. Mr. Dyer is in a meeting right now, and I can't leave my desk." Patsy was personal assistant and secretary to the agency's deputy director, and she was the only person who knew the personal conflict I was having about my job.

"Hey, guess what? A friend just called and told me about a vacancy announcement she had seen. It's for a managing editor for the *Arkansas State Press*."

My ears pricked up, immediately. I knew about the small, weekly newspaper that Daisy and L.C. Bates had started back in 1941, and how it became world famous during the 1957 crisis when the Bates helped integrate Little Rock's Central High School.

"You think they already hired someone, Patsy?"

She shook her head, "Nope, not yet. My friend checked before she called...but, you better hurry to make sure they don't."

I spent a large part of the morning revising my resume. In the late afternoon, I pulled my office door closed, nervously dialed the number advertised for the newspaper and listened to the hollow rings. I sat hunched over my desk, wondering but refusing to get my hopes too high. The voice on the other end of the phone jolted me back to the present.

"Hello...*Arkansas State Press?*" The young woman's voice was friendly enough, giving me impetus to go on.

"Yes, Hello...my name is Janis Lunon, and I was calling about the managing editor job...."

The woman on the other end of the line interrupted just as I was about to ask about an interview. "Hold on."

After a moment, a second voice came on, a male's deep bass. "Hello...may I help you?" I hoped my frown didn't come through the line. While the voice was friendly enough, I could sense a hurriedness, as if he was eager to get back to whatever it was he was doing.

"Hello...Yes, my name is Janis Lunon, and I was wondering if you're still interviewing for the managing editor position, there?" I held my breath, waiting.

"Yes, we are...can you tell me a little about your background and work experiences?" I imagined he was losing patience after asking that same question for the umpteenth time.

"Sure..." I went over my list—the three jobs I'd held since college; the fact that I worked for the university newspaper during my senior year; that I graduated from the University of Arkansas with a degree in Journalism and could offer references from past professors; and that I was a free-lance writer and had been published quite often in local newspapers. His gruntlike responses were noncommittal.

"Miss Lunon, can you fax a copy of your resume to me ... today?" I said I would, "...within the next 30 minutes." He offered a small chuckle, "Good. Can you come in for an interview tomorrow?"

I nodded with no thought to the fact the man couldn't see my head move so eagerly up and down. "Yes, yes I can. Do you think I could come around noon or at 12:30?"

He hesitated, then asked me to hold while he checked his calendar. I held my breath until he returned to the phone. The man's voice was miraculously calmer, friendlier when he returned to the phone. "Yes, if you can be here at 1 p.m. tomorrow, that'll be fine, Miss Lunon."

I thanked him and promptly hung up. That night, I told Darryl about the interview. While he was not excited, we talked about the possibility of me actually getting the job. By midnight, we were both too exhausted to go on. I knew I had not convinced him that what I was planning made sense. "I really think you should just keep your job and continue to do free-lance writing right now," he had said, shaking his head.

I couldn't be angry with him. I knew Darryl was being logical, and his concern was mostly about how the job change would affect our family and our bank account. I was grateful, though, that before he fell asleep he mumbled, "Janis, if this is really what you think you have to do, I'm behind you 100 percent." I'm sure it was his reluctant vote of confidence that allowed me to dream that night of what would eventually become reality.

Even though I understood Darryl's reservations, in truth, I was too far into my dreams by then to think seriously about turning back. I woke earlier than usual the next morning, knowing somehow that this would be the beginning of a new page in my life. I drove to the Migrant Data Bank as usual but told my supervisor I needed to take a late lunch to take care of personal business. Hardly looking up, Mack McCurry, a middle-aged farmer at heart, mumbled, "Sure, take as long as you need," and warmly waved me out of his office.

I sat in MacArthur Park, slowly eating my Rally's hamburger and fries and taking peeks at a watch I almost never wore. I slowly sipped a Dr Pepper, while my mind fast-forwarded to the interview just minutes away. I imagined the conversation, the questions and my brilliant answers. I took a deep breath, prayerful and confident the interview would go well.

At 12:45, I drove past Little Rock's black college, Philander Smith College, and over to 17th and Izard Streets. *The Arkansas State Press* was located in Village Square Apartments. As I parked, I realized the office sat among a barbershop, an interior designer's office and a handful of other small businesses in the Section Eight housing complex.

I parked one car space from the windowed entrance to the newspaper office and listened to classical music to soothe the raucous butterflies in the pit of my stomach. At 12:58, I clicked off the radio, left the car and walked into the large, comfortably disheveled newspaper office. Months later, I would realize the one-room office was only half as large as I imagined it that day.

I spied a tall, dark man sitting at a desk in the back and decided he must own the deep voice on the other end of the phone yesterday. Though he had not introduced himself, I also guessed the intense young man was the managing editor preparing to leave. He sat with a woman whose back was to me, and the two seemed to be in the middle of a serious conversation.

As I stared toward the back of the room, a petite young woman wearing a warm smile walked up and greeted me, "Hi, you here to see

Miss Bates?" I would later learn this was Rita, the office manager. I smiled, question marks dancing in my eyes. "Yes, I guess... I spoke to Don Trimble about an interview at one today." She nodded and guided me to a chair. "You can wait here," she said, already walking to the back. I looked down as she whispered near the man's ear.

A strange feeling passed over me, a strange, illogical sense of familiarity. I was offered a job at one of Little Rock's two daily newspapers ten years earlier, shortly after graduating from the university. I had turned the job down. My husband and I decided I needed more money to help pay for the cost of our three-year-old son's day care and to help defray the cost of my night graduate courses. Something told me a managing editor's job at this small newspaper was probably less than the entry-level reporter's job I was offered 10 years ago.

The young woman stood at her desk motioning me to walk to the back. "You can go on back, now...Don and Mrs. Bates are ready." Her smile told me she noticed the startled look in my eyes. When I walked back to the man's desk and looked in the woman's face, I realized the small, slightly stooped person was, indeed, Daisy Bates. The man caught the surprise in my eyes, too, and smiled softly as he stood. "Hi, I'm Don Trimble, the managing editor...and this is Mrs. Bates, the publisher." He offered his hand.

As we shook hands, I looked from the tall man's dark smiling face to Daisy Bates' girlishly mischievous smile. In due time, I would learn the innocent mischief and the smile were vintage Daisy Bates trademarks. "I'm Janis Lunon...it's so good to meet you again, Mrs. Bates." Her bright eyes narrowed some, and I knew she didn't recall meeting me so many years before. "Thank you both for inviting me in for an interview." The small, still beautiful Daisy Bates slowly offered her tiny hand to me. "Thank you for coming."

I sat facing her and the departing managing editor in the chair he had dragged near his desk. We waited in silence for the next minute. Mrs.

Bates, silent and with her hands perched under her chin, stared softly into my eyes as Don completed a phone call the woman up front had transferred to him.

As those still-piercing eyes stared into mine, I was remembering my first meeting with Daisy Bates, almost exactly 17 years ago. I was 16 years old, and she was unbelievably beautiful and full of life. It warmed me now to see that even with her age and her obvious ailments, she was still beautiful. Her eyes were still vibrant, and her spirit still alive.

I first met Daisy Bates in July 1969. It was two years after Gould schools officially integrated and twelve years after Daisy and L.C. Bates' and the nine black teenagers' courageous roles in the integration of Central High.

It was also two years after my brother Julius had been thrown into Gould's notoriously horrible jail.

While Daddy had spoken of Daisy Bates many times, I had never imagined actually meeting her. She was, after all, a celebrity in the same vein as Mary McCloud Bethune, Marian Anderson and Althea Davis. It was evident that Daisy Bates was even more special in Daddy's eyes because she was a homegrown celebrity. "That woman made a big difference up there in Little Rock—the way she stood up to the white folks who didn't want integration... black folks in Arkansas is lucky to have someone like her."

I once saw a picture of Daisy Bates in the *Pine Bluff Commercial* and compared her to my own mother, as I did most beautiful women—black or white. For the life of me, I couldn't see Daisy Bates ever picking or chopping cotton or hanging clothes on a wire line in the back yard as she yelled across the yard at her children. But there was also a deep contrast

271

between the beautiful Daisy Bates and women like Sojourner Truth and Harriet Tubman, heroines who wore their struggles on their faces.

During the summer of 1969, though, a few months before my junior year at Gould High School, I came face to face with history. As always, we spent the first half of the summer working Daddy's cotton crops and the second half hired out to white farmers—chopping their cotton or soybean fields for the going rate that spanned from four dollars to seven dollars per day.

My siblings and I looked forward to earning whatever amount it was. We knew we would divide that amount by half with our parents and squirrel the rest away for our one-day shopping spree in Pine Bluff the week before school began. By the time we were teenagers, we were expected to spend most of what we earned during the summer on school clothes and supplies for the next year.

That summer, however, Mama came up with the bright idea to introduce Jo Ann and me to office work. A friend had told her Mrs. Bates now lived in Mitchellville and was running a community project called Office of Employment Opportunities. "Lizzie Baker say Mrs. Bates is hiring teenagers for summer jobs," she had told Daddy, while we were within earshot of their conversation. We giggled at Daddy's grunt of a response, a hint that he wasn't warming to the idea.

"James, the girls got just a couple more years in school... we ought to let them try to work in somebody's office. They need to know more than just how to chop cotton when they leave home." Jo Ann and I listened silently as our parents talked back and forth in their bedroom about how we would spend the rest of the summer.

"Why don't you take the girls up to Mitchellville and see if Miss Bates got any work they could do for the summer?" Mitchellville was just ten miles south, off Highway 65. Daddy wasn't anxious to see us bypass a sure thing like a job in the cotton fields, but he didn't argue with Mama about those last few weeks of summer.

In spite of her never-ending role as mother and helpmate in my father's cotton crop, everyone knew Mama had an independent streak. She saw a woman like Daisy Bates as a wonderful role model for her girls. Jo Ann whispered to me, "I'm not going down there...you can."

The morning I was to visit Mrs. Bates' office, I awoke before dawn and already knew this would be one of the hottest days that summer. My sleeping gown was already damp from perspiration. I lay there for a minute, enjoying the quiet time before Jo Ann and the rest of my family started their day.

Jo Ann convinced my parents that both of us didn't need to go to Mrs. Bates for a job. "Let Faye go; I'll work in the fields to make some money for school." My parents didn't argue, agreeing that Mrs. Bates wouldn't likely hire both of us. Jo Ann whispered, outside Mama's hearing range, "Told you...I don't want to work for no Miss Bates...all cooped up in her office the rest of the summer!" She was happy to be off the hook and was looking forward to earning her four dollars a day from the white farmers.

I hurriedly dressed in my favorite yellow Sunday school dress Mama had sewed last year. It was a sleeveless shift with a pleated tail. "Oh Lord, there must be some boys down there," Jo Ann said, laughing. I pretended to ignore her as I smoothed a small pat of Royal Crown Hair Dressing through my hair and made a headband out of a yellow Christmas ribbon.

As I bounded out the front door, I hurried past Mama who was sitting on the steps with a silver pot of unshelled peas in her lap. She smiled up at me as she continued to shell peas and drop the hulls in a bucket near her feet. I skipped down the steps past Jo Ann who sat helping Mama. She looked up at me with a smirk on her face. "Have fun!"

"Faye, you talk up when Miss Bates speak to you. Don't act like the cat got your tongue," Mama offered. I nodded and mumbled my goodbyes before hurrying to Daddy's blue Chevrolet truck. I slammed the door just as Daddy began backing out of the driveway.

As usual, it took Daddy twice as long as it should to drive the ten miles to Mitchellville. In spite of his children's complaints, Daddy refused to drive faster than 30 miles per hour. This was one day I didn't complain. Instead, I was thankful for the extra time to think about what I would say to Miss Bates.

Even though Daddy had often sang the woman's praises in the past, he was amazingly quiet about Daisy Bates on the drive to Mitchellville. I remembered that he didn't really know Mrs. Bates, just read about her like most folk. I wondered now, what her reaction would be to my simply showing up unannounced at her office.

This would be my first real job, unless I counted the time when old Mr. Shooks from Cole Spur asked Daddy if Julius and I could help him and his wife out on their rice crop. But Daisy Bates was famous. The closest I had come to meeting anyone famous before were the gospel singers who drove from Little Rock to Rankin Chapel Church some Sundays with their guitars and tambourines.

Finally, Daddy was turning the truck off Highway 65, beside the sign that said "Welcome to Mitchellville." As he slowed the truck to a stop, he finally offered me advice. "You got to talk to Miss Bates like you got some sense, Faye. She's an important woman, and she talk to people from all over the country. Don't just shake your head when she asks you a question." I nodded, looking down and swallowing hard. I wondered if Daddy knew he was making me even more nervous than I already was.

The small fabricated building we parked beside looked a lot like a trailer house, but Daddy was sure it was Mrs. Bates' office building. He turned off his truck, and I took a deep breath, waiting for him to get out. "Daddy, you're not making me go in by myself, are you?" He started unfolding his *Pine Bluff Commercial* newspaper. "Now, Faye, it's no need for me to go in with you. Just do like your mama and me told you... you'll be all right."

I started to pout but somehow knew it wouldn't help. I knew Daddy was dying to meet Mrs. Daisy but was ashamed that he wasn't dressed better. With all his teaching his children about self-worth, Daddy didn't feel comfortable meeting a woman like Daisy Bates.

"OK, I'll be back...." I scooted out of the truck and took the few steps to the building. I held my breath as I knocked softly on the door. Thin streams of sweat trickled down my face. I hoped I wouldn't get sick on Miss Bates' white cement steps.

Just as I decided no one was there, the door swung open. "Come on in, you don't have to knock. This is an office. Don't you see the sign?" I had, but given my nervous state, it hadn't really registered. Mitchellville Office of Equal Opportunity was painted across the top of the white door. Too embarrassed to look at the person speaking, I tentatively followed the voice through the opened door, and the owner of that voice hurriedly pushed the door shut behind me.

As the door closed, I looked shyly up and saw this unbelievably beautiful woman smiling back at me. It's her, was the only thing I could think. She was even more beautiful than I'd expected, so much so that I completely forgot what I was doing there. Daisy Bates wore a magnanimous smile, and her bright eyes sparkled with humor. "Well, young lady... Are you here to see me?" I nodded, willing the words to come out of my mouth. "Yes ma'am. My mama sent me down here."

She laughed and gestured to me to sit in the chair sitting opposite her desk. As she walked around to her own chair, I took in the sleeveless summer shift skimming her thin, straight frame. Her light tan legs were bare and her child-size feet were clad in sandals. The small woman appeared six feet tall to me despite her five-foot frame. She was the epitome of the word I had discovered this past year in the school library's dictionary—elegant. She could easily have stepped out of the pages of *Look, Life* or *Ebony* magazines.

Daisy Bates walked to the cluttered desk and sat down. Crossing her legs, she then turned to me. "All right, now, child...Tell me why your mama sent you here." She waited a moment for my answer. "It's hot out there, isn't it? You want some water?" I shook my head, "No, ma'am." She casually pulled the jet black hair off her face, and I watched mesmerized as it fell back, softly framing her small face.

I wondered if Daddy knew just how beautiful Daisy Bates was when he talked about what a great leader she was. The newspaper picture had not done her justice, and the article had not mentioned the woman could have easily been a beauty queen or a movie star. I could not imagine any woman in southeast Arkansas—even Mama, who I considered so pretty—rivaling her beauty.

"Miss Bates...I'm...My mama wanted me to ask you if you had any summer jobs for girls...teenagers." Daisy Bates' small eyes brimmed with laughter as she rested her hands on her doll-like waist. She tilted her head and looked directly into my own huge, round eyes. When she had had enough of watching me, she asked, "How old are you, honey, and what kind of work can you do?"

"I'm 16, and I'll be in 11th grade next year," I said proudly. "I can help around the office and type some." She nodded. "And, who is your mama?"

It took me a minute. "Miss Ethel Kearney...in Gould. She wanted me to come down and see if you needed any help for the summer. My daddy drove me; he's in the truck." Miss Bates looked toward the door as if she was expecting someone to come in.

"Well, Miss Kearney. I don't think I know your mama, Miss Ethel." I swallowed hard, and she shook her head. "Anyway, the summer's halfway over, and the teen-agers were hired at the beginning of the summer."

"Oh, we always have to help Daddy in the cotton field the first part of the summer." She nodded, as if she understood and was about to speak when the black phone on her desk rang, loudly. Still nervous, I took a deep breath. I couldn't believe I was sitting, talking to Daisy Bates in her office. I drank in every inch of her office, taking each item in, separately—the desk, the typewriter, the chair, a long wooden table with stacks of folders, books and files; the file cabinets in the corner.

Daisy Bates' office was disheveled and messy, but an elegant messiness—not like everyone else's. What stood out most in the room was a beautifully framed portrait. I guessed without being sure that it was her husband. It was a larger than life photograph of a handsome, distinctive-looking man who didn't smile for the camera. His face was long and narrow—an intelligent man's face, made even more so by the black-rimmed glasses he wore.

I heard Mrs. Bates say goodbye to the caller while I was still staring at the man's photograph. "That's L.C., my husband...you ever hear of him?" I nodded my head, then remembering Daddy's words, answered, "Yes, ma'am, my daddy said you and him ran a newspaper."

She nodded, "Yep, we sure did...for eighteen years." Then with a rueful smile she added, "He is a great man, and a great newspaper publisher. Ours was the only black newspaper in Arkansas for many years."

I wondered if the man was smarter than Daddy. Though I was in awe of Mrs. Bates, I didn't think so. "Anyway, I'm sorry to tell you little Miss Kearney, but we just don't have anything this late in the summer. I have a girl that lives in the community come in part-time to do light office work."

The thought of the disappointment in Mama's face gave me courage. "But...don't you need someone to do some extra typing or some errands, sometimes? I can do anything, and I'm a hard worker..." She laughed, and I wasn't sure whether it was what I said, or the desperation in my voice. I didn't want to go home and tell Mama Miss Bates didn't hire me.

"I tell you what, why don't you sit down over there at that desk and let me see your typing." My heart lurched. The only typing I'd done was in my class last year. I had gotten a C from a teacher who almost always gave A's. I took a deep breath before I sat down, fed a lone sheet of white paper into the manual typewriter and prayed under my breath.

"What do you want me to type, Miss Bates?" I asked, shyly. "Oh...oh, here. Take this dictionary, and just type from a page...type for five minutes." She smiled, and walked to the back of the office. I turned to a page in the middle of the book and began typing. By the time Miss Bates walked back in, I was almost in tears. "Time's up, little Miss Kearney, let's see how you did."

She took the piece of paper from my damp hands and sat down at her desk with a pen. It didn't take her long. "Goodness...I don't think this is your strong point, is it?" She smiled and tilted her head, some. "I'm sorry. Why don't you take typing again this year and come back down and see me early next summer. If you've improved, I promise I'll give you a summer job."

I smiled, in spite of the sadness I was feeling. At least, now, I had some good news I could take to Mama. She stood and came around to where I was standing, offered me a motherly hug around my shoulders, then escorted me to the door. "You do good in school this year, Miss Kearney, and I'll look to see you next summer.

I smiled, said I would and thanked Mrs. Bates as I left the office. Daddy had finished reading his newspaper and was half-asleep when I returned to the truck. "How did it go?" he asked, straightening himself in his seat and starting the truck.

"She want me to come back next year...she already filled all her jobs," I told him, with just a hint of guilt.

Daddy nodded and backed out of the parking lot. We were halfway home when he turned to me and asked, "Was Miss Bates as pretty as her pictures?"

I looked over and smiled, "Yep, she sure is, Daddy."

Mrs. Bates' departing managing editor ended his phone conversation, hung up the phone and called out, "Rita, hold my calls until we finish." Rita was on another call but signaled that she had heard and would comply. Don apologized for the interruption before beginning the one-minute overview of the newspaper, most of which I already knew. I already knew the newspaper was closed in 1959 after white businesses pulled their advertisements. From newspaper accounts, I also knew Mrs. Bates reopened the newspaper in 1984, keeping a promise to her late husband, L.C.

Daisy Bates would later tell me how hard that decision had been, that she was neither financially nor physically fit to operate a newspaper. "I just used my bull-headed determination to keep my promise to L.C.," she had said. Independent all her life, Mrs. Bates' reopening of the newspaper would necessitate dependency on others to make it work. To assure that L.C. Bates' dream became a reality, she would have to depend on committed staff, loyal volunteers and advertisers and loyal subscribers.

Like Mrs. Bates, though, the *Arkansas State Press* had a memorable history and a place in the hearts of black Arkansans. Yet, it was also a struggling small business that had its good weeks and not so good weeks. The paper loosely claimed a circulation of ten thousand to assure consistent advertising from national companies.

Don was honest, telling me that the newspaper operated on a shoe-string budget, even with national ads from community-minded corporations, Arkansas' black corporate leaders and white businesses who now felt a sense of responsibility to the woman and the newspaper.

When my interview began that day in August, I realized to what extent the multiple strokes had left Mrs. Bates' speech and motor skills impaired. Mostly, though, I was amazed at her determination, in spite of her frailty, to do the job her husband asked of her. I listened intently to understand her meanings, relying on her eyes and gestures. Don

279

helped some, translating the unintelligible words.

Even with my rapt attention, it was difficult to understand the once eloquent woman's slurred, garbled speech. The same pride that pushed Daisy Bates to extraordinary feats made her blind to her physical shortcomings. Her mind and reasoning, after all, remained razor sharp.

I left my interview with Mrs. Bates that day with mixed emotions and with the realization that I desperately wanted the job. I was convinced that the historical newspaper was part of God's plan for me and that our meeting back in 1969 was all part of that same plan. Even so, as I drove back to the Migrant Data Bank that afternoon, I was less than pleased with the interview. I wasn't so sure Mrs. Bates thought I was the one.

The small woman's clear eyes had seemed to peer straight through me, and I was now petrified that whatever it was she was looking for had been missing. I imagined those bright, clear eyes saying, "This girl just isn't the one." After an almost sleepless night, I dragged myself to the National Old Line Building the next day still nervous about yesterday's interview. I would learn, later that morning, I had worried in vain.

Don Trimble called around eleven o'clock and offered me his job. "Mrs. Lunon, you got the job if you want it...Mrs. Bates likes you a lot, and she wants you to come to work for her." I could hear the smile in his voice, and I'm sure he could sense the surprise in mine. "Are you sure?" I asked, hardly believing what I heard...that she actually liked me. His booming laughter assured me he was on the up and up. "I'm sure. If you know Daisy Bates at all, you know she's real clear on exactly what she wants. She would never offer you the position unless she thought you were right for the job."

Don Trimble was a thirty-ish Vietnam War veteran whom Mrs. Bates had grown to trust and depend on during the two years he was managing editor. She would later tell me, in confidence, "You know Don Trimble reminded me a great deal of L.C." She had secretly hoped the young man would put law school on hold and stay on at the newspaper.

Before Don hung up, he asked me to hold for a minute. Before I knew it, Mrs. Bates was on the phone, laughing. "Hi! Are you ready to do newspaper work?" I would learn over the years that at times, Mrs. Bates' speech was amazingly clear, as if it had never been impaired. I imagined she was smiling from ear to ear. "Can you start next week?"

Guiltily, I told her I was in my brother's wedding in Pittsburgh, and I needed to give my current job at least two weeks' notice. "But I'll be there bright and early two weeks from today!" She sounded fine with that, especially the fact that I would be dropping by for a couple of hours during the next two weeks to shadow Don before his departure. "Okay...that sounds good. We're really glad you're on board!" I smiled, and nodded. "I am too, Miss Bates...and thank you for giving me this opportunity." I heard a quick "Bye!" The phone clicked. I guessed Mrs. Bates had gotten another call.

I floated through the rest of the day with a smile plastered on my face. That is, except for the time I spent in McCurry's office, making my official two-week departure notice. We had had a good working relationship, and I would miss that. I thanked him for his support over the years and assured him he could call me if he needed to. From there, I went immediately to Patsy's office and gave her the good news. "I can't believe it's happened this fast!" she said, as if she was hoping it would take a little longer. "Well, it's best to do it now...not put it off," I told her. She gave me a warm hug, and I knew she was genuinely happy for me. "How's Darryl with all this?" she asked, tentatively. I looked at her and shrugged. "He'll be fine." I returned to my office shortly after that to start my list of people to call and share my exciting news.

Friends who didn't know my lifelong dream of writing thought I had made a huge mistake leaving my middle management state job to become managing editor of a small newspaper. Others were sure I was having an early midlife crisis. Darryl was somewhere in between. "That's great, Sweetie," he had said, when I announced the good news that evening.

D.K. grinned and gave me a hug. "That's really good, Mama," before peppering me with lots of questions about what is it, exactly, that a managing editor does.

I knew my husband well enough to know that while he was happy that I was happy, he was nervous about this drastic change in our lives. Even with our ongoing discussions about the changes and even calculations of how we would get by with him carrying most of the load, there was still doubt and discomfort about what the career move could mean.

My week of shadowing Don Trimble quickly taught me that while managing editor was an impressive title, it was little more than that. In fact, I was now a certified Jill of all trades—responsible for everything from chasing after stories to hiring and firing staff to getting the paper laid out each week to overlooking the distribution of the paper.

Two days before he left for good, Don escorted me into the newspaper's dark room and gave me an invaluable lesson on photo development on a shoestring. I had never dreamed that I would one day learn to develop photos all by myself. Don suggested I spend the afternoon taking random photos on the office camera and the next day we would develop them.

After my eyes grew accustomed to the dark and I stopped gagging at the smell of the acid, I spent the next hours listening to Don and watching him go through each step of developing photos. "Now...it's your time." While he laughed, I knew he would not let me out of that dark room until I had successfully developed at least one photo.

Unfortunately, I ruined a couple of rolls of film before I saw success. I learned quickly that photo development depended mostly on patience and good timing. By the time he left, Don was confident I would do fine all alone. "You're a fast learner... that's good, because it's all yours after today."

The day I walked into the *Arkansas State Press* newspaper office as managing editor was the last day of the life I had known for 33 years. For the next five years, I would have little time to be bored or even time to do anything outside of newspaper work. After Don left, Mrs. Bates finished his job of training me on the intricacies of small newspaper management. She wrote lists each day for me, and we would spend part of the early morning going over the logistics of newspaper production, layout and design, editorial content, choosing the best free-lancers, newspaper distribution and the advertisement process.

I was sure Mrs. Bates felt sorry for the burden she knew I had let myself in for and exhibited more patience than she sometimes felt. She came in early each day and left at the end of the day. I couldn't have gotten through those early days without her invaluable wisdom and experience. By the end of my first week, I already knew the newspaper was woefully understaffed—with no extra funds to hire anyone. I was thankful for the workers we had. Though they had varying levels of skills, they were all hard workers which were most important in a small newspaper. Rita, the office manager, was invaluable.

At the end of my first few weeks, Mrs. Bates and I sat eating lunch when she asked, "So...do you now have an idea how hard it is to run a small Negro newspaper...with limited resources and staff?" I looked into her eyes, hesitating for a moment as the half-smile slid across her lips. "I think I had some idea, maybe not the full picture. I'm used to hard work, though...and I still don't think it could be harder than chopping or picking cotton all day in the middle of summer." Mrs. Bates laughed and thought a moment. "I don't know...it's more than just hard work, you have to use your brain and your brawn and sometimes that can be a lot on a person." I nodded in agreement.

"Do you remember when I met you back in 1969, Mrs. Bates?" I remembered she had had that questioning look on her face when I first indicated meeting her before. She dimmed her eyes, struggling to gather

her memories, as she folded her sweater and laid it on top of her stack of papers. "No...I really don't." she slowly shook her head, apologetically.

"Well, it was a long time ago. I was sixteen years old and you were living in Mitchellville at the time...running the OEO office, there." Her eyes lit up and she leaned back in her chair, tilting her head in that already familiar way. "I was looking for a summer job but came looking too late in the summer. It's just that I remember telling you how hard I could work that day. But my problem was that I couldn't type worth two cents!"

The still-beautiful, petite woman laughed; slapping her thin leg at a memory she hadn't held on to but still appreciated. "Is that so? Well, I guess it was just destiny that you would end up here, then." She smiled and answered the ringing phone at her desk.

Taking the job as managing editor at the *Arkansas State Press* turned out to be more of a critical decision than I ever would have dreamed. In October of 1987, just three months after starting at the newspaper, about the time I thought it was safe to exhale; Mrs. Bates came into the office one morning and asked if I had time to talk with her.

She beckoned me to sit at the chair next to her desk and within the next moment, she had dropped a bombshell. She was retiring—quitting and selling the newspaper. She sat for a minute, allowing me to take in what she had just told me.

"I had been thinking about it a long time, Janis, but I just wasn't sure...I'm just plain tired, and so many days I don't feel well enough to come. I've been talking to a number of people for some time...people who want to buy the paper, and I'm close to deciding."

Nothing Mrs. Bates had said or done over the last months suggested this would come to pass. I thought back, wondering if I had misread God's message to me. I had been so sure He had told me this was where I was supposed to be. I sat speechless for a time as Mrs. Bates looked into my face.

"I'm sorry I'm dropping this on you like this, Janis...but I just think it's time for me to go home. I'm just plain tired."

I understood, I just didn't know what to say to Mrs. Bates. I simply nodded my head. "I understand Mrs. Bates...of course, you have to do what's best for you." Her face was sad as she said one of the prerequisites with the new owners was that I stayed on. I smiled and touched her hand. "Thank you, Mrs. Bates...but I'm not sure it would be the same working for   someone else."

I left the office earlier than usual that day, asking Rita to take messages for me and tell callers I would return tomorrow. I needed to go home to think and to talk to Darryl about this new piece of news. Besides that, I was feeling sick as I tried to figure out how Darryl would react. I had been so gung-ho about getting myself out on this limb, against his better judgment. Closing my eyes to fight back the tears, I imagined his reaction.

I had been home just a few minutes when Darryl walked in the door. "You're home already...anything wrong?" He was smiling, happy to see me before the middle of the night for a change. I hurriedly sat him down before we ate or began   watching television. Without breathing, I told him what had transpired today. I sat, waiting to hear all the words of recrimination and "I told you so."

Instead, I was pleasantly surprised. Darryl was calm and empathetic. I guessed part of that was the hurt he detected in my face and in my voice. The other part, I figured out a little later was that he believed that was a sign. "Don't worry, Janis, everything happens for a reason. Besides, I bet you can probably go back to your old job or find another one." While I appreciated his empathy, I wasn't as excited about the prospect of returning to state government.

That week flew by because I filled every waking moment with work. I didn't want to think about the looming prospect of finding another job or working for another publisher. My nights were almost sleepless as I kept remembering things would soon be changing and I had no idea what that meant for me. Now, I realized that I simply had overlooked the conversations Mrs. Bates had had with potential buyers. Those same people I had seen before were still in and out of the office, taking Mrs. Bates to lunch and dinner or calling her on the phone. I watched silently as Mrs. Bates talked in hushed conversations with prospective future bosses.

I threw myself further into my work and kept my mind off the inevitable. Just as the work had helped me cope with the pain of my sister's death, I was now able to numb my depression over the sale of the newspaper by throwing myself into my work with complete abandon. I found the time to take lunch breaks outside the office, deciding I needed that time and space to think. I returned to MacArthur Park and began again asking God what he had in store for me.

His answer, I was convinced, finally came in the guise of a dream one night in November 1987. I woke before dawn that morning and lay there hardly believing that God would ask something so ludicrous of me. I hurriedly awoke Darryl who wasn't happy for the interruption from his sleep. I knew there were just a few more hours before he would be up and on his way to work with no time for a conversation.

"Darryl, we can buy the newspaper! We can ask Mrs. Bates to sell the newspaper to us. We can get a small loan. I can use my state pension, and we can ask her to let us pay the balance over the next few years!"

Darryl shook his head, "We can't do that, Janis." He looked at me as if I had lost my mind in my sleep, then laid back onto his pillow in hopes of getting the last few hours of sleep. "Go back to sleep, Janis, I can't talk about this now."

I heard his breathing settle back into slumber mode, but I couldn't go back to sleep. I slipped from the bed and found a pen and pad. Crawling back into bed beside my sleeping husband, I began outlining a business plan for the purchase of the newspaper.

With the seed of my campaign already planted in Darryl's mind, I didn't bother him with it the next morning. Instead, I worked frantically on my plans the next day during my lunch break, including looking into where I could get a small loan and what it would take to take my pension from the state. I also contacted my sister, who agreed to invest some funds into my plan.

It took a few days more of explaining and justifying my plan, but Darryl finally conceded. "Well, we can try it...we can see if it works." Like my job change, he never was completely convinced that this would work, but he didn't have the heart to keep fighting me on it.

Once we had finalized our paperwork and agreed on how we would handle the meeting, Darryl called in to tell his office he would be late that morning and we drove together to the newspaper office to talk to Mrs. Bates. We sat at Mrs. Bates' desk and gave her a copy of the business plan before beginning the discussion. "As I mentioned to you earlier this week, Darryl and I are interested in purchasing the newspaper," I told Mrs. Bates, more nervous than I thought I would be. She looked from one of our faces to the next, smiling, "You look like two college kids, my goodness." I laughed, feeling a lot less nervous, then.

She took a minute to read over the plan, then laid it on her desk in front of her, crossed her legs and settled her hands in her lap. "So...let me hear what you two have to say." Darryl started the conversation, then I talked for another 10 minutes. My appeal, I knew, was more emotional than logical. I was proud that Darryl actually sounded like he knew the business end of the transaction.

When we ran out of words, Mrs. Bates nodded, looked again at the plan, then told us she would think over everything we said and talk with her advisers. "I'll be able to tell you one way or another before the end of this week."

The next days were difficult ones for me. I felt as if I had placed my head on the chopping block and was just waiting for Daisy Bates to decide whether to let it remain on my body or send it rolling. By the end of the week, I was nervous beyond words. I was sure she had decided that selling the newspaper to Darryl and me wasn't a good business move.

The day had almost ended when she turned and beckoned for me to come and sit at her desk. This reminded me of sitting at a teacher's desk after I'd done something wrong in class. We sat for more than a moment, saying nothing. She was looking into my eyes, that penetrating stare that was so uniquely hers. Finally, she took both my hands in her small hands and asked, "Is this something you really want to do, and something you're confident you can do, Janis?" I nodded, the butterflies having a field day in my stomach. "More than anything I've ever wanted, Mrs. Bates." I answered. I wanted to tell her that more than what I wanted, I was convinced God wanted this for me but didn't want to go too far.

She nodded and sat quietly for another while. "All right, I'm going to do it...and, I'm doing it against most of my advisers' opinions. But I'm doing it for just one reason. I've been watching you over these three months, and I've been amazed and pleasantly surprised. You've proven to me that you have what it takes to run a small, Negro newspaper. You have what L.C. used to call that fire in the belly. You have to have that to do a job like this. I think you do."

I couldn't hold the tears back any longer. The emotion was overwhelming, and I was wishing Darryl was here with me then. I couldn't stop crying as I stood up and went to Mrs. Bates, hugging her for all my worth. "Thank you, Mrs. Bates, for having confidence in me. You won't be disappointed, I promise." I told her she would have her down payment first thing in the morning and a contract laying out our agreement to pay monthly installments over the next three years until the balance was cleared. We talked about the logistics of how the newspaper would be transferred legally, and I remembered I had to call Darryl to share the good news.

The next months were full of hard work mixed with business. I was seeing less and less of my husband and my son. The one thing I would begin to realize during those first months after purchasing the newspaper was that the things we seek in life almost always come in the form of trade-offs. Sadly, it wouldn't be long before I realized what I was losing in exchange for gaining what I wanted so much.

Certainly, my marriage hadn't been made in heaven, but we had made it work for almost fifteen years. There was a certain amount of stubborn pride in that for me. Though I believed I had made the most significant sacrifice—leaving a comfortable job, work environment and paycheck—the most crucial sacrifices weren't mine to make. My husband and son were the real sacrificial lambs in the bittersweet decision to spread my wings and fly.

D.K was entering his teenage years now. But for all of the years before now, he had grown up with the assurance of a comfortable home and a close relationship with both parents. Except for infrequent after-work meetings, I was almost always there when he needed me. I oftentimes dropped him off at Central High School in the mornings on my way to work and picked him up after work.

I had always been deeply involved in every aspect of his school life and enjoyed spending time with him and his friends. The epiphany that I had lost much of that in my efforts to create a niche for myself with the newspaper hit me like a cold splash of water. I had already missed out on some very important times in my son's life.

In the back of my mind, I had believed that my happiness with my career change would, somehow, resolve some of the issues with my marriage. In fact, it did just the opposite. It wasn't our decision, but mine to change careers. Unlike before, I had little time for myself or to work on a broken marriage. Both of us had always known that the marriage was a trade-off too, assuring a legal birth for our son.

To our credit, we had both tried to make it work for D.K.'s sake, and, in truth, in spite of everything, we truly loved each other. But love never cured our marriage's ailments, and my new career surely precipitated its unraveling. While I wouldn't give up on the newspaper and didn't want to give up on my marriage, by April 1989 it was evident to both Darryl and me that one of them wouldn't get through this.

After 15 years of marriage, Darryl and I agreed to a separation that we both knew would result in divorce. There wouldn't be any coming back this time, no gluing it back together for sake of appearances or our son. We had fallen in love, still children during that first year away from home. Sheltered from the realities of life outside Varner Road, I was green and innocent and naïve. My friends would jokingly say, "She's so green, she could've fallen off a turnip truck."

How right they were. How wrong I was in believing that falling in love gave me a right to be irresponsible. I didn't know the first thing about how to be responsible when it came to sex. I was pregnant within two weeks of losing my virginity in December 1972. I was married six months later at the age of 19, and I gave my beautiful son a proper birth exactly four months after Darryl and I said "I do." In retrospect, it would have truly taken a miracle to overcome the odds against our recipe for a doomed marriage. ℚ

PART VII

The
Last Reunion

(July 1987)

TWENTY-NINE

A Final
Gathering

The Kearney family reunion began in 1971. It was Mama's idea that the family begin celebrating with the annual get-togethers. Part of the impetus was that she'd seen the trend burgeoning in California where she visited her children each summer. But, more than that, she had awakened one morning and learned that tomorrow isn't promised to any of us. Mama was diagnosed with cancer a year earlier in the midst of a regular breast examination that included vague complaints of discomfort in her chest.

The Pine Bluff doctor examined my mother's breasts, found a lump, told her she should have a biopsy "to be sure" and came back with the horrible news. Cancer cells were already traveling into the lymph nodes of her arm and a radical mastectomy was the best option "to be sure."

To say losing a breast was life-changing for my mother, whose whole existence over the last 33 years was tied to her mammary glands, would be a gross understatement. The cancer, though, was what got Mama to thinking about the importance and fragility of life and family. From the start, Mama wanted it to be a yearly get-together for her family and always during the week of July Fourth.

Mama's joy was seeing all of her children together and her grandchildren quadruple over the years. The more people sleeping on pallets or two or three to a bed in our home, the happier Mama was. She never let the reunion come to an end without holding every newborn, talking to every toddler and gathering the birth dates of each of the new additions to the rapidly growing Kearney clan.

My siblings and I valued these family gatherings more as we grew older and had children of our own. This coming together allowed us the chance to peer into slightly distorted mirrors of ourselves. The reunions grounded those of us threatening to forget where it had all begun or who it was that allowed us the dreams that propelled us into our varied roles. Without the usual inability to express our emotions, during these reunions it was OK to hug or kiss or say "I love you" or "Thank you," especially to our parents for all they had sacrificed.

The front and center role Mama had played in our reunions made them surreal after her death. The annual gatherings were dotted with quiet moments, unexpected tears at unexpected times. Daddy struggled to be for us what she had been. He learned at the expense of our humor that he didn't have the patience of Job with his grandchildren, like Mama did. There was a limit to how long he could talk with them or listen to them cry throughout the night. His efforts, though, meant a lot to all of us.

After a sleepless night, Daddy would let us parents know we were not doing a very good job of raising disciplined children the way we had been raised. "Spare the rod, spoil the child," he would say after a long night of listening to grandchildren romping in the bedrooms and laughing loudly through the night. While the bottomless cans of soft drinks and voluminous bags of candy he shared with the children must have had something to do with their unabated energy, Daddy was sure we were simply raising a bunch of heathens. "You all got to do a better job of raising your children," he'd say.

But even with Daddy's early missteps as keeper of the reunion and his impatience with grandchildren, we never skipped a year celebrating our family reunion—not even those years when it was just as hard for us to be together as it was for us to stay home remembering.

We used the reunion to celebrate Daddy's birthday which fell on June 25th. Our gift was always a card filled with cash or checks and a birthday cake. We decided on cash after years of seeing my father stow away our gifts for that "rainy day" that never came. He had more blue shirts, ties, gloves, slippers and robes than he'd ever be able to use in his lifetime. During one year's Christmas cleaning, I'd discovered years of Christmas gifts packed neatly in his closest—the Christmas wrapping and bows still intact. "They're too nice to wear around every day..." he'd said sheepishly, when I asked him about them.

Daddy was proud of his family, even though you'd have to threaten him with bodily harm to get him to say it out loud. We all knew about neighbors' jokes and whispers that "the Kearney children won't ever amount to nothing...look what they come from...a poor sharecropper with not even a pot to piss in and a new baby every year." Mama's annual pregnancies for nearly 30 years straight were a subject of humor and ridicule throughout the community. "James Kearney ought not be so proud of having a wife pregnant every year and a house full of raggedy children already."

Our reunions redeemed James Kearney. They were proclamations of his and his family's worth. As if anyone might forget, he made a special announcement at Rankin Chapel to remind them. "My children will be in this weekend for our little reunion...they coming from all over the country."

"God is good" is how Daddy explained the way things had turned out—how his 17 children had turned out to "be something," taking his early admonitions that we all had to "do something with your lives" and make education work for us. He believed God understood and forgave his pride on those reunion Sundays when his children and their families filed into Rankin Chapel for Sunday school. He would look down and let just a shadow of a smile move across his lips as the congregation took in a glimpse of God's goodness.

It was 1987, the last reunion before Jo Ann's final goodbye. I had driven in early to plan Daddy's birthday party and was up early preparing to drive into town for last-minute shopping. Daddy, as usual, was the first one up. He was already outside pushing the old hand-mower across his back yard. It was so like him to hang on to what he knew best. His sons had bought him a tractor-mower the year before, but by the look of things, it was still sitting in the spot where they left it.

I pushed up the window and stuck my head out. "Good morning, Daddy...you up mighty early."

He stopped the mower, taking the opportunity to pull a clump of grass from the blade. "I thought I better go on and finish the grass before it get too hot...and 'fore the rest of the family come."

"I'm on my way to Failla's to pick up a few things...you need anything?"

Daddy shook his head and pulled the same tweed hat he'd worn for 20 years further down on his head. "Nah, I don't thank so." Before I pulled the window down, he turned and hollered, "Maybe you oughta get some more Sprites or 7-Ups?" I nodded and waved before pulling the window all the way down. I checked my purse and walked to the back door and out to my white Toyota.

Sprites and 7-Ups? Daddy's reversion to drinking soft drinks befuddled us. We hadn't grown up with soft drinks in the house because Daddy said soft drinks "bothered his stomach and made him light in the head." Since Mama's death, however, we'd noticed his slow re-introduction of soft drinks to his diet and grocery lists. It was humorous and odd and so Daddy. He had discovered that 7-Up was good for settling the stomach.

As I backed the car out of Daddy's yard and onto Varner Road, I imagined I could probably drive the eight-mile route with my eyes closed. How many times had I traveled those eight miles from our home to the town of Gould?

Daddy stood and watched me back out. I watched as he returned to his job and felt a catch in my heart as I realized he was moving slower this year than last year this time. Neither age nor slowed movement would keep Daddy from his outside work...his one-acre garden and the flowers he grew each year now that Mama wasn't there. I couldn't imagine Daddy sitting with people his age in a home for the elderly.

The wooden bridge over Bayou Bartholomew set a half-mile from Daddy's house. I remembered when they'd replaced the older iron bridge with this one 29 years ago. The original one still stood there, rusting as it reminded us of the years gone by.

Daddy complained that the new bridge needed repairing now. "It's just an accident waiting to happen...the foolish folk at the county didn't take into account about how many tractors and farming equipment pass over that bridge in planting and harvest seasons." Five years after it was built, Daddy said, the wood planks were already loosening and the frame sagging in the middle.

These two bridges held many memories—from the onset of tractors and farming equipment that took the place of the horses, mules and men; to the cotton trailers with the thick white bales of cotton peeking from beneath quickly placed tarpaulins; and men and women, black and white, on their way to the Saturday market; to truckloads of black youths half-asleep and quiet in their morning ride to the dew-drenched cotton or soybean fields.

I slowed the car to a stop and peered over into the shallow Bayou Bartholomew, still dark and murky after all these years. The bayou had once teemed with catfish, cod, grinners, perch and even the sharp-mouthed gar. But during that time farmers had used pesticides to rid their crops of boll weevils and worms, destroying generations of wildlife and fish, as well.

Later, through environmentalists we learned that the years of crop-dusting and manual pesticides also affected our health For many years, farmers and low-flying crop dusters would spray the dangerous chemicals onto the fields where men, women and children chopped cotton or soybeans. As the damp, acid-sweet odor blanketed us, we would hold our shirts and scarves to our noses, not realizing the extent of possible dangers from these chemicals.

I listened to the sound of loosened planks beneath the tires as I drove over the bridge. As I sped by the Calloways' old home, the large dog Daddy had warned me about jumped from the ditch toward my window. Daddy didn't really know the people who bought the Calloways' home, just that they hadn't "kept the house up" the way the Calloways' did all those years.

The house I remembered had been a sparkling white rambler sitting up on a hill. For years, it was a reminder to my parents of what their life could have been if they had owned their own land and had fewer children. Jo Ann and I were just as much in awe of the Calloway home as Mama was. It was so white and neatly kept inside. We looked forward to the infrequent visits there that Mama allowed. Phyllis, the Calloways' granddaughter, was younger than either Jo Ann or me. But we were the only girls near her age in the community, and Mrs. Calloway thought we should all be playmates.

We looked forward to the irresistible smell of just-cooked breakfast or dinner in the air as we walked into the expansive house. It was as if Mrs. Calloway spent every waking hour cooking in her big, white kitchen. That is, when she wasn't mopping the floor until it shined or dusting her furniture, leaving the fresh smell of lemon on it.

It was some years before either our parents or the Calloways discovered the secret Jo Ann and I kept for years—the countless times we stole into the Calloway home on Sundays and helped ourselves to the forbidden meals we knew Mrs. Calloway had prepared for her family's Sunday dinner.

Mrs. Calloway, a tall, big woman, would smile benevolently down at us as we walked through her spotless house with Phyllis, whom she had unofficially adopted from a daughter too young to be a mother. She was amazingly clean and freshly pressed, even when her hair seemed to have a mind of its own.

Guiltily, I compared her knack for cleaning and cooking to Mama. I didn't count the fact that Mama spent her days in the field beside Daddy...then her evenings in the kitchen preparing dinner for her tired and hungry husband and children. Mama devoted the little time she had left over after her day's work in the field to the upkeep of the house and us, while Mrs. Calloway never set foot in her husband's fields. Her house and children were her wifely responsibilities.

Mr. Calloway had fallen ill after a stroke some 10 years ago and never recovered. Mrs. Calloway suffered right along with him, continuing her downward spiral after "Wash's death." Finally, after she had lost her appetite and desire to go to church, her doctor diagnosed her with cancer. Her youngest son, Cornelius, or "Boot" as we called him, drove down to the big, white house and took her home with him.

Daddy was sad to lose his longtime neighbor and friend and to see the house go to strangers. He said a proper goodbye when Mrs. Calloway and Boot, who worked at the Pine Bluff paper mill since graduating from high school, stopped by his house on their way to her new home in Pine Bluff. Daddy promised he would visit—and he did. He also promised to look after the big, white house since no one would be in it for the time being. He did, until the new neighbors moved in.

The new neighbors' dog spent as much time around Daddy's house as he did at home. "They must not be treatin' that dog too good," Daddy had speculated. As I drove by, I noticed a big yellow school bus sitting in the back yard and guessed that meant someone there had a steady job. I wondered about the new inhabitants—Daddy's new neighbors.

Seeing the Calloway house in such shambles now, at least from the outside, made me sad. The front screen door was half off. The white paint had long since yellowed and was badly flaking, and the front lawn, once perfectly manicured, had grown into a small jungle.

Even in Gould things change, I thought, as I pressed the pedal down sending dust billowing up behind me. I let up some, though, when I remembered the number of cars that had flipped over in this very curb.

I saw Pat Failla standing at the clerk's counter as I walked into his brother Sam's general store. Pat had been my high school chemistry teacher and had been something of an oddity for white teachers at the integrated Gould High School that was 95 percent black. Pat Failla, though, had taken a genuine interest in his students and wanted to see them learn.

I smiled when he recognized me, remembering how kindly he'd treated Jo Ann and me during our senior year at Gould High. He and our English teacher had taken five black teen-age girls on a weekend college tour a few months before graduation.

"Well, I declare! Is that you?" I blushed, in spite of myself, and walked over to the checkout counter to accept the hug I knew was coming. "How are you, Mr. Failla? I can't believe it's been 10 years since I last saw you.... You still look the same."

He laughed and patted his stomach, "Yeah, plus about 20. Girl, you show 'nough look the same. Must be that good water and clean living up there in the big city of Little Rock," he laughed at his own joke. "Hey, how is Jo Ann doing? I heard she was having some problems.... Is she all right?"

I nodded, "She's doing a lot better. I'm expecting her at the reunion today."

He smiled and patted my shoulder. "Man...now that was a smart girl. She was amazing in my chemistry class." I smiled, remembering how Jo Ann would walk up to the blackboard and finish Mr. Failla's chemistry equations for him.

"Will you tell her I asked about her? I'd love to see her if you get a chance to drop back by." I waved as I walked down the aisle.

"Tell your Daddy hi for me, now." I nodded, again, saying I would.

"I saw Mr. Kearney just last week and was telling him how good he look for a man his age...what a blessing y'all are to him." I moved down the aisle in the opposite direction.

As I drove out of Failla's parking lot I scanned the city's streets to see how much things had changed, shaking my head to see so much was just as it was when I left. There were still few people here—probably less than the "Population: 1,600" portrayed on the sign coming into town. It was the same sign from 30 years ago.

Gould had been run by the Holtoff family for as long as most people there could remember. According to Daddy, "Mr. Howard" Holtoff owned most of the town—and the people in it. The bank was the Holtoffs', the cotton gin was theirs and the land the cotton was planted on was theirs.

After cotton lost its luster in towns like Gould and the Holtoffs lost most of their land over the years, Gould had continuously gone down. Since black families couldn't depend on making a living picking or chopping cotton with the onslaught of big, new farming equipment, the small town's population had also steadily declined. Unfortunately, the only thing keeping the numbers somewhat steady was the high rate of teen pregnancies.

Daddy described it as a town "gone to hell in a hand basket," and he relayed horror stories of youngsters succumbing to drugs and crime. He admitted he wasn't as brave as he once was, with all the crime taking place so close to his house. "It ain't nothing like it was when y'all lived at home...nothing but drug fiends and hoodlums in town now."

Like many small towns that showed no outward signs of change, Gould had obviously lost its small-town mentality and its citizens had somehow lost their concern for each other. Many of the youth in the town—without any jobs or an ample education—were lured into drugs and crime. The fact that Daddy lived so far outside town with so few neighbors was both a blessing and a concern for us.

When I arrived back home, Daddy was standing under the carport feeding bread to his dogs. "You made it back, already? You didn't have no trouble, did you?" Daddy had always been a worrier. He never stopped worrying about his children-even when the youngest of them was nearing 25.

"I just took my time getting back. I saw Pat Failla, and he wanted to talk all day. He said he saw you last week." Daddy nodded. He'd seen Mr. Failla, and they had talked enough for three or four visits.

It was already 1 o'clock, and the party was set for 4 p.m.. The balloons had to be blown up; the birthday table needed to be set. Where was the cake? That was always the downside of being the first one to show up for family events—everybody depended on you to have things ready when they got there. I frowned as I started to feel those all too-familiar butterfly wings twitching in my stomach. "Where is everybody?" I whispered.

As if in response to my question, two cars drove into the yard. Suddenly, I thought of the children and became excited at the thought that the balloons could now be blown up before the party began. Little girls...how they liked to emulate their mamas. With the children's help, I'd have the birthday table set in no time flat!

"Hey! You people sure took your own sweet time getting here!" I laughed as I greeted my brothers and their wives and children, realizing that my "old" Gould dialect had returned as I settled into being around family. How quickly that happened, I thought.

John, married to another Janice, was there with their four children. Julius and his wife, Lydia, my former classmate, drove up in their white Geo loaded with four children of their own. Lydia had been one of Jo Ann's and my best friends in high school, as well as part of the group of five that went to the university in 1971. The other two were Delois Arnold who had married a former pro football player and Linda Hokes who had moved away to Kansas City years ago.

The family joke was that Julius and Lydia transported more people cross-country in their Geo than Greyhound Bus Lines did. They seemed to never tire of loading the Geo with Sunday school classes or volunteers from Lydia's daycare or a few women from the nursing home for daylong trips around the country.

"Is the food ready?" John asked, as he passed me carrying packages into the house.

"It would be, if y'all had made it here on time," I said with as much sassiness as I could muster. John laughed at my attempt, "Uh huh."

Even with his gruff exterior, "Johnny," as he was called during our earlier years before he became a city attorney, was harmless. He usually said exactly what he thought and had an unending reservoir of jokes he shared with the family whenever we gathered. The dirtier ones, like the cups of beer they passed around later, were kept hidden when Daddy was around.

"I see you were successful in talking your sister into joining her family today," he said. I half-smiled and said I had little to do with Jo Ann's final decision to attend the family reunion. She had decided at the last minute.

"Well, I'm glad she's here...I never feel right when she's not." I patted John's shoulder, knowing it always took a lot for him to be honest about his feelings with the family. In fact, it was a Kearney trait to be honest about everything else in life except our emotions. We had learned that from Mama and Daddy, and none of us seemed able to shake it no matter how much we tried. Most of us admitted during our weaker moments that this characteristic wreaked havoc in our marriages and relationships—always causing more problems than it resolved.

The old adage "never let them see you sweat" must have been coined for my family. We could have added—never let them see you cry; never show you care; never grieve in public; never show your sadness; never allow your anger to show; and rarely exhibit your joy or happiness. Stoicism was a family virtue—not that we couldn't laugh and play. We could and we did. In fact, we probably laughed and joked to an unhealthy extent because we'd learned these were our only acceptable outlets for our emotions.

J ohnny was the smallest child Mama brought into the world. Growing up in a family of athletic brothers, Johnny's size would be the bane of his existence for many years. But later, it became the impetus for his adult work ethics and determination to succeed. He would more than make up for his small stature with a quick mind and daring attitude. When he wasn't bullying someone twice his size, Johnny would sometimes be found asleep under the bed, surrounded by books.

He loved his independence, measuring it by the money he had in his pockets. To assure that he always had money, he constantly sought out chores and errands from the neighbors, even though it was unusual at that time for children to expect or receive recompense for work they did for neighbors or adults.

After graduating at the top of his class, Johnny received a scholarship to AM&N College in Pine Bluff. There, he always kept a job, working to help pay his way through college. As a young man, he was dubbed the "black Elvis Presley" after winning a number of talent contests imitating Elvis Presley.

There was, however, another side to Johnny. From early on, he was known for his quick temper. Unfortunately this quite often landed him in trouble at home.

One such incident would mark him for life as "David" to Miss Mary Baldwin's "Goliath." According to Kearney legend, Johnny was no more than 12 years old but still looked nine or 10 when he ran afoul of Miss

Baldwin, a teacher at Fields Elementary School who also served as student-monitor for the school bus Johnny rode to and from school each day. At the time of the incident, Johnny was less than five feet tall and weighed 100 pounds soaking wet. Miss Baldwin was six feet tall and weighed 300 pounds on her light days.

According to the story, the incident happened during a normal bus ride home from school. On this particular day, according to Miss Baldwin, Johnny was particularly hyper and was "running his mouth even more than usual and moving from one seat to another while the bus was running." After watching Johnny's behavior for a short while, Miss Baldwin directed him to take his seat and "keep your voice down during the rest of the ride home."

According to Johnny, he did just that and besides he hadn't been talking any more or louder than anyone else that day.

Miss Baldwin, however, said young Johnny looked at her, mumbled something under his breath, rolled his eyes and continued to talk loudly and move from seat to seat. She raised her 300 pounds up off the front seat, which she always occupied alone. She walked back to where Johnny was and slapped him across the face. According to Johnny, the slap was completely unfair and uncalled for. He had not been talking or moving from seat to seat at the time.

After she walked back to her seat, Miss Baldwin said, Johnnie pulled from his pocket an old, rusty pocket knife. He then walked halfway to where the large woman sat and "threatened her life with that old, rusty pocket knife!"

Angry by then, Miss Baldwin threatened Johnny with a "butt-whipping" if he didn't go to his seat and sit down. "I'm gone show tell your parents 'bout your behavior when we get to your house...."

At that, Johnny was said to have turned and walked quietly and silently back to his seat. He said he remained there until the bus arrived home.

Miss Baldwin was much too large and slow to be the first one off the bus to apprise Mama and Daddy of Johnny's altercation. Johnny and five of his siblings had already made it to the house to relay the whole story by the time Miss Baldwin arrived at the front door. She slowly walked up our steps and greeted Mama who was by now standing on the front porch. After their greetings, Miss Baldwin sat for a while before offering my parents her version of the discourse between young Johnny and herself.

My parents were too embarrassed and horrified to question Miss Baldwin's version of the story and sheepishly apologized profusely for their child's disrespect. They tried to ignore Johnny's outbursts of dissension as Miss Baldwin talked, shushing his version of the incident.

"You best just be quiet now, boy. You in enough trouble all ready," Mama said, her eyes already glazing over with hurt and anger.

"Bless you, Miss Kearney...I'm sorry to have to bring you bad news," the woman said as she turned and made her way slowly back up on the bus.

For a long time after that, Johnny rode the bus without looking over at the large woman who always sat on the front seat immediately behind the bus driver. Years later when Johnny was an adult, Miss Baldwin would see him and laugh about the bus incident as if they had agreed to "let bygones be bygones. Johnny would smile cordially but rarely offered anything more.

Johnny shortened his name to John after he graduated from law school to became the first of nine Kearney attorneys. Jesse and Jack followed suit, then Julius, Jerome, Jude and Jeffrey after that. In fact, every male Kearney born after 1947 became a lawyer, and two female Kearneys—Janetta and Janeva—followed their lead.

J amie and her son Kevin had flown into Little Rock from California and rented a car to drive to Gould. Jo Ann sat in the back seat as they parked the rented Honda on the side of the road. Jamie, my parents' firstborn, had been the most independent of all the children, according to Daddy.

Daddy often told the story of how he and Mama had "lost" Jamie when she was just three years old. As young parents, they sometimes left their young daughter at the end of the cotton rows on a pallet of sacks as they picked cotton in the fall. They always left her homemade dolls or balls to play with and frequently checked on her.

Daddy recalled the fall day when they returned to the end of the cotton row. They walked over to the pallet to check on their baby girl and found her gone. Jamie was nowhere in sight.

"We were scared to death...we searched the fields and woods for hours—almost till night—and still hadn't found her. I was 'bout to go crazy, scared sick that something terrible had happened to her. We was feeling bad, too, about leaving the child alone-though we always left children at the end of the row like that. It was the only way we could get our cotton picked. It wasn't till I walked about a mile over to the old pump we used to get our water that I found her. There she lay...all curled up...sound asleep by the water pump.

"I couldn't believe it...she was laying there by the pump still holding on to that water bucket. She had walked to the pump to get some water! How she found that pump all by herself through that field, I'll never know."

That type of independence stayed with Jamie. She became the perfect little helper for Mama and for many years helped raise her younger siblings. Oftentimes she was given full authority, even to punish the younger ones, to keep us "in line" while our parents were away.

"What do we need to do to get the show on the road?" Jamie asked, as she and Jo Ann walked up to the house. Jamie told me later that day that she was pleasantly surprised when Jo Ann said she wanted to come to the reunion. Jo Ann usually found excuses not to attend the family gatherings.

I didn't mention how many times I'd asked Jo Ann in the past week to join us, to no avail. She had made it known, again, that family reunions were a long way down on her list of favorite things to do.

"I don't have time to go down and pretend with you all," she'd snapped back. "If anybody was interested in listening to the message I try to share with them, I wouldn't mind going...but you all get together to have fun and act foolish... celebrating yourselves, rather than celebrating God."

"I'm glad you changed your mind," I said to Jo Ann, smiling. I'd finally given up asking her to come a couple of days earlier and was happy to see her here. Jo Ann shrugged and gave me a half smile back. I quickly hugged my sister before she could walk away, then returned to the immediate task of getting Daddy's birthday party started by 4 o'clock. I began rotating the birthday card, passing it to John first.

"Girl, can I just donate half of whatever you give?"

Janice shook her head and laughed. "Don't even try it, Mr. Cheapskate!"

The children were more than excited to help. The boys helped with the balloons, while the girls helped set the table. Daddy, as usual, had mysteriously disappeared while we prepared for "his" day. He still liked to pretend he didn't have the foggiest idea what was going on.

At last, Daddy's front yard and roadside was filled with his children's cars. I was quite satisfied with how the day was coming together. Sheryl, Jesse's wife, had bought one of the largest and most beautiful birthday cakes I'd ever seen. When I asked where she'd bought it, she said a friend of the family who "just loves Mr. Kearney" made it for Daddy.

Since we all knew Daddy would put his age back a year or two, this year's birthday cake had written across it: "To Daddy Kearney, on his 80+ birthday!" Sheryl suggested Daddy fill in the blank, saving her the embarrassment of getting it wrong. Daddy laughed and said he'd fill it in later.

I remembered how, when we were growing up, there had never been a question about Daddy's "correct" age—we all knew he was eight years older than Mama. It wasn't until after Mama died that he admitted he wasn't sure of his exact age since his birth certificate was lost during his childhood.

The truth was, it didn't matter to us if Daddy was 65 or 105. It was just always funny when he'd remind us that the age we came up with wasn't necessarily his real age.

Before we knew it, the sun had made its way across the sky and now hovered just above the trees across the bayou. It was our first day of the family reunion, and Daddy's birthday party celebration was slowly coming to a close. We had eaten as much as our stomachs could hold and had successfully outdone ourselves in telling embellished truths.

It had been a good day, and as always we were ending it with a short tribute to Daddy. The beautiful cake set in the middle of the table, waiting to be cut. Each year a different sibling cut the first slice from Daddy's birthday cake and made the official birthday wish.

This year, Cecil, our half-brother, was given that honor. Cecil was the son Mama had when she was still a girl and living at home. Though we'd never learned the full truth behind Cecil's birth, over the years we'd heard a number of different pieces of myth.

Cecil had grown up in the Curry home in McNeil and was raised more like Mama's younger brother than her child. Big Mama, for all practical purposes, had treated him as her own son.

During our childhood, Cecil had been an infrequent visitor to our home. We had all resented the special treatment he had received from

Mama and were puzzled as to why our brother was being treated more like a guest than a family member.

While Cecil had been a consistent participant in our reunions over the years, our half-sister Clara, from Daddy's first marriage, had only attended a few times. Clara, almost 60 now, was a registered nurse living in California. Daddy said her job kept her away. Though they were our siblings, too, I always wondered whether Clara and Cecil felt comfortable around Daddy's large immediate family.

At the reunion, Cecil's birthday wish to Daddy was a simple and short one. "Well...Mr. James, I would like to take this opportunity to wish you many more birthdays like this one with your loving family...and also...I'd like to say how much I appreciate being a part of the Kearney family and how much I appreciate you always making me and my family feel as if we belong."

Daddy's grandchildren were given the task of making his birthday presentation. Self-consciously, they stood and made their brief speech before handing Daddy the oversized birthday card signed by his children and their children and the envelope filled with dollar bills. As always, Daddy was grateful for his children's generosity, even though we had been doing this same thing for a while now. We all chimed in for Daddy to have the last words. As usual, he seemed hesitant to talk in front of every one, though we knew he'd finally do so.

Daddy, once skinny and straight, was now a little stooped and carried a small pouch around his middle. He wore his still-thick hair down on his neck and slicked back from his face. It was curly and had been coal black for years and remained so-with a little help from a jet black coloring stick to "touch up the edges." You didn't have to look hard to see the prominence of Native American blood that ran in Daddy's veins—the thick, aquiline nose, high cheekbones and the wavy black hair. He often told us that his paternal grandmother was half-Cherokee.

Daddy looked slowly around the yard at all his children, grandchildren and great-grandchildren. He fidgeted with the envelope of money in his hand and cleared his throat. "I just want to say thank you to all my children and my grandchildren and great-grandchildren, too. I know Ethel would be so happy to have all of you here today. I feel so blessed to have all of you here with me—and I have to say especially Jo Ann. I'm so glad you came. And...I...just thank you."

From the sound of Daddy's voice, I could tell he was choked up. I looked over at Jo Ann and saw there was a very pensive look on her face. She was neither smiling nor frowning. It was as if Daddy's words had forced a crowd of thoughts to start moving around in her head. I started to walk over to try to shake her out of her pensive mood but decided against it.

We couldn't get over the fact that Jo Ann was here and were amazed at how "like her old self" she was that day, though none of us said it to her. She smiled a lot and hugged the sisters and brothers she hadn't seen in some years.

My older brothers and sisters seemed most happy to see her doing well. They had had to go by word of mouth from either us or Daddy on just how Jo Ann was doing from one year to the next. It was the first time in a while that all of the family members were able to attend. This had all the makings of a very special Kearney reunion.

———

During this reunion, Jo Ann and I spent time with old classmates. In spite of herself, she seemed excited to see our old friends Linda and Jimmy, whom she had a crush on during our high school years. She laughed when she learned he was married and had children. She carried on conversations with a number of people, asking questions of those she hadn't seen in a number of years.

Jo Ann started smoking the summer she graduated from high school and spent two weeks in Ohio. Since then, she smoked up to two packs of cigarettes a day and, when she was at her sickest, even more. During those times, Daddy complained that she "smoked like a chimney." This time, she swore she was giving it up before the year was out. At the same time, she was losing all her extra weight.

Jo Ann's weight had ballooned to over 200 pounds over the last 10 years. She blamed her weight gain on the medicine she took. Today, it looked as if she had lost as much as 30 pounds. And, as usual, her hair was impeccable. I never understood how, in spite of her illness, Jo Ann's hair always managed to look twice as well-cared-for as mine did. Though her face was rounder than it had been years ago, it was still flawless and beautiful.

She wore a tailored shirt-waist, khaki-colored dress that day. It flared at the tail and fit her tight across her breasts. Of all seven Kearney girls, Jo Ann was one of only two endowed with ample breasts. While we were all considered quite shapely by African-American beauty standards— small waists and healthily rounded hips and legs—when it came to breasts, most of ours were less than outstanding.

As a teenager, I'd been terribly jealous of Jo Ann's buxom breasts that were even more noticeable because she had slimmer hips compared to the rest of us. It wasn't until I gave birth to my only son that I was finally blessed with comparable breasts. Jo Ann had often joked that I'd gotten myself pregnant knowing my breasts would grow!

"I almost didn't come down, but I'm glad I did," she'd said softly, blowing smoke away from me and smiling as we sat out on Daddy's front porch. She talked easily with Daddy about Bible passages that day. As she'd gotten older, the Bible had become a passion. She carried her worn black leather Bible everywhere she went. Jo Ann, in fact, was as well-read in the Bible as Daddy had always been. That was saying a lot. We'd learned everything we knew about biblical characters and the wages of sin and the unending battle between good and evil from Daddy's weekly Sunday school lessons and class reviews.

He had always made the stories interesting and sometimes more horrible than we thought was necessary. But that day, Jo Ann's knowledge of the Bible at least mirrored Daddy's, and she easily repeated some of the same lessons he'd shared with us so many years ago. Daddy nodded as she spoke, chuckling softly with pride.

I smiled too, realizing that this time Jo Ann had actually left her battle gear at home, not wasting her energy arguing the facts of religion with Daddy.

Quite unlike her, though, Jo Ann didn't seem to find anything to argue with anyone about that day. She didn't question why the Kearney family needed to have reunions every year, like she usually did. She usually would say, "If we practiced family unity the whole year round, we wouldn't have to waste all this money and time coming down here to pretend we're such a close family!"

It warmed all of our hearts to see our sister interacting with the rest of the family, rather than sitting and reading her Bible off under a tree or in a room all by herself. So often, she'd been with us physically but not at all in spirit. This time, she'd played cards with her siblings and joked with her young nieces and nephews like she hadn't in a long, long time.

I found myself watching Jo Ann and smiling throughout the day, constantly thinking how normal Jo Ann seemed. She had been, for so many years, my competitor. Later, she became my best friend. It wasn't until we were adults that I realized I had lost my sister and friend. Today, she was the Jo Ann I had known and loved so long ago. The one I missed so much now.

Jo Ann asked if I she could ride back with me tomorrow for the cook out. I was so happy she was coming a second day that I couldn't stop smiling long enough to tell her yes. She laughed and admitted she had enjoyed herself more than she expected. "And thank goodness Daddy and I actually got along without getting into any arguments," she chuckled.

We talked about old times—boyfriends and jealousies and secrets we'd shared. Finally, she walked over and sat alone under Daddy's peach tree. She looked content. A smile hovered along her lips.

It was nearing dusk. The sun, large and a beautiful red-orange, was hovering over the woods. Daddy sighed as if he had just about talked himself out for the day. While his grandchildren continued their questions, he quieted them by saying, "Granddaddy's talked enough for tonight. I'll tell you some more stories tomorrow or the next day." He ruffled his great-grandson Michael's hair as the young boy hugged his grandfather's leg. "I think I'll go see what's showing on the television set before I go to bed tonight."

Traditionalists that we were, the groups also separated by the sexes. The women voluntarily returned to the kitchen for clean-up duty, while the men sauntered out to sit on the porch to talk, or down to the bayou toting Daddy's guns as if there was anything left in the woods to shoot these days.

Another year, I thought to myself. How fast the days are passing us by!

After cleaning up, the sisters took our turn to sit and gossip or talk about our families and jobs. After a while, I excused myself from the group and walked outside where the circle of males stood joking and laughing. I immediately recognized the old story about my younger brother Jude being retold. Jude half smiled and shook his head as he listened to his brothers retelling his story.

Jude was the most outgoing and vociferous of the family. The joke was that Jude would never run out of things to talk about. But he wasn't just talk, he was also extremely smart. A Harvard and Stanford graduate, Jude was now a partner in one of the largest law firms in Washington, D.C. He had met Lorraine, a former flight attendant from Pittsburgh, and married her just a few years ago.

I walked over to where Jo Ann sat listening. A half-smile lingered on her face. I tried to read her mood. "Want to go for a walk down to the bridge?" I whispered. I remembered how much we once loved those opportunities to get away from our parents and younger siblings. It had given us the freedom to talk about our lives, mostly about school and boys, and sometimes our parents.

She looked as if she could only vaguely remember that time in her life. "Can I smoke while I'm walking?" she asked. "Sure," I answered. I realized at that moment how much I missed the times Jo Ann and I had spent together during our earlier life and how much we were missing now.

I looked over and saw the woods I used to lose myself in when I needed time away from my family. While I didn't feel the need to venture quite that far today, it did bring back memories. Daddy's house still had the spirits of my childhood, and when I looked out the windows my long ago dreams were as clear to me as they were during that childhood.

We walked quietly for a while before Jo Ann laughed loudly and abruptly. "You remember the time I refused to wash the dishes and Mama whipped both of us? You were so mad at me you didn't speak to me or Mama for a whole week!"

I laughed in spite of myself. "I remember that like it happened yesterday. You were so much more stubborn and braver than I was."

Jo Ann shook her head. "No, it didn't have anything to do with being stubborn or brave. Sometimes it was just the principle of things. They sometimes asked us to do some of the stupidest stuff...I just refused to be treated like a fool."

I frowned and didn't respond. I thought I might be treading on thin ice, afraid of where the conversation might go. "Do you remember how we use to fight about whose side of the room we were on and who was sleeping on which side of the bed? It seems like we dreamed up things to fight about, sometimes."

"And do you remember the time I played with your Indian doll and tore it up on Christmas morning before you got a chance to play with it?"

I suddenly remembered that painful incident, surprised that there was still a hint of hurt attached to the memory.

Jo Ann looked closely at me. "I know I never told you I was sorry about that, but I am. I don't think I did it on purpose; but that didn't help your Christmas none."

I remembered that Christmas morning just as vividly as I remembered the dishwashing episode. How long did it take for hurts to just disappear, I wondered. I also wondered if Jo Ann knew just how hurtful those incidents had been for me. I remembered how she always had an uncanny ability to bring my hurts out when no one else even knew they existed.

"Were you sorry you caused me to be punished for your being stubborn?" I said, half-joking and half-serious.

Jo Ann looked at me for a brief moment, inhaled on her Winston and said, "No. Not really," without a smile.

"I think we better be getting back...I told Jamie I forgot to bring my medicine, and I have a 9 o'clock dosage." There was a faint smirk on her face. "I get so tired of taking pills...day in and day out. I guess I'll get used to it one of these days."

"It's just 6 o'clock. You've got plenty of time," I smiled. "Let's sit for a while. Remember how we used to come down here in the evenings and sit and talk?"

As Jo Ann lowered herself onto the edge of the wooden bridge, she was careful not to soil or wrinkle her dress. She quickly straightened out the wrinkles after she sat.

"I like your dress, Jo Ann. It really looks good on you."

She laughed loudly, saying, "I'll let you borrow it sometime."

As we sat on the bridge, the memory of the life we had shared for so many years loomed in my mind. I remembered how close we were during much of our adolescence and our teens. We'd slept in the same bed for most of those years and spent many a night talking and dreaming together until the wee hours.

We continued sitting on the bridge, staring down into the shallow bayou. I followed her gaze, expecting to see what it was that held her interest.

"I can't remember when I was the way you remember me, Faye. I've been trying, and I can't. Are you sure I was ever like you describe me? That sounds so different from...it sounds like somebody I never knew.

"But if I was that person, I'm not anymore...and I know that bothers you and I know it bothers Daddy and the rest of the family, but it's just the way things are. You all just have to learn to accept me, the same way I have to accept you the way you are."

I didn't know where this had come from, but I wanted to assure Jo Ann that we did accept her and love her just as she was. Before I could, though, she had scrambled up from the bridge where she'd sat and began walking fast back toward the house, the smoke from her Winston trailing behind. "Jo Ann! Jo Ann!" I hollered at her back. She refused to acknowledge she heard me.

I walked faster, afraid, remembering how good it was to have her with us today, to almost have the "old" Jo Ann. The tears streamed down my face as I tried to catch my sister without panicking.

Finally, she slowed her pace, throwing the half-smoked cigarette in the ditch. She sighed loudly and heavily before slowing, then turning around to look into my face. "I'm not going to change for anybody, Faye...not you, not Daddy, not nobody. If you all can't accept me in the shape I'm in, then...I don't guess you really have to...."

I was sad, out of breath and relieved that my sister had stopped and acknowledged me. "I do accept you, Jo Ann. I love you just the way you are."

She looked at me a long time, then hugged me briefly, lightly, before turning and walking slowly beside me the rest of the way home.

———————

On the second day of the reunion, I had awakened early and woke Judy to help me get things prepared for today's picnic. Today's event would be a cookout in the park. Judy hadn't kicked the cigarette habit she'd started while a youngster and took the opportunity of us working outside to light one up.

"Those things kill you, you know," I half smiled.

Judy smiled back and took a slow drag. "Yeah, so will too much working or playing."

We laughed, both because she was exaggerating and because we knew there was some truth to both our admonitions. I reminded her of Daddy's story about how she and our youngest brother Jeff had talked Daddy into stopping his smoking habit when they were younger. "I swear, after they scared me to death about smokin', convincin' me to throw all my cigarettes away, it wasn't a week passed before Judy and Jeff was down on the bayou smokin' up every package of cigarettes I threw away!" Daddy had said.

Out of all his children only three are smokers. We had all been so proud of Daddy quitting cold turkey like he did—after smoking since he was 11 years old.

Judy, mildly embarrassed, promised she'd think more seriously about quitting when she turned 55, too. Judy had often said she felt like an "only" child growing up. She didn't recall the house full of children that most of us had grown up with. She had been the last to leave the nest after Jeffrey. She still felt as if we couldn't accept her as an adult. It was easy to forget that she was no longer "our baby" even though she was now married and had a child of her own.

We both turned as the backdoor opened and laughed when we saw

Daddy's uncombed head peek around the door. "What y'all doin' up so early, here?"

"We're trying to get things ready for when everybody gets up and start moving. You know how your children are—so last-minute that nothing ever happens when it's supposed to. We're trying to remedy some of that."

Daddy walked out in the yard where we were packing bags of charcoal, chips, coolers, soft drinks and pots and pans in the back of cars. He was wearing a brand-new bathrobe that, at first glance, I thought I'd never seen before. It was only after a double take that I realized it was one of the many Christmas gifts he'd shown us last year before reboxing it and putting it at the top of his closet.

Daddy's two dogs must've heard his voice. They left their breakfast to come around front and join us. Daddy had always been a magnet to animals and children and it wasn't any different with these most recent pets. But just as they were galloping up to him, Daddy was directing them away. "Git on 'way from here." He shook his head, laughing. "Them ole mutts ain't good for nothing but eatin', I swear. I don't know why in the world I keep 'em 'round here."

Judy and I laughed. We knew he kept them for company and for some modicum of security at night. If nothing else, they barked when someone unusual came up at night.

"You sure looking spiffy in your new robe, Daddy." Judy smiled, having thrown her cigarette away the moment she heard Daddy open the door.

"Aw...this was one of my Christmas gifts last year. I don't remember who gave it to me."

Judy and I looked at each other. "Was it last year or 10 years ago, Daddy?" she joked. By now, Daddy had sat down on the front porch, enjoying the morning and the cool breeze.

Our picnic would be at Morning Star Park, five miles outside Pine

Bluff. We'd used the park a number of times for our reunions and liked it because of the pretty lake there. The smaller children always brought their fishing poles and bait. They liked fishing there, though the grown-ups were pretty assured we wouldn't catch a thing.

It would take us 30 minutes to drive to the park. That is, if everyone went straight there without making stops at the little grocery stores between Gould and Grady or detours to friends they hadn't seen "in ages" and just wanted to stop by and say hello. I estimated if we left by noon, we'd actually be ready to serve dinner between 2 p.m. and 2:30—a record for our family.

The coolness of the day began to disappear the later it got. By noon, I was rounding siblings and their families up. Those who were at other houses were called and directed to be on their way.

"Eating time is 2 p.m., which means we need to get the barbecuing started no later than 12:30." I listened to the grousing from siblings who'd stayed up all night chewing the fat and reminiscing. John's house was a magnet for those kinds of late-night gatherings. I figured at least half the family was there last night. I had opted to stay at Daddy's, along with Judy and Carlos. Daddy wanted and appreciated the company, though he wasn't as patient with children as he used to be. "I get along fine with them that still act like children and not grown folks," he'd said.

By noon, we had Judy's and Daddy's cars packed with all the necessary utensils and food. My husband, Darryl, had arrived for the day and was driving Daddy's car. Daddy sat up front in the passenger seat, and I climbed into the back seat.

Daddy made no bones about the fact that he preferred male drivers when he was in the passenger's seat. He didn't trust women drivers. I wondered if it had something to do with his one effort to teach Mama how to drive and her ending up in the ditch in front of our house. Then there's the fact that his other driver's education student, Miss Nola Mae Jackson, flunked his class, too, and ended up in the bayou. I always laughed to myself when I saw him cringing or grabbing the dashboard at the least little turn or bump when he was forced to ride with me.

By the time we made it to the park, there were a few cars already parked near the pavilion designated for the Kearney reunion. There were giant balloons and a huge banner reading, "16th Kearney Family Reunion!" I shook my head, thinking how fast time had passed since that first reunion in 1971 and how much older I was.

James and Martha had driven out with John and Janice, and they were already busy inside the screened-in pavilion dusting the benches, putting tablecloths on the tables and setting vases with flower sprigs on each one.

"My, how fancy we've gotten since way back there in the '70s when we'd just slap a hamburger between two buns and plop down on a blanket!" I laughed at my family's growing sophistication.

By 2:45, the food was prepared and everyone had arrived. The volunteer chefs carted in barbecued chicken, hot dogs, burgers and ribs. Daddy sat at the end of the table and opened a newspaper, just as he always did, using this opportunity to finish reading his paper. Family tradition had it that one of his daughters always prepared Daddy's plate before anyone else's was prepared. Mama had been the perpetrator of this old tradition, and we seemed unable to break it.

After we'd all filled our plates to the brim, Daddy laid his paper on the wood table, stood and asked us to bow our heads in prayer. Daddy's "blessing of the meal" had been another lifelong tradition for our family—not just for family reunions, but for holiday and Sunday meals, as well. There had been few times he had relegated this responsibility to his children; and the two he most often asked were James or Joseph. Unfortunately, the joke still sometimes surfaced that prayer was the only time anyone would be able to get the attention of all the Kearney family at one time, and Daddy strung it out for as long as he could.

Everyone had had their fill by the time "Desserts!" was yelled out across the pavilion. Daddy was the only one who had saved room. Someone cut the biggest, roundest melon out of the lot, handing a hefty slice to Daddy. One of the teenagers' boom box sent the soothing voice of Sam Cook, a favorite of the older Kearney children, clear across the park. I was remembering how I'd learned the singer was killed when I was in the sixth grade. It became a sing-along as my siblings swayed and sang along with Sam Cook's beautiful voice. Amazingly, most of the Kearney children were blessed with beautiful voices.

The day was changing to evening and finally cooling down. Everyone began to seek comfortable spots around the lake. A few siblings had stretched out on blankets near the bank. Some sat under the shaded trees and talked. A number of the females took walks around the lake, while the younger children cast out their fishing lines hoping to snare a fish. Daddy sat at a table under a tree talking with his older sons about the past.

The sun slowly dipped lower across the lake as the evening wore on, and we started packing up for the ride back home. It was agreed that the family would converge on Jesse's home in Pine Bluff for a night of more reminiscing, card playing and imbibing in something stronger than soft drinks and lemonade.

Even then, we still hid from Daddy the things he always preached against, namely smoking and drinking. Daddy pretended year-in and year-out that he wasn't aware that his children smoked or drank. Card playing had not been an issue since a few years back when Daddy had joined his sons on a trip to the Las Vegas casinos. "I guess what's right and wrong gets more gray than black or white as the old man gets older," John joked.

Jo Ann decided she would return to Daddy's house, rather than stop at Jesse's. "I left my medicine...and I need to take it and lay down for a while," she'd said.

I went with her, saying, "It gives me a chance to rest some, too."

Daddy was already home and busy out at the hog pen when we arrived. He was feeding the baby pigs Jesse had brought down a few weeks ago. I unpacked the car, put most of the things away and began clearing the dishes left from the morning. Jo Ann, quiet now, took a glass of water to the nearest guest bedroom to lie down. Through the kitchen window, I saw that darkness had fallen and it looked like we'd have another clear summer night.

I walked out on the front porch, sipping a glass of iced tea. The temperature was slowly falling, cooling the night air and accenting the sounds of the small creatures that made up country nights. Daddy walked out the screen door and sat down on the porch step. "I thought you might be ready to take a nap, too." I smiled over at him.

He shook his head and looked up into the darkening sky. "I was a little tired when I got here, but it didn't last long. I go to sleep and wake back up five or six times during the night."

I smiled and nodded. "Did you enjoy yourself today, Daddy?"

He smiled, and nodded as he looked over at me. "It was a good day...good to have all my children together. Really good to see Jo Ann doing better...I think that was the best part of all of it." I smiled and nodded, slowly.

"She look good," he continued, "and I really think she enjoyed herself. I've been praying all this time that she'd come back this way. It's so good having her part of the family, again. I guess I just don't see how..." Daddy's voice trailed off, and we sat in silence for some time.

"You, know, I still miss your mama at times like these. I know how much she would enjoy today with all of you and our grandchildren here." I smiled and looked up into the wide open sky I only seemed to find here at home.

"You're right. She would have been so happy to see all those grand-kids that are growing up so fast." More silence followed, and I finally realized Daddy was deciding whether to speak or not. I waited, enjoying the night and the final quiet.

"You remember the morning Ethel died? Course, you do...the hospital called you when it happened. It seems like I remember that morning a lot when the family gets together...just like it happened yesterday. I wonder why I can't remember that Indian doctor's name...."

I laughed and admitted that neither could I. I did remember his kindness.

Daddy went on, "I actually came to like him, once I decided he was right about keeping Ethel there. You know I wanted her to come on back home and told him we could come and go like we'd been doing all along. He didn't want your mama traveling back and forth between here and Little Rock...said Ethel was too sick for that. I remember that's when I knew to be scared.

"But, still, doctors don't always know...he gave us six months, and Ethel lived another 18 months. That morning when he called...something told me what it was. In fact, I know it was God that told me.

"I was getting dressed, getting ready to go out and feed the hogs and do some work in the garden since planting season was right on us. I was thinking about running out to Star City to pick up a few more peas and okra plants, just to be on the safe side.

"I remember thinking the night before how good it would be if Ethel could come home in time to see the garden and maybe even eat a few peas and okras that spring. I knew her appetite wasn't worth nothing, but maybe if she got home and smelled some real food cooking...maybe that would help her appetite."

My parents had celebrated their 45th anniversary two days before Mama's passing. It was as if she had held on long enough to give Daddy and us that.

Mama had been alert, beautiful and quiet that day. By then, we had all accepted that she would leave us. While that knowledge loomed in every crevice of the small, white hospital room, we ignored it, sending it as far back in our minds as we could—that and the fact that this would be our parents' last anniversary celebration.

"Forty-five years...sometimes I can't believe we had 45 years together. Take Ethel to make you remember to be thankful for all God's blessings, no matter what you got to be sad about...that's what she told me before I left that day. 'James, you oughta be shamed of yourself. Look at all we got to be thankful for. Look at your beautiful children we raised together. Look at how they turned out. How many other parents can claim that?' "

The hardest part of Mama's death, Daddy said, was having to live on without her—returning to a house where they'd shared so much of their lives.

"I still miss her, you know?" Daddy said.

I knew. We would never stop missing Mama. ℚ

THIRTY

Reunion Sunday

Sundays were always the last day of the Kearney reunion, and the only day we all worshipped together and openly thanked God for our blessings. The day always included our trek to Rankin Chapel, the family's church for the last 50 years, for Sunday school service.

As we worshipped there on reunion Sunday, I remembered the hundreds of Sundays Mama sat on the front-row pew and Daddy sat at the superintendent's table. This was one of the favorite parts of the reunion for Daddy. He enjoyed having his children join him at church and the opportunity to brag about our accomplishments with the now elderly congregation. It was like giving back one day of his past to him each year. He likely remembered, with nostalgia, the years when the Kearney family outnumbered others there.

Yet, the first order of the day was juggling Sunday morning breakfast and making sure everyone was dressed and ready for Sunday school by 9:30 that morning. Sunday was the most hectic day of the reunion, but no one dared not show up for church.

"I already got my biscuits in the oven, Faye. You might want to start the bacon and eggs, so it'll all be ready when the crowd gets here...we don't need nobody stragglin' in there late after Sunday school start." Daddy's Sunday breakfasts mirrored those we'd grown accustomed to when Mama was here.

While nobody much cared about eating a "real" breakfast during the rest of the reunion, we always looked forward to and expected one on

Sunday. It did Daddy's heart good to see us stuff ourselves on his hot biscuits, rice, bacon and homemade jelly before lighting out for Sunday school.

"You know, Daddy, I was about out of high school before I could actually tell my friends we had indoor plumbing," I laughed, as I rinsed Daddy's big iron skillet at the sink.

"Yeah," Daddy chuckled, "it wasn't but a few of you who grew up knowing any thing about flushing a stool." The children, barely awake, all snickered in surprise at Daddy's Sunday morning conversation.

"Whatever happened to that old pump we used out in the back yard all those years? Did you just pull it up and throw it away when you got water through pipes?" I asked him, scanning the yard, though I knew it was no longer there. Daddy scratched his head and looked out the window as if he might see the pump sitting in the yard somewhere.

"I don't rightly know what I did with that pump. I know we took it down...it's probably out there in one of them sheds, somewhere." I followed Daddy's eyes, out the window, seeing things as they were almost 20 years ago.

———

We all made it to Rankin Chapel before the final opening song was finished. The members looked back at the door each time it opened, knowing it was likely another one of Mr. Kearney's children walking through the door. They were curious to see who was here and to see what kind of grown-ups we'd turned out to be.

The neighbors never tired of telling us how proud they were of our accomplishments. We knew they really meant they were amazed we had all made something of ourselves. While none of them would have wished us bad fortune, they simply were not able to visualize anything except the worst of fortunes for the houseful of Kearney children. Daddy, puffed out with pride at his "show and tell" family, took the liberty as superintendent to call on his eldest son, James, to teach the adult class.

He looked over to see if another one would volunteer for the children's class. The congregation's congenial smile as I walked to the back of the church was their way of remembering my mother. According to some of the women, I was the spitting image of a young Ethel Kearney.

After Sunday school, the congregation merely moved from the church to the churchyard. We all felt obligated to say our hellos to the members we hadn't seen in a number of years. I asked some of the parents about the children I'd grown up with and learned they had either married and moved away or were still living on the same street... sometimes in the same house they had grown up in.

Daddy was already anxious to get home. He'd done his part. He'd gotten his clan to church on time, showed them off to the church, impressed us with the oratory skills he still possessed after all these years and even made sure we participated in the Sunday school activities. Now, he was ready to get home, eat dinner, watch the football game, and spend the last day of his family's reunion with his family.

"I'm ready, Faye. You gone ride back with me?" He carried his weathered Bible tucked under his arm. I smiled, knowing how easily bored Daddy had always been with small talk. "Yeah, Daddy, I'm riding with you. Just let me go say bye to Miss King." Without looking up, he kept moving toward the car, expecting me to catch up after my quick goodbyes.

On our way down the dusty road, Daddy was up to his usual, going twice as fast as he should. The poor cars behind us were catching hell trying to see through Daddy's dust. "It was a nice Sunday school service, wasn't it Daddy?" I asked, settling into my seat.

Our annual family visits to Rankin Chapel had always brought back memories of my childhood. I remembered the children I'd played with among the cars and the trees out in the churchyard. We'd hunted the brightly colored eggs together in the tall grass on Easter Sunday and licked ice cream under the trees on Children's Day until our stomachs felt as if they would burst.

How we'd looked forward to Children's Day—in the middle of the hot Arkansas summer and the promise of as much ice cream and cookies as our little stomachs could hold. This was our reward for standing in front of the grown-ups reciting our Children's Day speeches.

As we drove into Daddy's large front yard, I saw it was already half-filled with the family members who'd left the church before we did and the cars that were left behind.

There was already movement in the back yard. Joseph and James were busy setting up the barbecue pit. What I wanted most, though, was to get inside and take off my stockings and pumps. I'd never grown out of the pleasure of going barefoot inside the house when I was in Gould, and I rarely wore shoes once I was inside my own house.

There wasn't much to preparing dinner. My siblings who lived in Arkansas had already prepared most of the food. They simply brought it down in pots and pans that could be warmed up within minutes. They had divided the main dishes among themselves, each adding a dessert or their own specialty dish. John and Janice always found the most succulent hams for the Kearney family gatherings. Jack's specialty for the last decade had been hog mauls—the tender pieces of the hog's stomach that were indescribably delicious when Jack seasoned them just right.

The Kearney reunion continued to be the one time of the year when we all dropped our health regimens and on-again, off-again diets, vowing to return to them when we returned home. I'd prepared my reunion specialty—ambrosia salad made with unmeasured amounts of fruit, nuts, sour cream and cool whip. It was an especially hot July day, and Daddy's fans and window air conditioner were of little help in keeping the house cool, especially with a house full of adults and very mobile children.

"The children need to keep the doors closed or we won't be feeling a bit of coolness," Daddy said, growing impatient with the young grandchildren constantly slamming in and out the back door. Daddy brought out another floor fan and placed it on one of the tables in the dining room. "Let's see if this help."

By the time we'd finished dinner, the air had begun to cool. The sun was finally easing its way down beyond the trees. Most of the family had moved out onto the yard or on Daddy's porch. Daddy's two dogs lay comfortably under the shade of the peach tree, looking from one Kearney child to the next as if they didn't know what to make of a crowd such as this one.

"Don't get too comfortable before you come back in the kitchen and help clean up," Judy hollered out the back door. I was too comfortable to move from the pallet under Daddy's tree. "I'll be there in 10 minutes, Judy. Just give me 10 minutes." The rest of the females chimed in that they'd be there soon, just not this moment. Eating, as always, had taken more energy than we'd expected, and now we had to rest up to get ourselves moving again.

Daddy asked the children if they wanted to walk down on the bayou with him. "We'll see if it's too hot for them old fish to move around, too." He was a Pied Piper leading his band of eager grandchildren down on the bayou.

"Grandpa, can we fish while we down there?" Little Michael asked.

"We can't do no fishing on Sunday, Michael...we just gone see if the fish is moving around out there in that hot water. Then, we'll know where to fish tomorrow!" The children looked at each other and shrugged, as if their grandfather might have a pretty good plan after all.

The bayou behind our house had been a big part of our childhood. Not only did we fish in it on summer and spring days, but it served as my brothers' personal swimming hole as well. And during the few winters when it was cold enough for bayous and lakes and rivers to freeze over, it served as their own personal skating rink. Though I was always eager enough to follow them down to the bank of the bayou to see what devilment they got themselves into, I was never brave enough to join in that devilment-nor was I invited. It seemed that the boys at the Kearney home had all the fun, while the girls watched.

It was about an hour later that I heard Daddy and his band of grandchildren coming back from the bayou. They were all talking and laughing excitedly.

"But...was it a real snake, Granddaddy, like the ones they have on TV?"

Daddy shook his head. "Yeah, boy, it was a real snake. Didn't you see it sliding down in the water when we walked up?" The young boy's eyes were big as saucers as he ran toward the house. "We saw a real snake down in the bayou!"

Daddy had batted a thousand with his field trip. The children had seen turtles bobbing their head in the water and sleeping on top of logs; dragonflies—or snake doctors as we called them—flying above the water in search of snakes; big and little fish jumping up in the water; and minnows swimming at the top of the water. The children were mesmerized at the "real animals" they saw.

I stood at Daddy's kitchen sink when Jo Ann walked up behind me, holding a package of cigarettes in her hand. "Finished?" I nodded. "Wanna go out back and smoke, like we used to wish we could do growing up." I laughed, knowing it was the truth. But I'd never had the nerve to do it. "I'll finish putting the rest of the dishes away, then I'll come out. I'll pass on the cigarettes, though. I'll see if I can find my drug of choice, Dr Pepper."

"Hey, wait for me...I think I'll join you, give me a second," Judy hollered from the living room. I realized it was almost time to say goodbye...another year, come and gone, I thought. I wondered if Daddy felt the same way or if he was actually looking forward to his solitude again.

The Kearney men all stood around Jesse's truck whispering and drinking out of tissue-covered beer cans. They were all nearing middle-aged and still hiding beer from Daddy. Nobody smoked in front of him or cursed in front of him. I wondered if that was all out of respect or partly from our refusal to grow up or share our adulthood with Daddy. We talked briefly about next year's reunion, though we all knew the plans weren't made until the last few months before it was time for another reunion. An indelible Kearney trait was procrastination, which tended to drive some in-laws stock raving mad. Though it certainly wasn't a trait passed on from either of our parents, it was one that most of us held on to all our lives.

I walked out the back door in search of Jo Ann and Judy and found them sitting under the walnut tree. I stood there a second, taking the tree in, remembering how it had nurtured my dreams and fears and questions during my youth. It was old, many of its limbs blown away by strong winds and storms. I slowly walked to the place my sisters had staked out for their last smoke here.

"Well, everybody's getting ready to go...it's kind of sad, you know?"

Judy nodded and smiled. "At least we have something to look forward to every year, and Daddy can be sure he'll see us all at least once each year."

Jo Ann nodded without speaking. "I can't believe I stayed for the whole three days...every day I said I was leaving, but for some reason...well, here I am." She chuckled, a puzzled look on her face. "I admit I actually enjoyed myself, but...I really hadn't planned to stay."

Daddy walked to the back door and looked out. When he saw what we were up to, he laughed and turned around and walked back into the house.

"Daddy's scared if he come out here, he might pick up his old cigarette habit again," Judy joked. We all laughed.

333

"Wow, after all these years...if he still wants a cigarette, I definitely want to stay away from them," I said.

Jo Ann smoked quietly. I had seen her in this mood, smoking one cigarette after another just halfway to the filter before throwing it away and starting another one. "I was just thinking about Mama...I'm just sorry we never were able to realize just how much we're probably alike...when we had the chance," she said.

Saying goodbye was still awkward for us, even after all these years of saying goodbye after family reunions. Some of my brothers found it easier to skip it altogether, simply jump in their cars without saying a word and wave as they drove off.

There was poignancy to watching Daddy say goodbye to Jo Ann. He had been surprised at how much he enjoyed her company. "I'm so glad you came this year, Jo Ann. I hope you'll start coming every year. It makes it so much better when you here with us."

Jo Ann smiled her bright smile but didn't make a promise. "I enjoyed myself, too, Daddy...it was really nice." She was riding back to Little Rock with our brother Jack and his family. "Call me when you get home, Faye," she said as she waved back at us.

"This was a good reunion, wasn't it?" Daddy said, after the last car drove slowly around the bend and up the road. I nodded, "Yes." We walked back to the porch and sat there.

"I think everybody really enjoyed themselves and was real glad to see you," I said. He smiled and looked up the road at the dust still swirling from the last car, then over at his two dogs who were watching him.

I was the last of his children to leave. I wanted to make sure the house was left intact and Daddy's leftovers were securely wrapped and packed to last him a while. As I walked out the front door carrying my one bag, Daddy smiled, hugging me goodbye.

"Same time, next year, Daddy."

He laughed and waved until I couldn't see him through the dust swirling around my car. ℚ

Epilogue

At the End
of The Day

The sun was at its brightest now, hard glints of yellow breaking through the trees just before it waned. The air had cooled, a welcome relief from the relentless heat that shadowed us throughout the day.

The hardest part of this day was the two surreal hours devoted to Jo Ann's funeral. We'd all made it through—even Daddy, who seemed still wrapped in some protective fog. The hurting wouldn't end today, but healing would begin.

I hurried into Daddy's house and into the guest bedroom, dispersing what I could of the funeral attire and donning an old faded shirt Daddy probably still wore.

"Faye, you find something to put on?" Daddy had sat on the edge of his sofa and was reaching for the television monitor.

"Yeah, Daddy, I'm fine." I lightly rubbed his shoulder as I passed through the crowded living room. "We'll prepare something to eat in just a minute," I told him. "Just not right now."

As I walked out onto his front porch, I recognized the measured throbs of pain shooting through my head...just as I knew they would. I was thankful they'd waited until now but wondered that it had taken them this long. My migraines began the day we buried Mama and had never gone away.

The gray concrete steps were one of the late additions to Daddy's home; one more sign of how Daddy had kept himself busy after we all left home. I sat and practiced the slow breathing that sometimes helped the pain subside. It would be useless today, I knew. I snapped the cap on the already fizzing Dr Pepper and pushed the Tylenols into my mouth.

"Bottom's up." I closed my eyes and sighed. I was grateful that the pain had taken a weeklong vacation.

As I walked gingerly back into the house to help my sisters prepare dinner, I peeked into Daddy's room and saw him lying across his bed. It was only the second time in my lifetime I'd seen my father lie down in the middle of the day. My sisters had already taken over the kitchen. More structured than I'd ever be, Janeva and Jamie washed the dishes before beginning to cook.

Most times when his children were around, Daddy's kitchen would be bustling with laughter and jokes. There was quiet except for the perfunctory requests and responses and the clanging and banging of cooking utensils and cupboard doors.

The unspoken edict: today is not a time for discussions. We had always been an introverted group of people when it came to matters of the heart. Jo Ann's death would most certainly fit that description. We would have to figure it all out inside ourselves before we shared it with each other. That would take some time. None of us were ready to go to that place inside ourselves, not just yet, not with the wounds being so new and raw.

I would wait to help out I decided as I walked back through the front door and reclaimed my place on the hard concrete that was Daddy's front steps. I lay back, waiting for the Tylenol to do its job. As I began to doze, the smell of roast beef, chicken and collard greens came through the screen door. For a scant second, I imagined Jo Ann's laughing face at the dinner table last year. How her face lit up when she laughed; how rich and wonderful was that laughter we had heard for the last time.

Why had God chosen Jo Ann as the first Kearney child to die? I wondered. Out of all the ones he had to choose from, why Jo Ann? Or was it really his choosing? I wiped the stream of sweat beginning a path down my face. It was safer, I decided, to rest here rather than in the bedroom I'd shared with Jo Ann all those years.

The sound of voices and quiet laughter woke me. Daddy's large brood of children and their spouses and children were spread all over his house, his back yard and the nooks and crannies inside. Some brave soul would later suggest a family photo. None of us could think of a reason not to take one, and I certainly thought of one why we should.

I had actually slept, and the sun that had shone so bright just minutes earlier was now peeking dully from behind the trees. It was dusk. Daddy's dogs sat in a semicircle staring up at me. I felt his presence before I turned to see Daddy sitting on the side of the porch, sipping Sprite from a can.

"My goodness, I can't believe I actually fell asleep."

He half smiled. "I did too...I guess we all could use some rest."

"I do feel a lot better, and my headache is about gone." I took a deep breath and straightened myself. The dark dress beneath the old shirt reminded me of today. "Did you eat, something, Daddy?" He shook his head and said he wasn't hungry. "You really need to try to eat something. You haven't eaten a real meal in a few days now."

He stared into the can of Sprite and mumbled he'd try to eat something later.

Did I dream what had happened today? Did we all gather at the funeral chapel and bid farewell to my beautiful sister? Had the minister actually recalled things from our past that I had all but forgotten—of that younger, innocent Jo Ann we all could love and despise so easily?

"I think I better start back home before it gets too late, Daddy. Remember how you used to worry about me zipping up and down the highway? Well, you should be happy to know that I don't enjoy driving half as much anymore." Especially not today, I thought. Daddy nodded slowly and cleared his throat.

"Faye, you know, I was thinking...just how much I hate what happened...how sad it makes me that Jo Ann died the way she did. I still can't hardly believe it.

"I just wonder...if maybe there was something I should've done...or should have known. Your mama always worried so much about Jo Ann. She hated knowing one of her children was sick like that.... I guess the truth is I'm glad she's not here to see how Jo Ann ...died. That would have been just too much for her to take."

I knew Daddy was grappling with the same guilt we all were.

"You both always did all you could for Jo Ann, Daddy. You weren't supposed to know everything that was going on with her. None of us did, and I was probably closer to her for a long time than anyone else. But...none of us could have saved her from herself."

I stood and turned to go into the house, deciding it was time for me to go to my own home and check on my own family. I hesitated but decided there were no right words at a time like this.

"Daddy, listen, you have to start making sure you take care of yourself. What's happened, happened, and none of us can change that. The worst thing we can do is not keep our own lives on track. For the last few days, you just stopped doing the things it takes to live a healthy life, and I understand that...but you can't continue doing that...not after today. You just have to keep doing what you always did in your life...the best you can." I gave him a hug, knowing that he needed it.

"Besides, we don't need you to be getting sick, giving us one more thing to worry about. We can't bring Jo Ann back, and we can't change what happened. We all feel guilty and sad and angry and confused about her death, but we can't let it take over our lives...OK?"

Daddy sighed and nodded slowly. Quiet for a minute or so, he looked up and out across the fields.

"That cotton is getting ripe early this year; just about time for somebody to start picking it, already."

I looked out at the snow white cotton sticking out of the partially opened bowls.

"I remember when my hands would start burning, just knowing it was getting close to cotton picking time," I chuckled.

Daddy smiled back. "Well, nobody have to worry about that no more. The machines took care of that." Daddy raised himself up from the porch and walked around to the back of the house. "I better check on my new pigs...I don't think I've fed 'em in a couple of days."

I decided a walk was what I needed before the sun set and I began my drive home. I'd check to see if Bayou Bartholomew was the same—if the wood bridge still had wobbly slats. I'd feel the crunch of gravel under my shoes and know I was on Varner Road. I'd cry and think of Jo Ann...remember the Jo Ann I loved and resented and wished was still here.

Like Daddy, I didn't have an appetite, though the food looked especially good as I walked through the kitchen. I quickly grabbed up my things and walked through the house, offering hugs and goodbyes to the family. I stopped at the door of the bedroom I'd shared so many years with Jo Ann. There on the wall hung an oil painting some anonymous Pine Bluff artist had painted from Jo Ann's high school graduation picture. The artist had captured the sophisticated and glamorous Jo Ann that didn't quite fit here on Varner Road. She had been only 16 then but already wise beyond her years and impatient with the world.

I walked with Daddy to my car. "Take care of yourself, Daddy. I'll call and check on you tomorrow." I was ready to put this day behind me, at least until I was better able to understand. As I turned onto the gravel road, I turned the "oldies but goodies" station on. I passed Daddy's corn-field, and I smiled, remembering the summer days Jo Ann and I spent combing and curling the corn silk.

As I turned the corner where tall Fred Lack once lived, I remembered the many nights Jo Ann and I lay awake, sharing secrets and promises. I treasured those memories as I did the picture Daddy kept on the bedroom wall. Passing the rows of cotton, I remembered our dreams and vowed to never forget.   Somehow, I knew that the Jo Ann I loved and remembered would never let me. ℚ

— The End —

James Thomas and Ethel V. Curry Kearney Family
(Chronological listing)

Cecil Green

Clara Harper

Jamie Kearney Young

James Kearney, Jr.

Jerrel Kearney

Janeva Kearney-King

John L. Kearney

Janetta Kearney

Joseph Kearney

Joyce Kearney Richardson

Jesse L. Kearney

Jack R. Kearney

Julius D. Kearney

Janis F. Kearney

Jo Ann Kearney (deceased)

Jerome T. Kearney

Jude D. Kearney

Jeffery H. Kearney

Judy C. Kearney-Ramos